Contents

Preface

This book was written for the benefit of all students of AutoCAD, be they members of an educational establishment, practising artisans of industry, or simply those individuals excited by the potential of current personal computers.

The book is not intended to be a comprehensive account of 3D design using AutoCAD. It is intended to fill a growing need for the design process to be communicated from concept to customer in a 3D format, and as such, complement existing books in the AutoCAD series by avoiding unnecessary duplication and concentrating instead on original material that extends the current existing publications.

The book is arranged in three basic parts. Part One starts with an overview of the user coordinate system (UCS); this is followed by a series of structured practical exercises designed to build up a wide range of written and practical competences in 3D design, relating at all times to the needs of education and industry. This section also contains a helpful set of rules for beginners of 3D design. There are five specific exercises in Part One, each containing tasks at the end to enable the reader to test and apply each new competence.

I make no apology for starting the first exercise with wire frame modelling, as this is still the preferred method for the teaching of spatial concepts. It also plays a valuable role providing construction lines for complex solid model constructions. Surface modelling is also a necessary technique in the '3D' design process, if for no other reason than the current limitations of the AutoCAD editing facilities.

Part One is intended to offer a quick introduction to 3D design by working through five exercises on different subjects, with the sole purpose of motivating the reader to consider the potential of these different time compression technologies, so important to the efficiency of modern commercial activities. I recognise the more advanced nature of Exercise 5 and invite those less experienced users of AutoCAD to proceed to Part Two with a view to returning to this exercise at a later date.

Part Two has been developed to act as a link between Part One (a quick introduction to 3D design) and Part Three (the 3D design project), by means of a series of progressively arranged practical exercises. These exercises give the reader the opportunity to try out some of the AutoCAD commands without the

A Practical Guide to
AutoCAD 3D Design

Trevor Bousfield

LONGMAN

Pearson Education Limited
Edinburgh Gate, Harlow
Essex CM20 2JE
England
and Associated Companies throughout the world

© Pearson Education Limited 1999

First published 1999

British Library Cataloguing-in-Publication Data
A catalogue entry for this title is available from the British Library.

ISBN 0-582-36935-5

Set by 24 in 10/13pt Times
Printed in Singapore (KKP)

A PRACTICAL GUIDE TO AUTOCAD 3D DESIGN

full 'parrot fashion' approach used in Part One, and develop the surface/solid modelling competences necessary for those readers wishing to progress to the level required in Part Three.

Part Three is designed to encourage the reader to apply the full range of 3D design competences to a realistic practical project. The project can be conducted on PCs without undue delay in processing time when performed on current processor technology. This project offers the opportunity to apply a wide range of AutoCAD 3D design competences, extend the knowledge of basic optical theory, apply design solutions to practical problems and to realise the design concepts by manufacturing the project using a range of 'deskilled' solutions.

The option to develop the completed model using rendering technologies for enhanced photo-realistic coloured images also helps with the realisation of the design process. It must be remembered that this is a design book, and by its very nature, design is a decision-making process. Certain detail omissions in the design project are deliberate with a view to the development of decision-making skills.

By using this project as an example of 3D design, the author's intention is to motivate readers to apply these solutions to their working environment, and as such, hasten the inevitable day when concept to customer consists entirely of 3D communications.

The author's thanks are due to Neville Cumberland for his contribution towards a number of exercises in Part Two of the book and to Denise Rowntree for the colour rendering. I wish also to acknowledge the support given over many years by Joan, Ian and Howard.

Trevor Bousfield
York, 1998

Introduction

Purpose

It is assumed that the reader has a basic knowledge of 2D AutoCAD. This book is a natural progression for those students possessing the C&G 4351–01 qualification (whilst advisable, it is not essential). The content of the book is directed towards the needs of those studying for the new City and Guilds Three Dimensional Design, Solid Modelling and Rendering qualification at both NVQ levels 2, 3 and 4, and also for students taking the new National and Higher National BTEC units in design (including SCOTVEC) studying such subjects as engineering, construction, interior design and so on.

Many GNVQ students will benefit from this book as will a great many more CAD users engaged in industry and commerce, all wishing to take that important first step from 2D to 3D design.

The book forms a natural progression of knowledge and practical competences, linked by a series of exercises and problems, each progressing the reader by a logical sequence of events, unrestricted by boundaries of 'subject departmentalisation'.

Background

Release 13 AutoCAD, like its predecessor, made considerable improvements to the development of its 3D capabilities, and with the improvement in computer hardware it is now a realistic option to consider 3D design using the current range of PCs and software. Gone are the days when a simple HIDE command meant an invitation to take the dog for a walk in the hope that the regeneration would be complete on your return.

There are three different methods of representing 3D models on a computer.

■ **Wire frame** – This is a very simple representation. I think of the old-fashioned tailor's dummy, made from wire, as the analogy for a wire frame model. Wire frame models are created with the normal 2D drawing entities or objects such as LINE, PLINE, ARC, CIRCLE.

■ **Surface model** – This model is more complex than wire frame models, requiring surfaces to be created on the facets of the model bounded by the wire frame in our analogy. Think now of placing clothing on the tailor's dummy in such a way that contact is made with the wire frame or wire mesh. The clothing represents a series of 2D faces all joined together. This type of model gives better visual appearance and can be subjected to the HIDE command as well as rendering and shading for a better and more realistic representation.

The 3D drawings shown here form part of a technical illustration describing various mechanical functions. They were produced by conventional draughting methods using French curves to draw the arcs. All the necessary information required to produce the pictorial drawings was gathered from 2D detail drawings. The time taken to produce these three drawings was two-and-a-half working days.

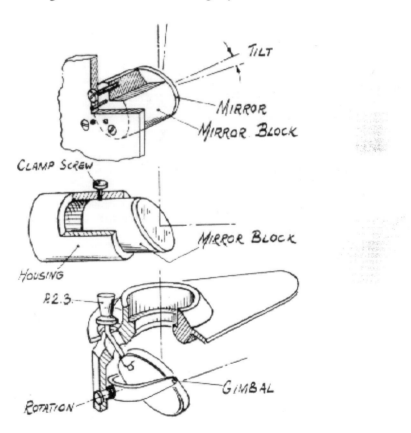

Had computerised isometric projection been available at the time when these drawings were produced, a less tedious six hours' work would have been necessary.

If, instead of using 2D detail drawings to gather information, the details had been constructed in 3D on a computer system. This electronic data could have been inserted into the drawing editor, reducing the overall time to produce the 3D drawing from two-and-a-half working days to two-and-a-half hours, producing a more professional result with the possibility of further enhancement.

- **Solid model** – This is the highest level of 3D modelling. The tailor's dummy in our analogy becomes a real person, having solid form with internal properties and attributes such as mass, volume, mobility and response to stresses, resulting in a considerably enhanced appearance.

Why 3D design?

It does not seem over ten years since the doubters scorned the claim that 'All detail drawings in the future will be created on a CAD system.' Sadly, for many of those doubters, they are like the tee-squares and set-squares put to the back of the drawer as a thing of the past.

The above statement was referring to 2D drawings and was considered a replacement method for the conventional orthographic projections. The only 3D representation at the time on PCs was isometric projection, a pictorial method which had satisfied the draughtsman or woman over many years as a means of conveying solutions that would otherwise be complicated and prone to error in orthographic projection. Isometric projection was used as an emergency when urgently recruited female labour was employed in the munitions factories during the Second World War. Isometric projections have also been found useful for spare parts manuals and do-it-yourself instruction material. There is no doubt that the 3D drawing communicates with greater clarity than the 2D drawing.

The two diagrams shown here illustrate the use of isometric projection to communicate with a non-technical reader.

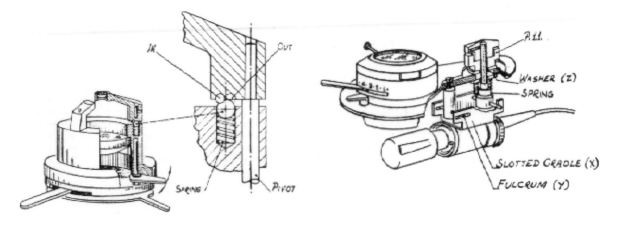

Once CAD software had introduced a 'Z' value to the 'x,y' coordinate system (even if 'Z' were equal to zero), a new world of possibilities was opened up to the designer, giving true 3D entities (or objects) and relegating isometric projection to $2\frac{1}{2}$D, becoming the poor relation of 3D computer graphics and entering into the pages of history.

It is now time to see the future design process in terms of 3D computer graphics. 'This is to be the destiny of the majority of designers.' As with the historical case of 2D computer graphics, this statement too has its doubters. Only time will confirm to them that the new breed of young designers will be trained to think and communicate designs directly in 3D computer graphics.

The design process

The design process is a creative activity dependent upon the ability to visualise problems and solutions as a mental image in a 3D state. To enhance and stimulate this mental process, the designer sketches in 3D prior to formulating the solution in 2D (orthographic projection).

To assist in this design process, some designers use models. My particular favourite modelling method was the use of a large piece of plasticine sculptured with the aid of a penknife. These traditional methods have been taught to design students over many generations. The above helps to illustrate the limitations of a 2D design process: certain complicated designs are only clearly realised at the *pattern-making* stage or the *prototype* stage. It is also important to remember that not everyone in the design approval chain is an expert reader of 2D drawings and some prefer to await the above stages before contributing to the design process (hopefully before the design has entered the manufacturing stage).

This traditional *design/manufacture* process can be described in three basic stages:

- Stage 1 – The designer visualises the solution as a 3D image.
- Stage 2 – This 3D mental image is translated into a series of different views, drawn to a particular convention in 2D.
- Stage 3 – The craftsman or woman translates the 2D drawing into a 3D product.

Now that the technology exists to eliminate stage 2, it will become increasingly difficult to justify its continued existence.

The advantages of the design process being conducted in 3D are numerous. Consider:

- How would you like to give your potential customer a photo-realistic coloured image of the finished product without even making a prototype?
- How would you like to drastically reduce your leadtime (concept to customer), by time compression technologies?
- How would you like to satisfy those outdated requests for orthographic projections in the time it would take to sharpen a pencil, by 3D view associativity?

■ How would you like to produce exploded views for service manuals within minutes of the request?

■ How would you like to check your design for assembly interference without leaving the screen?

All this and more can be yours once the designs are created in 3D computer graphics. Remember, good designs to the market late are dead designs; there is no better example than the British shipbuilders, designing and building some of the best ships in the world (still celebrated in the words of a popular song played at the 'Last Night of the Proms' every year). Unfortunately, this industry responded to the challenge of leadtime slower than its competitors.

The new breed of designers will input design solutions directly in 3D without ever resorting to 2D graphics, gaining all the above benefits with true electronic data for downloading to the CAD/CAM process, and maintaining a competitive edge and a future for their industries.

Part One
A quick introduction to 3D design

Contents

Part One contains a series of structured exercises to build up the user's competences in 3D design.

For the sake of simplicity, Part One restricts the commands to direct keyboard entry, thus avoiding the problem of searching menus or icons in different versions of AutoCAD. It is therefore a suitable starting point for beginners in 3D design.

Objectives

- The general objective of Part One is to build up a range of written and practical competences in 3D design to serve the needs of education and industry.
- The specific objectives of Part One – the individual competences as they apply to the particular exercise – are set out in detail at the start of Exercises 1 to 5.

User coordinate system

What's in an icon?

The sign in Figure 1 was displayed in a shop window, in a narrow village street, in a very popular tourist area of the Yorkshire Dales. I am reminded of it whenever I advise beginners of 3D design.

Figure 1

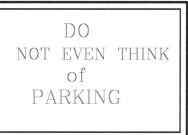

Do not even think of starting before you have mastered the art of UCS manipulation. The introduction of the UCSICON (Release 10 of AutoCAD) was a most important development for the benefit of 3D design. Here lies the key to all surface and solid modelling. Without a sound knowledge of the UCS system and the ability to place the UCSICON anywhere in space, progress in 3D design will be slow and limited.

The user coordinate system (UCS) is, as the words imply, a coordinate system defined by the user. The default location (or datum) for the UCS is called the world coordinate system (WCS) and has a 'W' in the 'icon'.

The icon in Figure 2 indicates the default location with the 'origin' in the bottom left-hand corner of the screen. In the diagram:

Figure 2

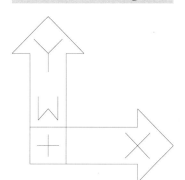

W = WCS
+ = Icon located on the origin
□ = View in the positive 'z' direction

Once the UCSICON is moved from the default location the 'W' in the icon disappears. (To return to the WCS, enter UCS at the command prompt and press 'Enter' twice.)

The first lesson in 3D design is to place your right hand on a horizontal surface such as a rectangular table with the palm of your hand facing upwards and your fingers and thumb closed as a clenched fist. Make sure that your right arm is parallel with one of the sides of the table. This side will then represent the 'Y' axis, with the 'X' axis being the side of the table nearest to your body. Now:

1. Extend your thumb outwards until it hurts. This represents the positive 'X' axis. ('No pain – no gain'.)
2. Extend your index finger towards the horizontal surface to represent the positive 'Y' axis at 90º to the 'X' axis.
3. Finally, extend the second finger 90º to the horizontal surface; this finger represents the positive 'Z' axis.

This finger and thumb configuration is often referred to as the 'right hand rule' and, in the case of beginners in 3D design, must become permanent – as if set by rigor mortis – for the benefit of this exercise.

4. Look directly down the 'Z' axis.

This view now represents the ideal screen configuration for constructing entities in 3D (see Figure 3, and later, Rule 1). It is exactly the same configuration as you have been using for 2D graphics. Remember that many 2D commands are used to create 3D objects.

If you imagine the intersection of both fingers and thumb to coincide at a common point, then this point becomes the 'origin' having coordinate values of 0, 0, 0. The view you are seeing when looking at (4) above is called the 'plan'.

Figure 3

POSITIVE DIRECTIONS

Whenever you wish to look down the positive 'Z' axis, use the command PLAN (in the current UCS). All entities or objects constructed in this configuration will have their positive 'x' and 'y' coordinates in the direction of your thumb and index finger respectively, with the 'Z' axis normal to the screen. This process can be achieved automatically by using the UCSFOLLOW command (useful when using two or more viewports).

Moving the UCS

There are a number of subcommands within the UCS command to help define a new coordinate system. These subcommands relate to the current UCS configuration (unless preceded by an asterisk).

Note: You will notice on your system that the AutoCAD screen prompts present these (and other) subcommands in mixed upper and lower case letters. the upper case letters indicate the shorthand form of the option which can be entered from the keyboard.

To illustrate these subcommands we will move the right hand in relation to the rectangular horizontal table in Figure 4 in terms of certain constraints. The UCSICON will now represent your right hand.

Figure 4

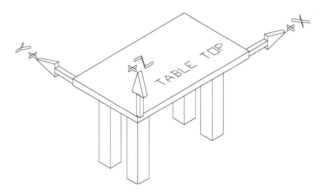

1. Option O (origin)

Move your hand anywhere on the horizontal surface, keeping the back of the hand in contact with the surface and the index finger and thumb parallel to the sides of the table (Figure 5). This is called moving the UCS origin. The intersection point of your fingers and thumb becomes the new origin, i.e. $(0, 0, 0)$.

The ability to control the movement of the UCS in this way is the key to success in 3D design. Resist the temptation to construct 3D objects until you have mastered the following.

Remove one constraint by freeing your hand from contact with the horizontal surface, placing your hand anywhere in space parallel to the horizontal surface with the index finger and thumb parallel with the sides of the horizontal surface

Figure 5

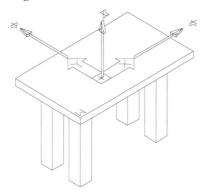

(Figure 6). This movement is also governed by the origin subcommand by entering values for 'z' coordinate. Any movement above the table is positive, any below the table is negative.

Figure 6

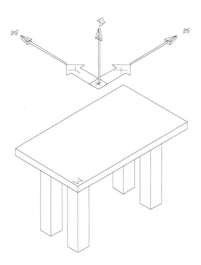

The 'x,y' plane of the table represents the 'x,y' plane of the screen. Keep this finger and thumb configuration the same and place the back of your hand on the surface of the screen. This now represents the basic 2D configuration and the one that most CAD users will be familiar with, namely looking down the positive 'Z' axis. What you may not have realised is that your entity or object points were constructed in 3D, having (in most cases) a 'z' value of zero.

Move your wrist and arm (like a robot arm) to any new location in space above the table free of any constraints (Figure 7). The intersection of both fingers and thumb represent the origin point (0, 0, 0) with the 2D plane 'x,y' positive coordinates represented by your index finger and thumb respectively. It is this ability to locate the UCS in any degree of freedom in space that holds the key to your success. The remaining subcommand options of the UCS command help to achieve this goal.

Figure 7

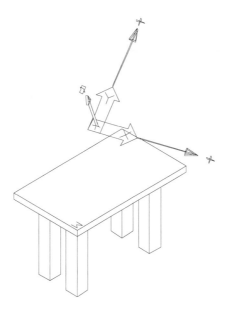

2. Option ZA ('Z' axis)

Consider placing a goblet on the horizontal surface. If the goblet is to be drawn as shown in Figure 8, consideration must be given to the correct orientation of the goblet during its construction. It is most likely that a 2D plane ('x,y') will be used to construct the profile of the goblet, followed by the surface model or solid model commands to generate the object. If the orientation of the 'Z' axis is ignored then the goblet will spill its contents when viewed in a direction similar to the viewpoint 1,1,1 (as many students of CAD have experienced).

Figure 8

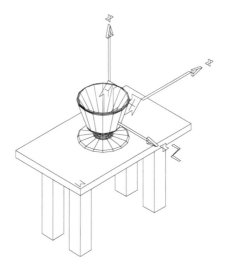

There are two solutions to the problem. Solution 1 involves the use of the subcommand ZA (this defines the 'Z' axis – do not confuse this process with rotation about the 'Z' axis, i.e. subcommand Z). Look at the 'Z' axis in Figure 8 and, once more using your right hand configuration, place your hand in the correct orientation in the horizontal surface (with the 'Z' axis facing your body). Now (with extreme pain) move your hand to represent the screen configuration by moving the wrist 90° towards your body. Notice that the new 'Z' axis is represented by the current 'Y' axis.

3. Option X ('X' axis rotation)

Figure 9

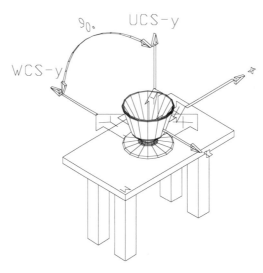

This is solution 2 to the above problem. Notice the 90° relationship between the WCS-'Y' axis and the desired 'Y' axis to construct the goblet (Figure 9). The second method of rotating the UCS about the 'X' axis is probably the easier (and less painful). The direction of rotation coincides with the direction of the remaining two fingers of your right hand. The direction of rotation is anti-clockwise when looking down the positive axis of rotation. (**Note**: If clockwise rotation is required, enter a negative angle.)

The rotated 'x,y' plane becomes the plane of the front elevation (orthographic projection) and is an important consideration when using standard graphic icons to create different orthographic views. (You cannot use standard graphic icons to create a side or end elevation from an orthographic plan view.)

4. Option 3 (3 point)

Randomly place an object on the table, as in Figure 10. If we wished to enter text on the side of the box shown, it would be necessary to locate the UCS on this face in preparation for this 2D command. A suitable subcommand in this case would be the 3POINT option entered in the following order:

```
ORIGIN: INT OF A (bottom left-hand corner of box)
X AXIS: END OF B
Y AXIS: END OF C
```

Figure 10

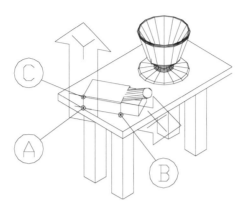

5. Option Y ('Y' axis rotation)

Rotate the UCS 90° about the 'Y' axis (see Figure 11). With your right hand in the agreed configuration, close the palm of your left hand around the index finger of your right hand to create a bearing (clearance fit) and rotate your right wrist 90°. If it doesn't hurt then you are rotating in the wrong direction.

Figure 11

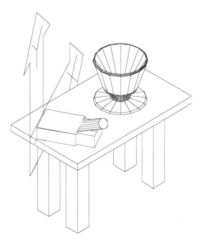

6. Option Z ('Z' axis rotation)

Rotate the UCS 45° about the 'Z' axis (see Figure 12) using both hands as in (5) above (this should be less painful). Note that option ZA defines the 'Z' axis; option Z rotates the 'Z' axis.

Figure 12

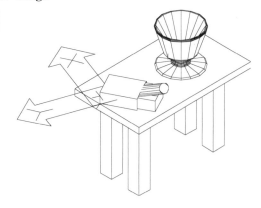

7. Option OB or E (object or entity)

This is a very useful subcommand which prompts you to select the desired object (or entity) for the UCS location. You may also find this subcommand useful when error messages on the screen inform you of reasons for terminating certain commands. Figure 13 shows the object circle selected.

The centre of the circle becomes the new UCS origin with the 'X' axis passing through the selected point, the positive 'Z' axis or 'extrusion' direction is the same as the selected circle. Not all objects can be selected in this way for locating the UCS (e.g. region, spline, 3D polyline etc).

Figure 13

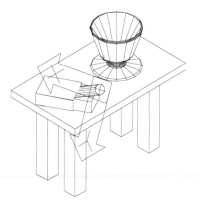

8. Option V (view)

This UCS option is required when the 'Z' axis is to coincide with the direction of view, very often the case when you wish to add text such as 'FINISHED' to the view, as in Figure 14. (The UCS origin remains the same.)

Relax your right hand (before rigor mortis takes over). This short exposition covers all the options you need in order to locate the UCSICON in any 'x,y' plane in space.

Figure 14

AutoCAD offers a dialogue box selection of a number of basic preset UCS orientations such as the previous VIEW subcommand (Command: DPUCSP). However, as this method is confusing to beginners in 3D design, if the current UCS is not in the WCS, resist this temptation for the moment.

In general, if entities or objects exist (in your drawing) then use the subcommands OBJECT or 3POINT to change the location of the UCS. When no predefined entity or object exists, use the subcommands to rotate the UCS about the 'X', 'Y' or 'Z' axis. If the start- and end-points of the 'Z' axis are known, use the ZA subcommand.

The following exercises will help to reinforce your use of UCS movement. Remember to use your right hand as a visual aid when learning to construct 3D designs. Figure 15 shows details of the microscope monocular head which will be used to illustrate Exercises 1 to 4 before being incorporated into the design project of Part Three.

Figure 15

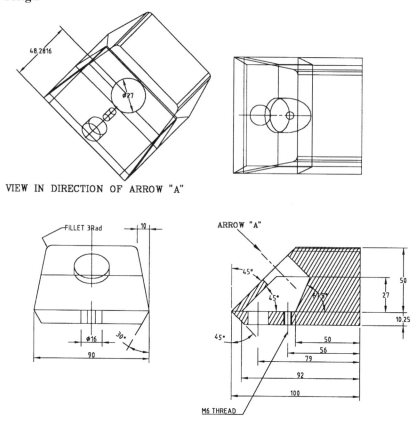

VIEW IN DIRECTION OF ARROW "A"

Exercise 1
Simple wire frame construction

On completion of this exercise the reader shall be able to:

- Set the user coordinate system in 3D space using the eight standard subcommands.
- Demonstrate spatial concepts by means of wire frame construction.
- Manipulate the UCSICON by means of wire frame construction.
- Manipulate by means of vectors and save 3D views.
- Create and restore previously named views and UCSs.
- State the first four rules of 3D design.
- Apply point selection in space.
- Change properties in the 'Z' axis.
- Use the PLAN command to display views of the current UCS.

A wire-frame model is a skeletal description of a 3D object consisting of vectors or lines describing the edges of an object, very similar to the way that we construct objects when making drawings with a pencil. The wire frame model is created by locating these lines anywhere in space by specifying the 'x', 'y' and 'z' coordinates of the start and end-points of each different line.

Because a wire frame model does not respond to the HIDE or SHADE command its use is often restricted to that of construction lines. However, wire frame drawings are very useful for 3D electrical wiring diagrams. Does Figure 16 convey a 2D hexagon or a 3D cube?

You can create wire frame models by locating any 2D planar object in space using several different methods:

- **Method 1** – Entering points by defining the coordinate values for 'x', 'y' and 'z'. (3D cartesian coordinates), e.g. 'P1/P2' in Figure 17.
- **Method 2** – Positioning the UCS in the appropriate 2D plane in space, e.g. 'P1' in Figure 17.
- **Method 3** – Creating the object in the WCS (x1,y1,0/x2,y2,0) and moving (or 3D rotate) the object to its correct location in space when complete.

For this exercise we will use the problem set in my earlier Longman publication *A Practical Guide to AutoCAD AutoLISP* to construct a microscope

Figure 16

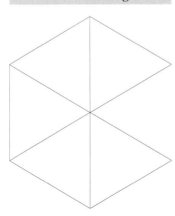

monocular head (see Appendix A at the end of this book). Instead of using the 3DMESH command within an AutoLISP routine, we will build the model in stages from a wire frame (this exercise) to a surface model (3DFACE, Exercise 2) and use this model to illustrate the UCS and VIEW commands.

Figure 17

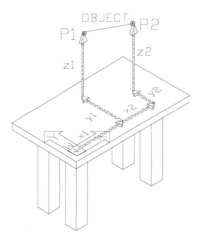

In this exercise we are going to construct the wire frame model shown in Figure 18, incorporating the three different methods (described below) of locating 2D planar objects in space.

Figure 18   **Figure 19**

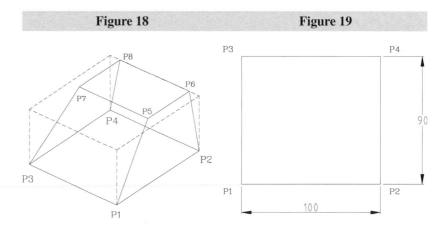

■ **Method 1** – Open a new drawing and create a new layer called CONS (short for 'construction'). Make this layer current.

With the UCS in the WCS, draw the rectangle 'P1/P2/P3/P4' of Figure 19 using the LINE or PLINE command to the values given. (Select 'P1' as the start-point anywhere on the screen.)
Move the UCS by entering:

COMMAND: UCS

Prompt Origin/ZAxis/3point/OBject/View/X/Y/Z/Prev/
Restore/Save/Del/?/<World>: *enter* O *for Origin*
origin point: *enter* INT *and select 'P2'*

If the ICON does not move to the new origin enter:

COMMAND: UCSICON

Prompt ON/OFF/All/NOORIGIN/ORigin<Current>: *enter* OR *to
move the icon to its new origin*

Notice that the coordinates at 'P2' are 0,0,0.

■ **Method 2** – We are going to position the UCS in the appropriate 2D plane to construct the rectangle 'P5/P6/P7/P8' (Figure 20).

COMMAND: UCS

(Same prompt): *enter* O *for Origin*
origin point: *enter* 0,10,50

This will move the UCS to point 'P6' in space (slightly similar to the ELEVATION command). Using the LINE or PLINE command, draw the rectangle 'P5/P6/P7/P8' to the dimensions given. (See Part Two for further details.)

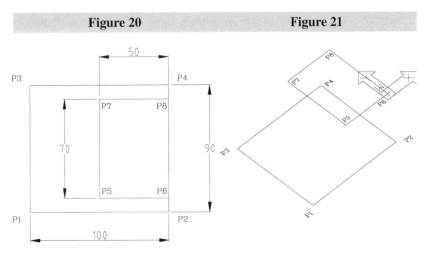

Figure 20	Figure 21

■ **Method 3** – We could have drawn rectangle 'P5/P6/P7/P8' in the previous UCS setting or even in the WCS using the MOVE command to place the rectangle in its correct location in space (Figure 21).

In order to obtain a 3D view of our current progress, the command VPOINT will give a 3D visualisation of the drawing from any specified point in space. There are three different methods of achieving this result, but for beginners in 3D design it is important to restrict the choice to keyboard input, using your right hand to predetermine the outcome, giving vector manipulation rather than graphical means of viewing models, reserving such activities for section two.

COMMAND: VPOINT
Prompt Rotate/<Viewpoint> <Current>: *enter* -1,-1,1

Using your right hand in a configuration coinciding with the current UCS, imagine a point created by the following coordinates: one unit movement in the opposite direction to your thumb; one unit movement in the opposite direction to your index finger; and one unit movement in the direction of your second finger. From this imaginary point, look in the directions of the UCS origin (intersection of both fingers and thumb). Relate this view to the view on the screen.

Experiment with different values for the VPOINT command using your right hand to predetermine the expected view before entering the command. Finally, return to the viewpoint –1,–1,1.

You do not have to keep entering viewpoint coordinates as it is possible to save particular views by naming them and restoring the view when required.

It is important to understand the difference between a view and a UCS, as experience has shown this to be a source of confusion with some students of 3D design.

Both views and UCSs can be saved and restored at any time in the drawing editor, and doing so is a basic requirement when developing a 3D model. There are usually more UCS locations than views in the finished model. You are therefore advised to use numbers as the name of views, such as 1, 2, 3 and short descriptive names for the different UCS locations when entering commands from the keyboard. For example:

COMMAND: UCS
(*Prompt as before*): *enter* S *for Save*
Prompt name: *enter* TOP
COMMAND: VIEW
Prompt ?/Delete/Restore/Save/Window: *enter* S *for Save*
View name to save: *enter* 1
COMMAND: UCS

Press the 'Enter' twice to restore the UCS to the world position (or datum).

COMMAND: PLAN

The PLAN command provides a convenient means of viewing the drawing down the positive 'Z' axis and is the same as the command VPOINT 0,0,1 (use your right hand as a visual aid).

Prompt <Current UCS>UCS/World: *accept the default setting by pressing 'Enter'*

The system variable UCSFOLLOW can be set to generate a plan view whenever you change from one UCS to another. This feature is best suited to multiple viewpoints, as you will see later on.

COMMAND: VIEW

Restore the screen view to number 1. Notice that the changed UCS location does not in any way affect the saved view. This view will remain in the same direction. It is not the view in terms of vectors that has been saved; it is not the view related to the UCS that has been saved. It is the *direction of the view in relation to the object* that has been saved.

COMMAND: UCS

Restore the UCS to TOP. Use the LINE command to complete the model by constructing lines between the end-points (END) of 'P1/P5', 'P2/P6', 'P3/P7', and 'P4/P8' (Figure 22). This is where 'free-hand sketching' comes into its own in 3D design and introduces the first rule of 3D.

Figure 22

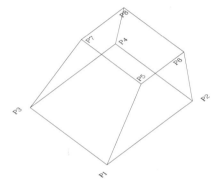

Rule 1

Always construct objects in the desired 2D plane by looking directly down the positive 'Z' axis, unless objects already exist to assist the *exact* location in a 3D view.

Let us confirm Rule 1 by erasing line 'P1/P5' in Figure 22 and drawing a new line from 'P1' to 'P5', judging by eye (without any snap points) the start- and end-points (i.e. free-hand sketching). When complete, change the viewpoint to note the error in line 'P1/P5'. Restore the view to 1 and correct the line 'P1/P5' by using the OSNAP (Object SNAP) tools.

COMMAND: HIDE

This will regenerate a 3D drawing with hidden lines (faces and solids) suppressed (see Figure 23). Notice that the model has not changed. This is because you have drawn a 'wire frame' model. (Save this drawing for use in Exercise 2.)

Figure 23

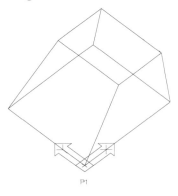

Move the UCSICON to 'P1' using the ORIGIN subcommand. We will now use this wire frame model to reinforce the use of UCS movement subcommands.

UCS manipulation

Experiment with the following procedures:

```
COMMAND: UCS
    Prompt: enter X to rotate about the 'X' axis
          : enter 90
```

This will rotate the UCS 90° anticlockwise about the 'X' axis when looking down the positive 'X' axis, i.e. in the direction of the third and fourth fingers of your right hand when held in a manner explained previously. (See Figure 24.)

Figure 24   **Figure 25**

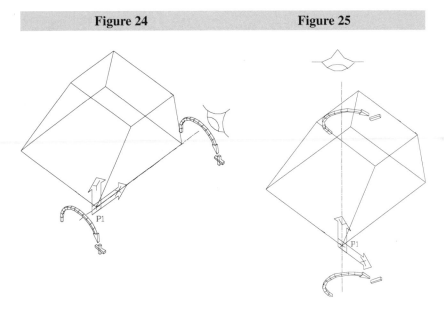

```
COMMAND: UCS
    Prompt: enter Y to rotate about the 'Y' axis
        : -90
```

This will rotate the UCS 90° clockwise about the 'Y' axis when looking down the positive 'Y' axis (Figure 25).

```
COMMAND: UCS
    Prompt: enter P for Previous
```

Note the result and enter 'U' for Undo to reverse the last operation.

```
COMMAND: UCS
    Prompt: enter Z to rotate about the 'Z' axis
        : enter 45
```

This will rotate the UCS 45° anti-clockwise about the 'Z' axis when looking down the positive 'Z' axis (Figure 26).

```
            COMMAND: UCS
                Prompt: enter 3 to select three points
origin point <0,0,0>: enter INT for Intersection
                    of: select 'A'
        Positive X axis: END
                    of: select 'B'
    Positive Y portion: NEA for Nearest
                    of: select 'C'
```

This is illustrated in Figure 27.

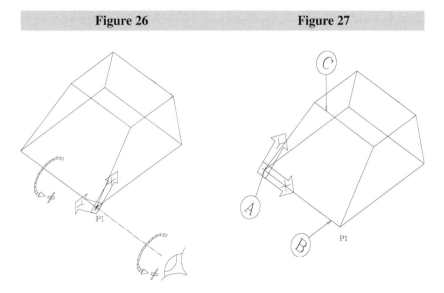

Figure 26   **Figure 27**

This will create the 2D 'x,y' plane on the front face of the monocular head in preparation for the 2D command CIRCLE which is required to have its centre point in the middle of the front face. Create a new layer called FACE.

On layer CONS draw a construction line between the mid-points (MID) of the two parallel lines on the front face to help locate the centre of the circle (Figure 28). We will use point filters in Exercise 2.

Figure 28

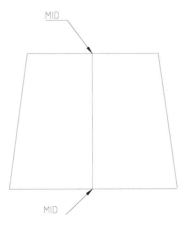

Rule 2
Always use a special layer for construction purposes.

Make layer FACE the current layer and use the PLAN command with the current UCS.

COMMAND: CIRCLE
Prompt centre point: *enter* MID *for Mid-point*
                    of: *select the construction line*
    <Radius>: 15

The result is illustrated in Figure 29.

Figure 29

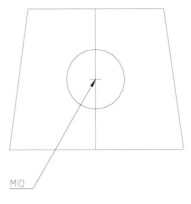

> **Rule 3**
>
> Make sure that there is no overriding OBJECT SNAP mode active when
> selecting objects or entities.

Failure to observe the above rule has been the cause of many mysterious
results with students of 3D design.

COMMAND: UCS
    Prompt: *enter* OB *for Object (or* E *for Entity)*
        : *select the CIRCLE*

Note that the centre of the circle becomes the new UCS origin with the 'X' axis
passing through the point you selected on the circle (Figure 30). The new UCS
has the same positive 'Z' axis as the selected object.

Note also that the 2D object is extruded along the positive 'Z' axis, normal
to the inclined face (Figure 31).

Figure 30

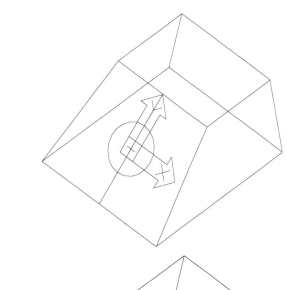

Figure 31

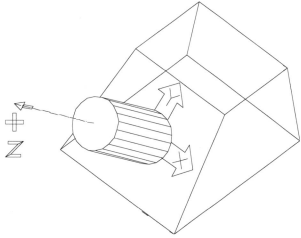

```
COMMAND: HIDE or SHADE

COMMAND: UCS
    Prompt: enter S for Save
      name: FRONT
```

Rule 4

Remember as you build up 3D models to save by number useful views and by name UCSs.

```
COMMAND: VIEW
      Prompt: enter R for Restore
        name: 1

COMMAND: CHPROP
Prompt Select objects: select the circle or enter L for Last
Change what property: enter T for Thickness
    new thickness <0>: enter 60
```

UCS problem with solution

Consider the problem of producing a cylinder similar to the extrudal circle when the 'Z' axis is known but the 'x,y' plane does not exist on the model.

To make this into a practical problem, consider a drilled hole parallel to the inclined face (see Figure 32).

Figure 32

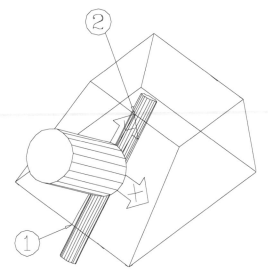

```
COMMAND: UCS
    Prompt: ZAxis
origin point:
```
select the end of the construction line at '1'
```
point on positive Z axis:
```
select the end of the construction line at '2'

This will place the UCS 'Z' axis normal to the required 'x,y' plane to enable 2D objects such as the CIRCLE command to be used for the drilled hole. What other method of UCS movement could we have used to achieve the same result?

Tasks

1. Construct a cylinder to represent a dowel placed parallel to and some distance from the inclined front face.
2. Using the UCS VIEW option, enter your name on the drawing.
3. Freeze layer CONS and hide (or shade) the drawing. (You should have two cylinders and your name displayed.)
4. Does the cylinder look like a polygon?
5. Move the UCS 'x,y' plane to coincide with the plane created by 'P1/P2/P5/P6'.

Exercise 2
Simple surface model construction

On completion of this exercise the reader shall be able to:

- Define edges and surfaces in 3D space using the SOLID, 3DFACE, REVSURF and RULESURF commands.
- Use the system variable THICKNESS to give an extrusion thickness to a 2D object.
- Specify multiple faces within the 3DFACE command loop.
- Use point filters to locate points in 3D space.
- Perform hidden line removal on a 3D view (including text).
- Use 2D objects on different user coordinate planes to produce 3D objects.
- State a further seven basic rules of 3D design.
- Demonstrate the use of the system variables SURFTAB1 and SURFTAB2.
- Control the use of invisible lines within the 3DFACE command.
- Define and use a region.
- Use the SUBTRACT command.
- Use the SHADE command.
- Perform calculations within a command loop and use the CAL command.
- Use the AREA and MASSPROP commands.
- Use AutoLISP functions to define points.
- Create a WBLOCK in 3D space by writing a block to a drawing file.

Figure 33

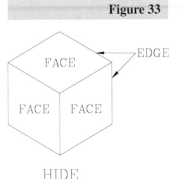

Surface modelling is more sophisticated than wire frame modelling in that it defines both the edges and surfaces of 3D objects in space (Figure 33). These faceted surfaces will respond to the HIDE command and can be edited by specific software to create smooth colour-rendered photo-realistic images of very complex surface designs. For faceted surfaces think of a polished diamond, for smooth surfaces think of a modern car body.

The command SOLID is a strange command to start an exercise in surface modelling in that the name implies a solid but the command is used to create surfaces. The area created by the SOLID command is only filled when the FILLMODE system variable is set to ON and the view is set to PLAN (looking down the 'Z' axis). However, the area is filled with the SHADE command irrespective of the FILLMODE value.

Surface model construction

Open a new drawing using the drawing saved in Exercise 1 as the prototype (or TEMPLATE from Release 14). Create a new layer called FACES (make use of colour), and make the CONS layer current. At the command prompt enter:

```
COMMAND: FILLMODE
       : OFF
COMMAND: UCS
       : WCS
```

Using the SOLID command (with filters)

```
              COMMAND: ELEV
Prompt new elevation: 0 (zero)
      new thickness: enter 10.25    the thickness sets the
                                    distance of extrusion above or below the
                                    elevation
              COMMAND: SOLID
```

The results are shown in Figure 34.

Figure 34

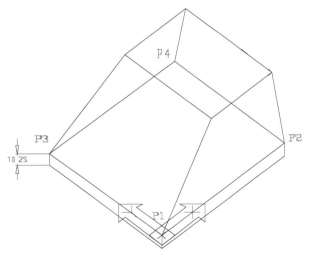

When you create quadrilateral shapes the sequence of the third and fourth points determines the resultant shape. If you select points in a clockwise or anticlockwise direction the result will be a 'bow tie' shape and not a rectangle as we require (Figures 35 and 36).

To work out the order of selection, build your shape in a series of triangles such as triangle 'P1/P2/P3' and triangle 'P2/P3/P4', resulting in the following order 'P1/P2/P3/P4'. In this way very complex filled shapes ('multiple connected triangles') can be created. Use the SOLID command within an AutoLISP macro

Figure 35	Figure 36

ORDER OF SELECTION
P1/P2/P4/P5

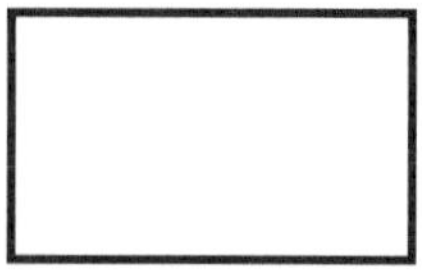

ORDER OF SELECTION
P1/P2/P3/P4

to solve complex 2D shapes to fill areas of colour, such as company logos and the British Standard pipe symbol. We continue as follows:

Prompt first point: *enter* .XY *(don't forget the dot)*
            .xy of: *select the intersection ('INT') of 'P1'*
    needs a Z value: -10.25
        second point: @ 100,0

You do not need to specify a 'z' value for the remaining points as the solid is constructed parallel to the current UCS (or WCS), in our case the 'x,y' plane located by 'P1'.

    third point: *select the intersection of 'P3'*
  fourth point: @ 100,0
    third point: *press 'Enter'*
        COMMAND: HIDE *or* SHADE

Notice the faces created on the sides, top and bottom (needs a new viewpoint to confirm the bottom surface).

Rule 5

When a beginner to 3D design and starting a new drawing, try to create a wire frame box or CRATE with the 2D 'x,y' plane in the WCS as your first drawing command. (Save this as a 3D view.)

Rule 5 is helpful in viewing the movement of the UCS (from its WCS location) in terms of some concrete object as the model is being constructed and viewed in '3D'. Experience will tell you when to dispense with this practice.

As we already have a wire frame model created in Exercise 1, erase the solid box.

Using the 3DFACE command (single and combined planes)

We are going to use the 3DFACE command to create a surface model of the monocular head. This command creates a three- or four-sided opaque surface anywhere in space. The 3DFACE command does not give an extruded thickness and ignores any current thickness settings. Unlike the SOLID command, these points must be entered in a clockwise or anticlockwise direction. The 3DFACE command will cover up any entity or object that lies under it, giving the same appearance as the SOLID command.

COMMAND: 3DFACE
      : *creates a 3D triangular or quadrilateral plane section*
Prompt first point: *select 'P1' using 'INT' (intersection) or 'END' (end of)*
second point: *select 'P5' using 'INT' or 'END'*
third point: *select 'P7' using 'INT' or 'END'*
fourth point: *select 'P3' using 'INT' or 'END'*
third point: *press 'Enter' to disengage the command loop*

COMMAND: CHPROP
Prompt Select object: *select the 3D face from layer CONS to FACES*

The result is shown in Figure 37.

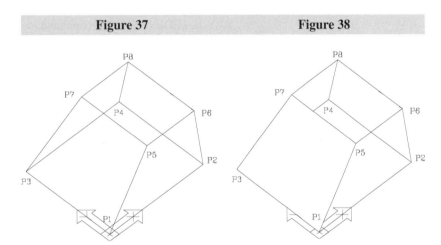

Figure 37   **Figure 38**

This technique of creating a face in the CONS layer and moving the face to another layer helps with the selection of coinciding lines and faces. By freezing the layer containing the faces until the model is complete, the wire frame model can be selected without the interference of faces occupying the same space.

Finally, use the Hide command to obtain the view shown in Figure 38.

With the 3DFACE command, AutoCAD repeats the third and fourth point prompts enabling you to specify multiple adjacent faces within the command loop, instead of restricting the command to a single face as we did previously.

COMMAND: 3DFACE
Prompt first point: *select 'P1' (using the OSNAP tools as above).*

Figure 39

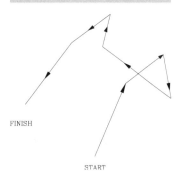

FINISH

START

<raw>*If you have not frozen layer FACES you will*
experience the above selection problem</raw>

```
  second point:
```
select 'P5'
```
   third point:
```
select 'P6'
```
 fourth point:
```
select 'P2'
```
   third point:
```
select 'P4'
```
 fourth point:
```
select 'P8'
```
   third point:
```
select 'P7'
```
 fourth point:
```
select 'P3'
```
   third point:
```
Press 'Enter' to break the loop

Notice in Figure 39 how the four points or corners of each quadrilateral face is selected in either clockwise or anticlockwise direction:

Face 1 = P1/P5/P6/P2
Face 2 = P6/P2/P4/P8
Face 3 = P4/P8/P7/P3

This method is much quicker than creating individual faces, one at a time, but can only be used when there is a common or connecting edge between two faces.

Use the HIDE or SHADE command to confirm your results.

We now need the UCS placing in the middle of the front inclined face (Figure 40). Unfortunately we saved this UCS (FRONT) in Exercise 1 but only after we had saved the drawing. This was deliberate as I now wish to introduce another rule.

Figure 40

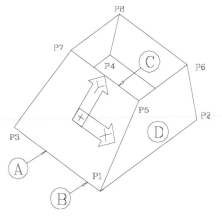

Rule 6

Make full use of point filters to locate points relative to existing objects. (Release 14 'Tracking' system will help in this respect.)

Point filter location

For a better view, zoom into the inclined front face. At the command prompt enter:

```
COMMAND: UCS
    Prompt: enter 3 for three points.
```

As a change to Exercise 1, enter MID at 'A', END at 'B' and NEA at 'C'. This sets the UCS 'x,y' plane in the same plane as the front face.

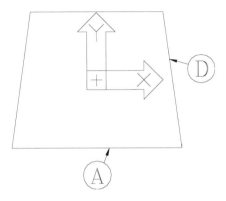

Figure 41

To move the UCS to the middle of the front face by means of point filters enter:

```
COMMAND: UCS
    Prompt: O for Origin
          : enter .X
     .X of: MID
    MID of: select line 'A'
 needs YZ: enter .Y
     .Y of: MID
    MID of: select line 'D'
 needs Z: enter 0 (zero)
COMMAND: UCS
    Prompt: S for Save
      name: FRONT (learn by experience)
```

Using the rulesurf command

We are now going to create a truncated cone as a polygon mesh, normal to the front face using the RULESURF command. This command creates a ruled surface between any two entities or objects such as points, lines, polylines, circles or arcs. (**Note**: All surfaces that are generated by straight lines are ruled surfaces.)

> **Rule 7**
>
> When using the RULESURF command, if one of the two objects used as a
> boundary is closed, then the other boundary must be closed. (Select open
> boundaries at the same ends.)

According to Rule 7, Figure 42 is correct because both the two objects used
as a boundary are closed (CIRCLE). Figure 43, however, is wrong because one
of the selected boundaries is open and the other closed. Solve the problem by
breaking the circle at two quadrant points into two connecting arcs.

When selecting the two edges within the RULESURF command, pick points
at corresponding ends of the objects for normal ruled surfaces if you wish to
avoid cross-line ruled faces.

Figure 42	Figure 43

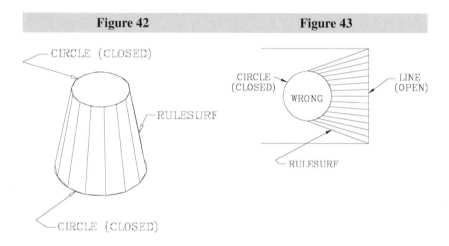

To create a truncated cone on the front face of the monocular head we need
to locate two circles in space.

One method would be to construct two concentric circles on the front face
and with the MOVE command move the inner circle along the positive 'Z' axis.
However, as an exercise in point filters, enter the following:

```
               COMMAND: CIRCLE
   Prompt centre point: enter 0,0
            <Radius>: 16.5
               COMMAND: CIRCLE
   Prompt centre point: enter .XY (don't forget
                        the dot)
              .XY of: CEN for Centre
              CEN of: select the existing
                        circle
             needs Z: 50
            <Radius>: 14
```

COMMAND: RULESURF
Prompt Select first defining curve: *select the large circle*
Select second defining curve: *select the smaller circle*

The result is shown in Figure 44.

Figure 44

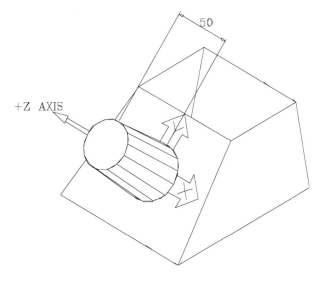

+Z AXIS

50

Mesh density

You can control the number of lines or surfaces in the polygon mesh by the system variable SURFTAB1. SURFTAB1 determines the mesh density in the 'M' direction (all mesh commands). SURFTAB2 determines the mesh density in the 'N' direction such as REVSURF and EDGESURF. Enter:

COMMAND: HIDE

Note the problem with HIDE at the interface between the bottom of the cone and the front face. When objects are drawn as if occupying the same space (no two objects can actually occupy the same space) such as touching or intersecting objects, problems may occur with the HIDE command.

Rule 8
Avoid objects occupying the same space.

To avoid the above problem, move the truncated cylinder a small amount (0.001) in the positive 'z' direction. (Move one object relative to another by a small amount.)

COMMAND: HIDE *to confirm the results*
COMMAND: CHPROP *to move the polygon mesh to the layer FACES*

If you feel the need to alter the SURFTAB1 value, you will need to erase the polygon mesh using the ERASE command and repeat the RULESURF command. (A regeneration does not alter the SURFTAB1 value.) Remember, there is a price to pay for increasing this system variable in terms of time and storage.

The four basic surface-generating commands are illustrated in Figure 45. They are:

RULESURF   TABSURF   REVSURF   EDGESURF

Figure 45

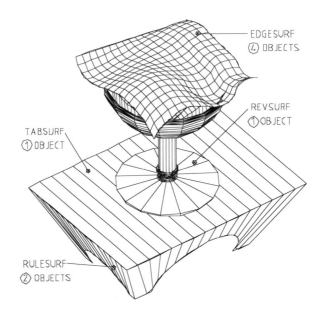

4 BASIC SURFACE GENERATING COMMANDS

a| RULED SURFACES
b| TABULATED SURFACES
c| SURFACES of REVOLUTION AND
d| EDGE-DEFINED SURFACE PATCHES

Modelling surfaces with holes (visible/invisible edges)

You may have noticed that we did not create a 3D face on the top of the monocular head. That was because this face needs a hole in the surface (Figure 46) and requires a slightly different process.

Because the 3DFACE command operates as three- or four-sided figures, certain lines need to be invisible in our model as we combine these faces to model the top surface.

Figure 46

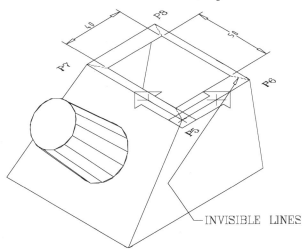

INVISIBLE LINES

Figure 47

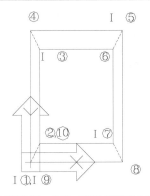

ORDER OF SELECTION

- Restore the UCS called TOP and move its origin to 'P5', or
- Return to WCS and move its origin to 'P5'.

Using the 3DFACE command, select the points in the order shown in Figure 47 from 1 to 10. When an 'I' (for Invisible) appears before a number, it indicates the start-point of a line that is invisible. You will see from Figure 47 that the combined faces consist of four four-sided surfaces:

Surface No. 1 = 1, 2, 3, 4
Surface No. 2 = 3, 4, 5, 6
Surface No. 3 = 5, 6, 7, 8
Surface No. 4 = 7, 8, 9, 10

```
          COMMAND: 3DFACE
Prompt first point: enter I for Invisible
       first point: 0,0 (or select the intersection of 'P5')
      second point: 5,10
       third point: I
       third point: 5,60
      fourth point: 0,70 (or select the intersection of 'P7')
       third point: I
       third point: 50,70 (or select the intersection of 'P8')
      fourth point: 45,60
       third point: I
       third point: 45,10
      fourth point: 50,0 (or select the intersection of 'P6')
       third point: I
       third point: 0,0 (or select the intersection of 'P5')
      fourth point: 5,10
       third point: press 'Enter' to close the loop
          COMMAND: HIDE or SHADE
```

If, when using the 3DFACE command, you fail to define certain invisible edges, it is not as great a problem as it used to be when you had to load an AutoLISP macro (HEDGE). Use the EDGE command to change the visibility of selected 3D face edges or to highlight invisible edges. Alternatively, use the DDMODIFY command by selecting the face to modify, responding to the 3D face dialogue box options for edge visibility.

The system variable SPLFRAME turns on or off the display of invisible edges. It is often useful to have the edges of 3D face visible for 'picking' whilst constructing the model: you need to be able to see the edges of a 3D face in order to select it for such commands as STRETCH, COPY, MIRROR. Return to a SPLFRAME value of zero when all 3DFACE editing is complete.

Using the REGION command

If you found this method of constructing faces with holes in them a little tedious and have at least Release 12 of AutoCAD, then consider creating 'regions'.

A region is a bounded planar object that may or may not contain holes. Regions will respond to Boolean operations as well as hatching, shading and mass property computations. Regions are created from geometry forming a closed loop. (This is only a first look at the REGION command: there is more to follow.)

Figure 48

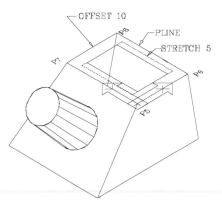

Now, with reference to Figure 48, enter:

COMMAND: ERASE
Prompt Select: *select the top face created by the 3DFACE command or enter* L *for Last*
COMMAND: PLINE
       : *create a closed polyline of rectangle 'P5/P6/P7/P8'*

COMMAND: OFFSET
Prompt offset distance: *enter* 10
Select object to offset: *select the polyline*
: *select the inside of the polyline*
COMMAND: STRETCH
: *select part of the inner rectangle to*
stretch 5 mm in the '+x' and '–x'
directions
COMMAND: REGION
Prompt Select objects: *select rectangle 'P5/P6/P7/P8'*

repeat the REGION command for the inner rectangle.

A first look at Boolean operations

Figure 49

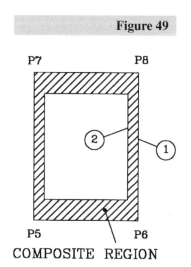

COMPOSITE REGION

We are now going to create a composite region by subtracting one rectangle from the other by using the SUBTRACT command. This command creates composite regions by subtracting one face (or solid as you will see in Exercise 3) from another (Figure 49). The term 'face' refers to a solid of zero thickness.

COMMAND: SUBTRACT
Prompt Select objects: *select PLINE '1' and press 'Enter'*
Select objects: *select PLINE '2'*

When using the SUBTRACT command the object to subtract '2' can partly overlap the object to subtract from '1' and is not restricted to the above example. REGION objects are rigid bodies and cannot be stretched.

COMMAND: HIDE *or* SHADE

This gives the same result as the more complicated 3DFACE command.

In order to encourage exact or perfect graphical constructions, all sources of error (like 'free-hand sketching') should be avoided if possible. One source of error is the possibility of making mistakes when performing calculations.

> **Rule 9**
>
> Let the computer perform any necessary calculations.

A simple example of the above rule would be the avoidance of calculating a radius value when only the value of the circle diameter is known. Use 'D' to change the default value from <radius> to diameter. Alternatively, enter the diameter value divided by two such as 25.176/2 for a diameter of 25.176. You can also use this method when prompted for 'x,y' coordinates such as 41.63/3, 2.43*1.621 (see *A Practical Guide to AutoCAD AutoLISP* for direct keyboard calculations in AutoLISP).

Further explanations of Boolean operations are given on page 63.

Using the CAL command

A more recent solution to the problems of calculations is to use the CAL command. This is a built-in calculator that evaluates expressions. The expressions can access existing points by means of the CEN, END and INT object snap functions within the transparent calculator (`CAL). This helps to simplify the determination of points when mathematical or geometrical evaluations are required. It is also possible to integrate AutoLISP variables into the arithmetic expressions.

Use these expressions in commands that expect 'points', 'vectors' or 'numbers'. If this is beginning to sound complicated, let's put it into practice with our surface model.

Figure 50

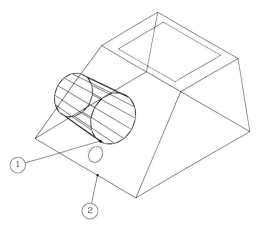

We require a circle midway between the bottom of the large circle and line 2 (Figure 50), having a diameter 1/4.5 of the large circle:

```
       COMMAND: UCS
         Prompt: restore to FRONT
       COMMAND: CIRCLE
Prompt centre point: `CAL
      expression: (QUA+MID)/2
      Select QUA : pick lower part of circle shown as '1'
      Select MID: pick the lower line shown as '2'
        <Radius>: `CAL
      expression: 1/4.5*RAD
   Select circle: select circle shown as '1'
```

Test to see if this new relationship between the two circles is associative by moving the large circle with the MOVE command or GRIPS. Remember to return the circle to the original location.

Use the TEXT command to place the letter 'T' in the centre of this new circle and, by using a VPOINT of 1,0,0, hide the drawing with the HIDE command to see if the text is hidden.

Rule 10
When attaching text to 3D objects, give the text a thickness otherwise the text will not hide.

AutoCAD as a calculator (using AutoLISP variables)

'Back to maths' – we are going to locate points 'P9' to 'P12' in Figure 51 to illustrate further use of AutoCAD as a calculator.

Figure 51

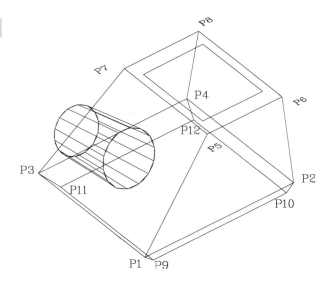

First, return to the WCS. In Figure 52,

Length $A = \dfrac{10.25}{\sqrt{3}}$

Figure 52

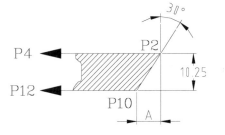

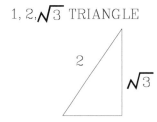

The calculation proceeds as follows:

> COMMAND: CAL
> *Prompt* expression: *enter* A = 10.25/SQRT(3)
> : *shows the answer*

This now is the value held by variable 'A'. Test this value by entering:

> COMMAND: !A

This should give the same answer (5.91784).

Assigning values to AutoLISP variables can also be achieved with the aid of the CAL command. A variable name such as 'P5' precedes the arithmetic expression followed by the equals sign such as 'P5='.Once this variable has been established, it becomes available throughout the drawing editor for further calculations as long as it is not redefined.

We have already defined the value of variable 'A' and will make use of this in our next expression as we defined the point 'P10'(see Figure 53). Remember that the values of these variables and points are relative to a particular UCS.

Figure 53

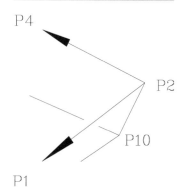

P4

P2

P10

P1

> COMMAND: CAL
> *Prompt* expression: P10=END+[0,A,-10.25] *(don't use spaces*
> *in the expression)*
> Select END of: *pick a point near the end of line 'P2'*
> *Variable 'P10' now contains the 'x,y,z'*
> *coordinates of the required location i.e. [0 in the*
> *'x' direction, 'A' in the 'y' direction, −10.25 in*
> *the 'z' direction] relative to 'P2' in the WCS*

Check this value by entering:

> COMMAND: !P10

Even though we can pick 'P2' from the screen, let us define it as a variable to draw the line 'P2/P10' using AutoLISP variables (Figure 54). The calculation goes as follows:

Figure 54

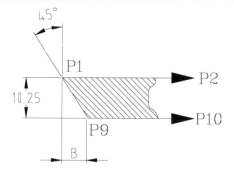

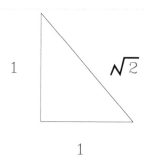

```
          COMMAND: CAL
Prompt expression: P2=END
   Select END of: pick a point near 'P2'
          COMMAND: LINE
Prompt from point: !P2
        to point: !P10
```

We know that length 'B'=10.25. Therefore:

```
          COMMAND: CAL
Prompt expression: B=10.25

          COMMAND: CAL
Prompt expression: P9=END+[10.25,A,-10.25] but it is
                   much easier to use P9=END+[B,A-B] (no
                   spaces)
       Select END: pick a point near the end of line 'P1'

          COMMAND: LINES
Prompt from point: !P10
        to point: !P9
        to point: END to save time
           END of: select near a 'P1'
```

The remaining points 'P11' and 'P12' can be determined as above to complete the wire frame (or construction lines). Those not wishing to continue with this calculation exercise can use the MIRROR command to complete the drawing.

To determine the distance between the AutoLISP variables 'P9' and 'P10' use:

```
          COMMAND: CAL
Prompt expression: DIST(P9,P10) this gives the answer which
                   can be checked with the LIST command
```

Remember that these points created by AutoLISP variables ('P9','P10', etc.) were defined in the WCS. Any changes in the UCS will change the location of these points for further use. (If you wish to use them again, return to the WCS).

Change the viewpoint to (−1,−1,0.4) and create a 3D face between:

Face: P1/P9/P10/P2
Face: P3/P11/P4/P12
Face: P2/P10/P12/P4

Using the 3DFACE command, try to complete the three faces within a single command loop; do not copy the order of selection from above. Those CAD users less confident with this command can create three faces using the 3DFACE command individually.

Using AutoLISP variables

To continue our exercise in AutoLISP variables, erase the truncated cone leaving only the large-diameter circle. We will now construct three arcs between 'P3' and 'P1' (Figure 55) *assuming all necessary values to be unknown*.

Figure 55

VPOINT −1,−1,0.4

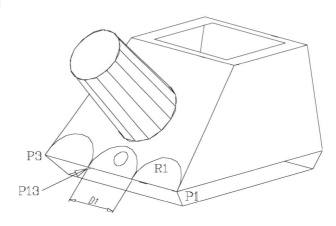

```
            COMMAND: CAL
Prompt expression: D1=DIST(END,END)/3
          Select END: pick near 'P1'
          Select END: pick near 'P3'

            COMMAND: CAL
Prompt expression: R1=D1/2

            COMMAND: UCS
                   : restore FRONT

            COMMAND: CAL
Prompt expression: P13=END+[D1,,]
                   : '[D1,,]' is the same as '[D1,0,0]'
          Select END: pick near 'P3'

            COMMAND: ARC
                   : use START, END, RADIUS option
Prompt start point: !P13
          end-point: END
            END of: pick near 'P3'
          <Radius>: !R1
                   : notice how we use the AutoLISP variables 'D1'
                     and 'R1' to determine the start-point and the
                     radius of the arc
```

```
COMMAND: ARRAY
       : use a rectangle array, 1
         row, 3 columns, with equal
         distance between the
         columns
```
Prompt `distance between columns: !D1`

We now need to rotate the middle arc of Figure 56 onto face 'P1/P9/P11/P3', as shown in Figure 57. The ROTATE command is a 2D command that rotates objects about the current 'Z' axis. The ROTATE3D command enables you to rotate objects anywhere in space once the rotation axis has been defined. To continue our exercise in the use of the UCS command, we will select the 2D option.

Figure 56	Figure 57

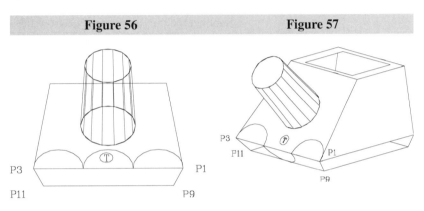

```
COMMAND: UCS
        Prompt: enter Y  to rotate about the 'Y' axis
rotation angle: 90 use your right hand configuration to confirm
                the positive axis of rotation
```

Figure 58 will remind you of the right hand rule.

Figure 58

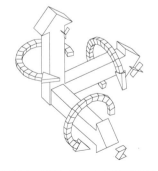

POSITIVE DIRECTIONS

```
          COMMAND: ROTATE
Prompt Select objects: select the middle arc
          base point: CEN
             CEN of: pick the middle arc
   <Rotation angle>: 270 once more use the right hand rule to
                     determine the positive axis rotation
```

It is possible to remove holes in a 3D face once that face has been defined as a region. The profiles of the holes should also be regions, and even circles need defining as a region before subtracting from the face. Remember that the selected regions must be coplanar.

If you try to create holes in faces created by the THICKNESS command (extruded in the 'z' direction) you will encounter the coplanar problem.

Putting the above into practice:

```
COMMAND: UCS
    Prompt: enter E or OB
          : select the rotated arc
COMMAND: LINE
          : create a line between the two end-points of the arc
COMMAND: PEDIT
          : enter L for Last and join this line to the arc
```

Create a 3D face between 'P1/P9/P11/P3' with the same UCS setting as the polyline arc, thus making sure that both objects are coplanar:

```
COMMAND: REGION
          : create a region of the polyline arc and repeat the command
            for the face 'P1/P9/P11/P3'
```

Subtract the polyline arc region from this new 3D face and used the SHADE command to confirm the results (see Figure 59).

Figure 59

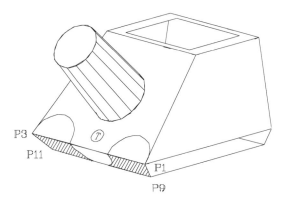

Using the AREA command

'Back to the maths' – Let us determine the area of the front face 'P1/P3/P7/P5' excluding the two circles (Figure 60).

Figure 60

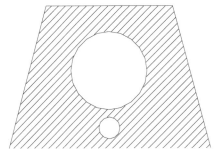

```
COMMAND: UCS
  Prompt: restore the UCS FRONT. It is good practice
          to place the UCS 2D plane in the same
          plane as the edited objects (often this is a
          necessity)
COMMAND: PLINE
        : make 'P1/P3/P7/P5' into a closed polyline
COMMAND: AREA
        : enter A for Add
  Prompt <First point>/Object/Add/Subtract
        : enter O for object
Select objects: select the front face
              : enter S for Subtract
Select objects: select the two circles
              : press 'Enter'
```

You will have noticed that the screen displays a running total as you subtract one area from another. You can define the area by specifying points or by selecting objects (as above) such as circles, ellipses, polylines, splines, regions and solids.

Intersection and centroid points

As a further exercise in maths we will now use AutoLISP to determine the intersection point ('P14' in Figure 61) and centroid ('P15') of the triangle constructed from the front face.

Figure 61

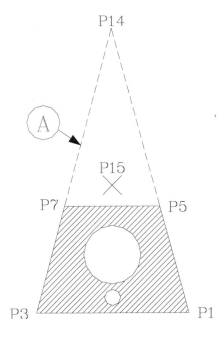

```
       COMMAND: CAL
```
Prompt `expression: P14=ILL(P1,P5,P3,P7)` *ILL is short for intersection of two lines. Problem: 'P1', 'P5', 'P3', 'P7' are not defined as AutoLISP variables*
       `SOLUTION:` *enter* `P14=ILLE(END,END,END,END)`
Prompt `Select END:` *select 'P1', 'P5', 'P3', 'P7'*
       `COMMAND: !P14` *to confirm the coordinate values*

The centroid of a triangle is (END,END,END)/3 when the end-points are the corners of the triangle.

```
       COMMAND: CAL
```
Prompt `expression: P15=(END+END+P14)/3`
       `END of:` *pick near 'P1' and 'P3'*

Set the POINT DISPLAY mode (PDMODE) to 3, or:

```
       COMMAND: DDTYPE
```
              `:` *specifies the display mode and size*
       `DIALOGUE BOX:` *pick the cross icon and set the size*

```
       COMMAND: POINT
```
Prompt `specify a point: !P15` *this will display the centroid of the triangle 'P1/P3/P14'*

```
       COMMAND: PLINE
```
              `:` *construct a polyline between 'P1', 'P3' and 'P14' and change this into a region*

Once the front face triangle is defined as a region we can use the MASSPROP command to determine (amongst other things) the centroid of the region. This centre of area is given as a 2D point when the current UCS is coplanar with the region, otherwise the centroid is defined as a 3D point.

Using the MASSPROP command

At the command prompt enter:

```
       COMMAND: MASSPROP
```
Prompt `Select objects:` *select the triangle 'A'*

Note the centroid value: it should be given as 'x,y' coordinates and should be exactly the same as 'P15' (to recall this value, enter !P15 at the command prompt). Do not write to file. We will return to this command in Exercise 3.

Component assembly

The monocular head now requires the eyepiece tube to be located normal to the front face. The lower part of the tube acts as a spigot location into the monocular head. In order to create a surface model of the eyepiece tube it is first necessary to created 2D polyline section of the tube (Figure 62) so as to rotate the section about the axis of rotation through 360° using the REVSURF command (Figure 63).

Figure 62

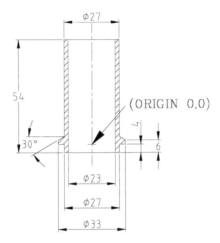

EYEPIECE TUBE

Figure 63

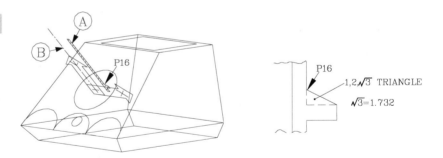

```
COMMAND: UCS
    Prompt: x
Rotation angle: 90

        COMMAND: PLAN (IF UCSFOLLOW=0)
                : accept the default value

        COMMAND: PLINE
            Prompt: 23/2,-4
                : 27/2,-4
```

```
                                  : 27/2,0
                                  : 33/2,0
                                  : 33/2,4
                                  : `CAL
                    expression: A=27/2
                                  : `CAL
                    expression: B=4+(3/1.732)
                                  : `CAL
                    expression: P16=[A,B,0]
                                  : !16
                                  : 27/2,50
                                  : 23/2,50
                                  : C  to close loop


              COMMAND: LINE
                                  : draw a centreline about the axis of rotation
```

Using the REVSURF command

```
                    COMMAND: REVSURF
                                  : constructs a polyline mesh
                                    approximating a surface of
                                    revolution about a selected axis
      Prompt Select path curve: select the polyline 'A'
   Select axis of revolution: select the centre line 'B'
               start angle<0>: press 'Enter' to accept the
                                    default value
   included angle<Full circle>: press 'Enter'
                    COMMAND: HIDE  to confirm the result
```

The number of surfaces generated by the REVSURF command is controlled by the system variable SURFTAB1. Alter this value if the results show a need. Remember, large values for SURFTAB1 may improve the appearance but there is a price to pay in terms of time and storage.

If you alter the value of the system variable SURFTAB1, erase the polygon mesh and repeat the REVSURF command.

It is also possible to use swept primitives as above to create 3D solids, as we will see in the next exercise.

Reflect for a moment on the friendly face of AutoLISP. Notice how when 'P15' was defined by the CAL command, and how, by using the transparent CAL command to define 'P16', a list of three values '[x,y,z]' was assigned to the variables 'P15' and 'P16' respectively, i.e. P16=[x,y,z]. Once the AutoLISP variable has been defined, it can be used within the AutoCAD command loop such as !P16 at any time during the editing session.

Figure 64

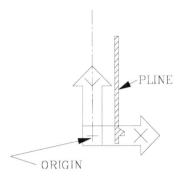

Reflect also on the previous HIDE command in relation to Rule 8: Avoid objects occupying the same space.

To help with Exercise 3, save the polyline as a WBLOCK. Make the WBLOCK insertion points as shown in Figure 64. Name the WBLOCK EPTUBE (eyepiece tube).

Rule 11
When creating a WBLOCK make sure that the UCS 'Z' axis is normal to the required 2D plane.

The mistake implied by Rule 11 is to think of the 'Z' axis of the view (in 3D) and not in the 'Z' axis of the UCS when they are not the same. Many AutoCAD students (prior to viewports) created three different views of a 3D model and saved the views PLAN, END and FRONT as WBLOCKs only to find on insertion that each inserted WBLOCK was identical.

Tasks

1. Use the monocular head wire frame model to create a 3D face as shown in Figure 65 using the RULESURF command with the correct SURFTAB1 setting. (**Hint**: Break the circle at the four quadrant points and rotate the circle 45°.)

2. Use the REGION command to create a face 'P9/P10/P12/P11' having a six-sided regular polygon hole located in line with the middle of the rectangle in the top face using point filters 'x', 'y' and 'z', as shown in Figure 66. (**Hint**: Use the SUBTRACT command with an appropriate VPOINT to confirm the results.)

Figure 65	**Figure 66**

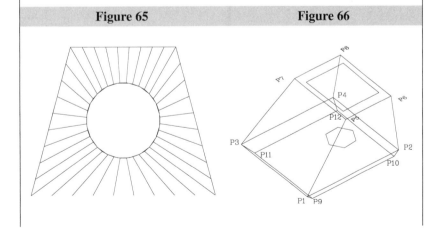

3. Using the PLINE (or SPLINE) command, construct a profile of a goblet, creating a surface mesh with the aid of the REVSURF command to give a view as shown in the WCS (Figure 67). Save this drawing for use in Part Two. (**Hint**: Set the 'Z' axis before constructing the profile.)

Figure 67

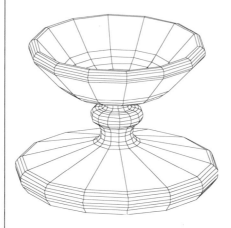

4. Create a region of the shroud as shown in Figure 68.

Figure 68

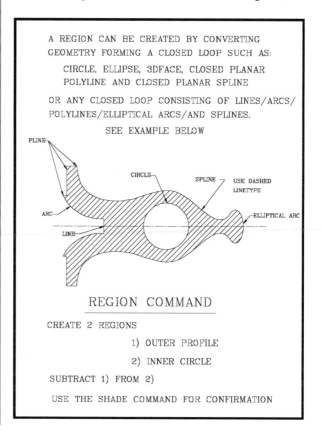

A REGION CAN BE CREATED BY CONVERTING GEOMETRY FORMING A CLOSED LOOP SUCH AS:

CIRCLE, ELLIPSE, 3DFACE, CLOSED PLANAR POLYLINE AND CLOSED PLANAR SPLINE

OR ANY CLOSED LOOP CONSISTING OF LINES/ARCS/ POLYLINES/ELLIPTICAL ARCS/AND SPLINES.

SEE EXAMPLE BELOW

PLINE

CIRCLE   SPLINE   USE DASHED LINETYPE

ARC   ELLIPTICAL ARC

LINE

REGION COMMAND

CREATE 2 REGIONS

1) OUTER PROFILE

2) INNER CIRCLE

SUBTRACT 1) FROM 2)

USE THE SHADE COMMAND FOR CONFIRMATION

5. Using the PLINE command, construct a curve $y = 0.256x^2$ for 'x' values of 1.5, 3.25, 5.15 and 7.171 (Figure 69). Smooth the resultant curve. (**Hint**: Use the transparent CAL command within the PLINE command.)

Figure 69

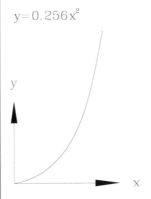

$$y = 0.256x^2$$

6. Explore the 3D command for future reference by entering 3D at the command prompt. (**Hint**: See Figure 70 for help.)

PREDEFINED 3D SURFACE MESH

Figure 70

THE 3D COMMAND OFFERS THE FOLLOWING 9 BASIC SHAPES.

COMMAND: 3D

: Box/Cone/Dish/DOme/Mesh/Pyramid/Sphere/Torus/Wedge

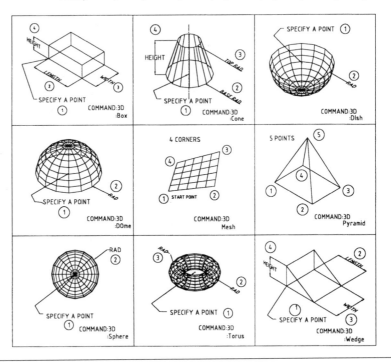

Exercise 3
Simple solid model construction

On completion of this exercise the reader shall be able to:

- Use the BOX, CHAMFER, CYLINDER, FILLET, EXTRUDE and REVOLVE commands for the construction of solid models.
- Describe the use of the EXPLODE command with solid models.
- Describe the use of the system variable ISOLINES to control the density of the wire frame model and the use of the system variable DISPSILH to show silhouette lines.
- Describe and use the system variable FACETRES to control the 3D mesh density for a curved surface.
- Define a composite solid by constructive solid geometry (CSG).
- Describe and use the INTERFERE and UNION commands.
- Select an appropriate construction method for solid modelling.
- Select and use shortcut functions as appropriate.
- Use the SECTION and SLICE commands.
- Use the MASSPROP and MATLIB commands.
- Understand and apply the RENDER command.
- State three further rules of 3D design.
- Insert a 3D block into a drawing with a specified orientation in space.

Solid modelling will become the preferred choice when creating objects in 3D as it is the easiest to construct and has many additional attributes when compared with the other two methods of creating objects in 3D.

At present, AutoCAD does not offer sufficient facilities to enable every different type of model to be constructed entirely by solid modelling (hence the need for surface and solid modelling techniques). However, as the present range of solid modelling editing facilities are extended, so the use of solid modelling will replace surface modelling for the construction of objects.

For direct comparison between surface and solid modelling we will construct a microscope monocular head as Exercise 2. The model is constructed by editing or building up a series of primitive solids by such means as joining, subtracting or overlapping. It is possible with solid modelling to 'edit downwards', i.e. from solid to surface models, however, there is no facility to 'edit upwards'.

It's time to consider the configuration of the screen when creating 3D models. The use of 'viewports' is recommended for CAD users with screens of 17 inches or more (using windows). The use of viewports will be explained in later exercises. For CAD users still using 14 inch monitors and consequently restricted by size of screen (and drawing) to a single viewport, create a 3D view for quick reference.

Rule 12

Immediately after applying Rule 5, create a view (–1,1,1) and save this view.

I always use a short name such as 1 for this view. In this way it can be quickly restored from the keyboard as a rapid check to the accuracy of progress when constructing entities or objects in a conventional 2D viewport looking down the 'Z' axis. Use the U command to return to the previous view.

Solid model construction

Open a new drawing in the WCS. Create layers CONS and MODEL with layer MODEL current.

Using the BOX command (classic geometry primitive)

The BOX command creates a solid box by prompting the user to input the length, width and height having located the first corner or centre point of the box. For instance, to create the box in Figure 71:

Figure 71

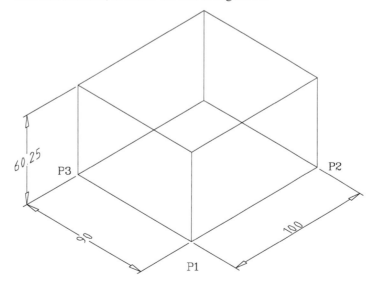

```
                      COMMAND: BOX
```
Prompt `Centre/<Corner of box><0,0,0>:` *pick a suitable point for 'P1'*
```
         Cube/Length/<Other>:
```
enter L *for Length*
```
                 Length:
```
enter 100
```
                  Width:
```
enter 90
```
                 Height:
```
enter 60.25
```
                COMMAND: VPOINT
                      :
```
enter -1,-1,1
```
                COMMAND: ZOOM
                      :
```
enter 1
```
                COMMAND: VIEW
                      :
```
(there is also a transparent view for certain commands)
```
                      :
```
S *for Save*

Prompt `View name to save:` *enter* 1

Once you have created a box, you cannot stretch, change the size or change its shape. Try using the GRIPS command to alter the location of any point.

You can explode the box to create regions of all the planar surfaces using the EXPLODE and REGION commands. The EXPLODE command breaks a compound object such as polylines, multi-lines, 3D solids, regions, meshes, blocks and so on.

```
         COMMAND: EXPLODE
```
Prompt `Select objects:` *select the box*

To test this command, use the ERASE command on one of the regions or faces, followed by a HIDE or SHADE command. When complete, use the UNDO command to reverse the effect of EXPLODE as follows:

```
         Command: UNDO
```
Prompt `<Number>:` *enter* 3

Using the CHAMFER command (Edge primitive)

From Release 13 of AutoCAD, the CHAMFER command works on solids in a similar way to the results when using this command to edit 2D lines and polylines, the major difference is that of selecting surfaces, not lines.

```
         COMMAND: CHAMFER
```
Prompt `Polyline/Distance/Angle/Trim/Method<Select first line>:`

Figure 72

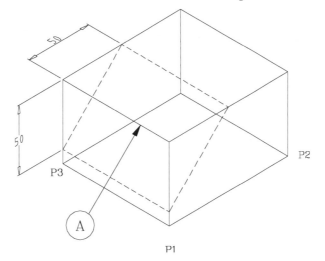

Figure 73

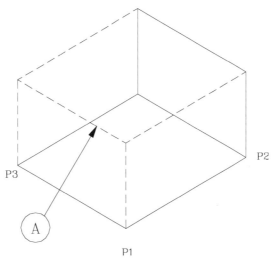

With the METHOD subcommand this enables you to use two distances or a distance and an angle to create the chamfer. Use two distances (Figure 72). Respond with:

: *select 'A'*

By selecting an edge on a 3D solid, you must indicate which one of two adjacent surfaces is to be the base surface:

```
Select base surface:
```

By entering N for Next you can toggle between the two adjacent surfaces. These two highlighted surfaces represent the faces to be chamfered (Figure 73). Pressing the 'Enter' key accepts the current highlighted surface. Make sure that 'P1' and 'P3' form part of the highlighted surface. Then:

```
              Enter base surface distance: 50
         Enter other surface distance <50>: 50
                      Loop <Select edge>: pick edge 'A' once
                                          more
                      Loop <Select edge>: press 'Enter' and
                                          regenerate the
                                          drawing for a clearer
                                          picture
                           COMMAND: CHAMFER
                                 : chamfer edges 'B' and
                                   'C'
```

Chamfer edges 'B' and 'C' by defining the base surface and distances to the dimensions shown in Figure 74.

Figure 74

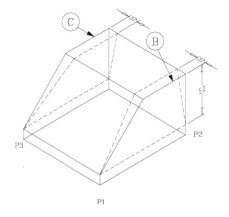

Do the same to edge 'D':

```
COMMAND: CHAMFER
      : chamfer edge D
```

Figure 75   **Figure 76**

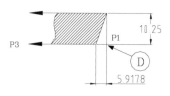

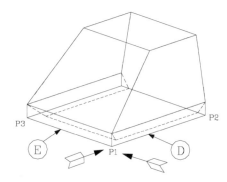

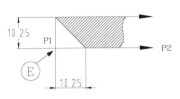

Figure 77

When chamfering edge D, make sure that the side surface is the base surface when you enter the distance 10.25, with the other surface distance being 5.9178 (this value was determined in Exercise 2). This is shown in Figures 75 and 76.

Repeat the CHAMFER command on the faces opposite to edge D. Finally, chamfer edge E using 10.25 as the value for both surface distances (Figure 77).

An alternative approach to the construction of the monocular head would have been to use the primitives BOX and WEDGE to create a composite solid by using the UNION command to join them together.

You may have noticed that we have almost completed the solid model without moving the UCS from the WCS. (Don't be lulled into a false sense of security.) We now need to construct a cylinder normal to the front face, as shown Figure 78.

Figure 78

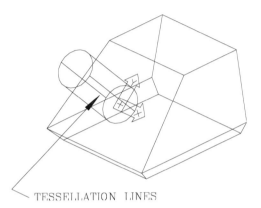

TESSELLATION LINES

```
COMMAND: VPOINT
        : enter -1,-1,0.75
COMMAND: ZOOM
        : zoom into the inclined front face
COMMAND: UCS
```

Create a UCS with the 'x,y' plane in the same plane as the inclined front face with the origin in the middle of this face, as we did in Exercise 2. Save this UCS with the name 'FRONT'.

Using the CYLINDER command

The CYLINDER command creates a solid column with an elliptical or circular base (see Figure 79).

```
                              COMMAND: CYLINDER
Prompt Elliptical/<Centre point><0,0,0>: press 'Enter' to
                                         accept the
                                         default value
            Diameter/<Radius>: 13.5
```

Centre of other end/<Height>: 60
COMMAND: HIDE *or*
SHADE *to*
confirm the
results

Figure 79

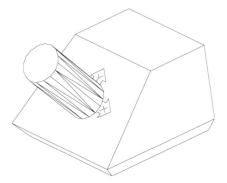

Surface visualisation (tessellation lines)

When a solid is created, it is initially displayed as a wire frame model with tessellation lines to help with the visualisation, such as the lines shown in the cylinder in Figure 78. However, when the SHADE command is invoked, the smoothness of the shaded curved surface responds in a different way (Figure 79). The display of solid objects is controlled by three different system variables: ISOLINES, DISPSILH and FACETRES (linked to the value of VIEWRES).

For the moment we will restrict our activities to the system variable ISOLINES. The ISOLINES system variable, controls the density of the wire frame, having an initial setting of 4, i.e. tessellation lines displayed on the cylinder extrusion. These lines are to help with the visualisation of the model only and have no function when editing the model. For a better visualisation of the cylinder, increase the value of the system variable ISOLINES and invoke the REGEN command to observe the results (more on this subject later). Remember, the greater the number of tessellation lines, the greater the regeneration time.

In Exercise 2 we created a composite region by subtracting one rectangular region from another. The same command (SUBTRACT) can be used to subtract the volume of one set of solids from another.

Solid model primitives

There are three basic groups of primitives used to create solid models:

■ Group 1 – Classic geometrical primitives: BOX, WEDGE, CYLINDER, CONE, SPHERE, TORUS.

■ Group 2 – Swept primitives: EXTRUSION, REVOLVE.
These primitives can be edited with edge primitives (see Group 3).
■ Group 3 – Edge primitives: CHAMFER, FILLET.

These primitive solids are used as basic building blocks to create the more complex finished design. In this exercise we will experience all the 3 basic groups.

■ Group 1 – Classic geometry primitives (basic): BOX for the basic body of the monocular head, and CYLINDER to create a hole in the monocular head.
■ Group 2 – Swept geometry primitive: REVOLVE for the generation of the eyepiece tube.
■ Group 3 – Edge primitive: CHAMFER to create the inclined faces of the monocular head, and FILLET to smooth the sharp edges of the monocular head.

Composite solids

When a solid consists of two or more primitives, related by union, subtraction or intersection, it is referred to as a composite solid.

This relationship between different primitives is performed by Boolean operations. The introduction of Boolean operations to the AutoCAD software was the next major step (after UCS) in the ongoing development of computer 3D design.

Constructive solid geometry

The process of building composite solids from primitives using Boolean operations is termed 'constructive solid geometry' (CSG). We are now going to use the recently created CYLINDER primitive to create a hole in the monocular head. (Make sure that your 'Z' axis is in the correct plane – see Figure 80.)

Figure 80

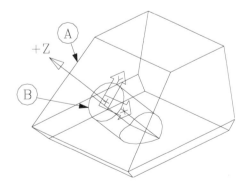

```
                              COMMAND: MOVE
         Prompt Select objects: select the cylinder
  base point of displacement: 0,0,0
second point of displacement: 0,0,-50
                              COMMAND: SUBTRACT
Prompt Select object to subtract from: select 'A'
     Select the object to subtract: select 'B'
```

Use the HIDE or SHADE commands to confirm the results. Remember to regenerate, using the REGEN command, before proceeding.

Figure 81

We now need to use this hole as a spigot location for the eyepiece tube, created as a sectional profile in Exercise 2. Consider your next move before inserting the WBLOCK named EPTUBE. In the event of an error, revisit Rule 11 on page 47.

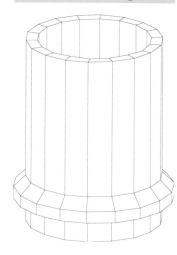

Swept geometry primitive

A swept geometry primitive can be used to create a 'swept solid' of the eyepiece tube (Figure 81).

Swept solids are created from such planar objects as circles, ellipses, closed polylines or splines and regions making for far greater flexibility of design than the basic primitives such as BOX and CYLINDER. Complex shapes can be constructed in 2D and extruded along the 'Z' axis of the object's coordinate system, or revolved around an axis of rotation such as the eyepiece tube. Rule 13 sounds a note of caution though.

Rule 13

Avoid using intersecting profiles (i.e. a figure of eight) to create swept solids, use a single loop.

Because you cannot revolve objects contained within a block, you need to explode the WBLOCK, insert the eyepiece tube (EPTUBE), and revolve the polyline.

Using the REVOLVE command

The REVOLVE command creates a solid revolution (Figure 82). At the command prompt enter:

```
                       COMMAND: REVOLVE
      Prompt Select objects: select polyline 'A'
Axis of revolution<Start point>: enter 0,0
           Axis<End point>: with 'F8' (ORTHO)
                           active, select any point
                           in the 'y' direction
```

```
Angle of Revolution<Full circle>:
```
accept the default value by pressing 'Enter'
```
COMMAND: HIDE
```
or `SHADE`

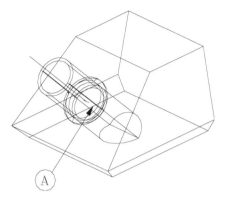

Figure 82

If the eyepiece tube is correctly located in relation to the monocular head, the spigot location of the tube should not be visible.

Whenever the HIDE (SHADE or RENDER) command is used on a solid, the result is a 3D mesh, returning to a wire frame when regeneration is performed (Figure 83).

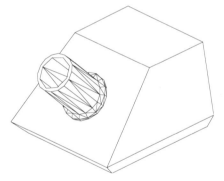

Figure 83

Solid model assemblies

One very important advantage of creating an assembly from a series of individual solid models by importing the objects to the assembly insertion points is the facility to use the INTERFERE command.

The INTERFERE command can be used to check the accuracy of each individual dimension when related in an assembly with other parts in their working positions. Interference fits can be used in an assembly when two or more parts are not intended to move relative to each other (such as a steel tire in a cast-iron wheel or a journal ball bearing). However, interference in assemblies is often due to error, only detected at the end of the production process.

Screen interference

Screen interference or overlap can be highlighted on the screen by simply selecting a set of solids as part of the INTERFERE command, eliminating the need to produce a prototype if this is the only reason for building a production prototype.

Using the INTERFERE command

At the command prompt enter:

COMMAND: INTERFERE

Prompt Select the first set of solids: *select the monocular head*

Select the second set of solids: *select the eyepiece tube*

The two selected sets are then compared for any interference. Because the spigot dimensions of both the male and female parts are the same, both contacting surfaces are common and as such are not considered to be an interference fit, hence no highlight appears on these objects. AutoCAD reports this fact. If, however, there is an error in the relative location of the two parts, then interference highlight becomes a possibility.

In practice this is not quite accurate, as both parts occupy the same space. If a precision hardened and ground 'plug guage' (male) is introduced to a precision hardened and ground 'ring gauge' (female) of identical size, they do not form a union without interference.

Wire frame

The system variable DISPSILH controls whether silhouette lines are drawn along with the isolines on tessellation lines.

The silhouette lines are determined by the current view. Notice in Figures 84 and 85 how the outside edge of the cylinder is shown by the lines when the system variable DISPSILH is set to 1, to help with the visualisation of the model.

By setting DISPSILH equal to 1, the time to regenerate the drawing is increased. (**Note**: Beware of viewpoint 1,1,1 with ISOLINES set to 4.)

3D mesh

When using the HIDE, SHADE or RENDER command, the wire frame is automatically converted to a 3D mesh. The system variable FACETRES (facet resolution) controls the density or smoothness of this 3D mesh curved surface. Valid values for FACETRES are from 0.01 to 10 with the initial value set at 0.5. Increasing the value produces a finer mesh; decreasing the value produces a coarser mesh (Figure 86).

Figure 84

Figure 85

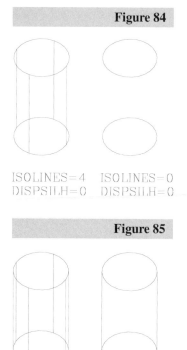

ISOLINES=4   ISOLINES=0
DISPSILH=0   DISPSILH=0

ISOLINES=4   ISOLINES=0
DISPSILH=1   DISPSILH=1

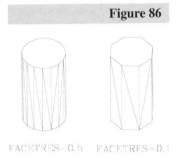

Figure 86

FACETRES=0.5   FACETRES=0.1

The FACETRES system variable is linked to the VIEWRES command (most readers will have used the VIEWRES command to improve the screen image of various shapes). When FACETRES is set to 1, there is a one-to-one correspondence between VIEWRES and the FACETRES tessellations. When FACETRES is set to 2, the resulting tessellations are twice the tessellations set by VIEWRES .

- **VIEWRES** – Controls the resolution of objects and affects the number of tessellations when using HIDE, SHADE or RENDER. (Draw with a low value; render with a high value.)
- **FACETRES** – Affects only solid objects and has no control over the VIEWRES command.

Experiment with both system variables, noting the results on the regenerated wire frame eyepiece tube and the shaded eyepiece tube.

Methods of construction

When deciding how best to build up your solid model, it is wise to keep Rule 14 in mind.

Rule 14
Keep the number of solid primitives as small as possible. Use swept primitives if further editing is not anticipated.

In Exercise 2 we constructed the monocular head and the bottom plate separately (Figure 87). However, in the case of this solid model exercise we created both objects from one edited BOX primitive. If now we wished to edit the bottom plate, as was the case with this particular design, it would have been better to have used two individual BOX primitives. (You cannot stretch or change the size of the BOX once it has been created.)

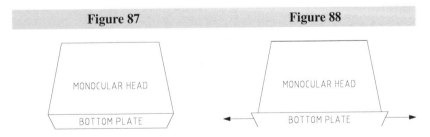

Figure 87   Figure 88

MONOCULAR HEAD   MONOCULAR HEAD

BOTTOM PLATE   BOTTOM PLATE

Alternatively we could have used a swept primitive to extrude the section in Figure 88 (PLINE), subtracting the front faces with wedge primitives.

If now we wish to edit the section in any way, the entire swept polyline would have to be re-created. Hence, whilst there are many different ways of constructing a solid model, consideration should be given at the earliest possible stage of the design process to the future possibility of any editing. (See Figure 89 for examples of solid model constructions.)

Figure 89

EXAMPLE	METHOD 1	METHOD 2
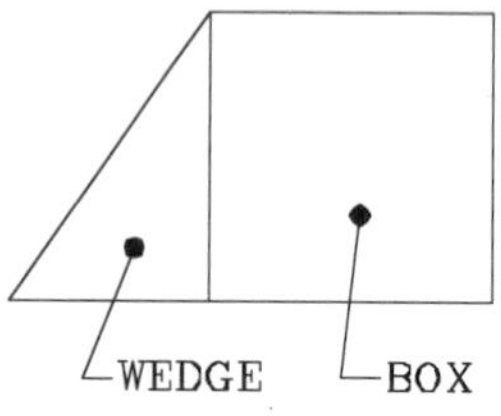 WEDGE BOX	UNION BOX AND WEDGE	BOX EDIT WITH CHAMFER
	PRIMITIVES GROUP 1	PRIMITIVES GROUP 1 AND GROUP 3
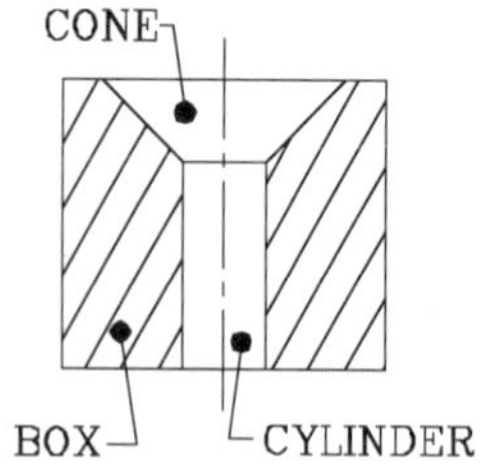 CONE BOX CYLINDER	SUBTRACT FROM THE BOX A CONE AND CYLINDER	SUBTRACT FROM THE BOX A CYLINDER EDIT CYLINDER WITH CHAMFER
	PRIMITIVES GROUP 1	PRIMITIVES GROUP 1 AND GROUP 3
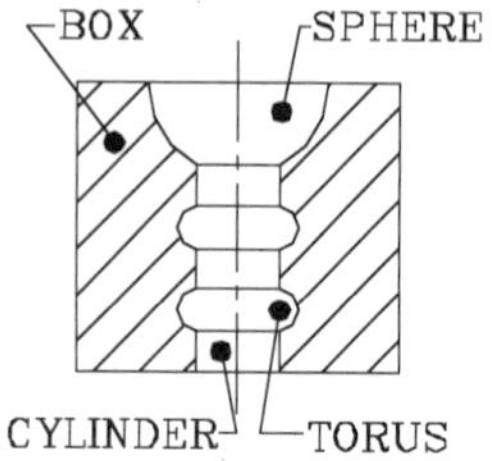 BOX SPHERE CYLINDER TORUS	SUBTRACT FROM THE BOX A SPHERE, CYLINDER AND TORUS	SUBTRACT FROM THE BOX A REVOLVED PLINE OR REGION
	PRIMITIVES GROUP 1	PRIMITIVES GROUP 1 AND GROUP 2
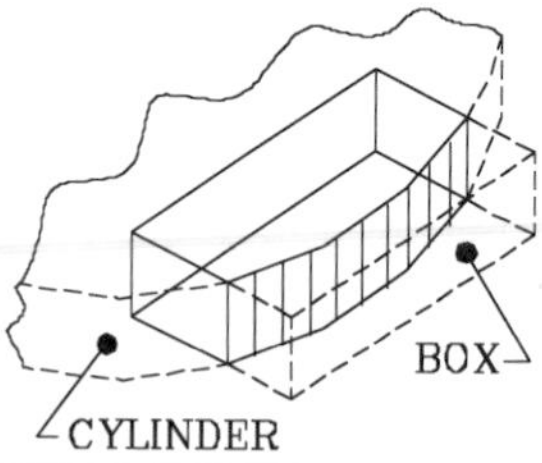 BOX CYLINDER	INTERSECT A CYLINDER AND A BOX	EXTRUDE THE SECTION PLINE OR REGION SEE RULE NO 14
	PRIMITIVES GROUP 1	PRIMITIVES

DIFFERENT METHODS OF CONSTRUCTING SOLID MODELS.

Filleting solid models

The sharp edges on top of the monocular head need to be smoothed with the FILLET command. The filleting capabilities of solids were improved in AutoCAD Release 13. The FILLET command used on lines, polylines and arcs will now work on 3D solids, with improved facilities for filleting edges with different radii, all within the same command loop. It is also possible to select a chain of edges from a single pick for filleting.

Figure 90

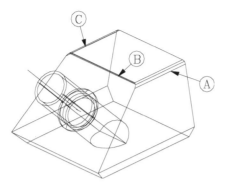

With reference to Figure 90, enter the following:

```
                COMMAND: FILLET
Prompts (Trim mode) current fillet radius = 0.50 (or
  any other value) Polyline/Radius/Trim<Select first
                object>: select edge 'A'
            Enter radius: 3
Chain/Radius<Select edge>: enter R for radius
            Enter Radius: 1.5
Chain/Radius<Select edge>: select edge 'B'
Chain/Radius<Select edge>: enter R
            Enter Radius: 3
Chain/Radius<Select edge>: select edge 'C'
Chain/Radius<Select edge>: press 'Enter' to close the loop
```

To reduce the length of the command loop, 'C' could have been selected immediately after selecting 'A', this was only an exercise in changing radii. Edges 'A', 'B' and 'C' are external fillets. Internal fillets are when a fillet is joined to the internal edges by the Boolean operation UNION. Chamfered edges can also be external or internal. It is time to have a closer look at Boolean operations.

Boolean operations

As we have seen, primitive solids are used as building blocks to create more complex 3D designs. These complex solids are called composite solids when they consist of two or more primitive solids, created with the aid of Boolean operations.

Composite solids are created using three basic Boolean operations:

- Union (UNION)
- Difference (SUBTRACT)
- Intersection (INTERFERE/INTERSECT)

These operations can be applied to solids and regions (since a region is a solid of zero thickness). Venn diagrams are often used to explain Boolean operations because of their direct relationship with mathematics. As 2D diagrams they are best suited to the application of regions.

The union operation

The union operation is the process of joining two or more solids to form a new solid or composite solid. This is not the same as addition, as addition would include the sum of both the squares shown in Figure 91(a), whilst UNION represents only the hatched area.

Both adjacent and non-overlapping examples can be considered as addition since then there are no common or overlapping areas (or solids).

It is not necessary for the objects to be in contact with each other to form a union. The solid show as a bolt head in Figure 91(b) is created by two adjacent or touching solids joined by UNION. The hexagon solid was created by extrusion, and the body of the bolt by a a CYLINDER primitive joined together by the Boolean operation UNION. The washer, as a non-overlapping object, could also be joined by UNION with the bolt.

Figure 91

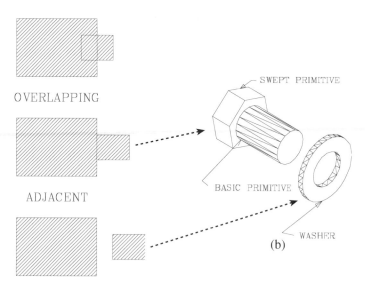

OVERLAPPING

ADJACENT

NON−OVERLAPPING

(a)

SWEPT PRIMITIVE

BASIC PRIMITIVE

WASHER

(b)

The difference operation

The difference operation involves the removal of one solid from another that is common to both solids (not restricted to two solids as in Figure 92(a)) resulting in a composite shown by the hatched area in the figure. The AutoCAD command for this operation is SUBTRACT, as we saw when we created holes in the monocular head.

Figure 92

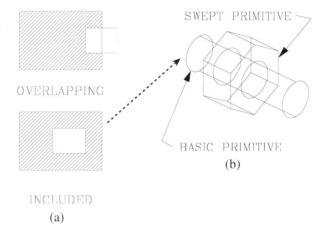

Subtraction involves the removal of only those parts of the volume contained within the subtracted objects that are common with the object to subtract from.

The solid shown as a nut in Figure 92(b) is created with two included solids by subtraction. The hexagon solid is created by extrusion; the hole in the nut by a CYLINDER primitive, subtracted by the Boolean operation.

The intersection operation

The intersection operation is the process of generating composite solids from the volume that is common to the two (or more) solids shown in Figure 93(a) by hatching. It is obviously necessary for one solid to be overlapping the other, either partially or wholly, to perform the intersection operation.

Figure 93

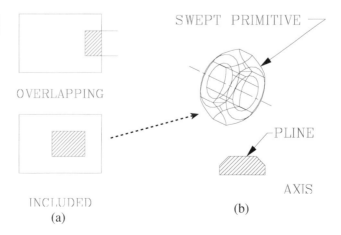

The solid shown as a nut in Figure 93(b) is created with two included solids by the INTERSECT operation. The hexagon solid is created by extrusion as above. The body of the nut, shown hatched, is created by revolving the polyline about the axis.

See Figure 94 for a practical example of Boolean operations.

Figure 94

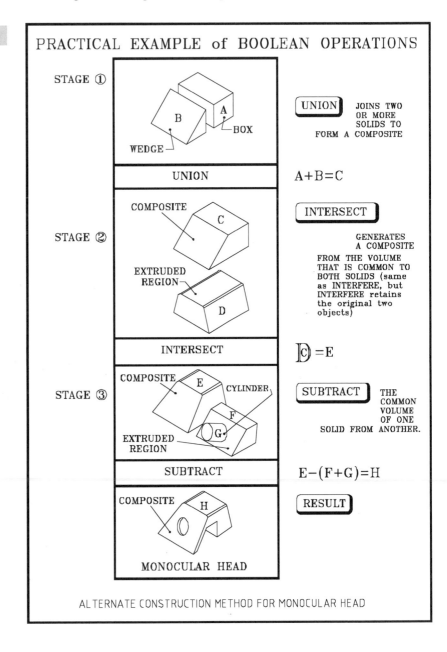

PRACTICAL EXAMPLE of BOOLEAN OPERATIONS

STAGE ①

WEDGE   B   A   BOX

UNION   JOINS TWO OR MORE SOLIDS TO FORM A COMPOSITE

UNION   A+B=C

STAGE ②

COMPOSITE   C

EXTRUDED REGION   D

INTERSECT   GENERATES A COMPOSITE FROM THE VOLUME THAT IS COMMON TO BOTH SOLIDS (same as INTERFERE, but INTERFERE retains the original two objects)

INTERSECT   C=E

STAGE ③

COMPOSITE   E   CYLINDER

F

EXTRUDED REGION   G

SUBTRACT   THE COMMON VOLUME OF ONE SOLID FROM ANOTHER.

SUBTRACT   E−(F+G)=H

COMPOSITE   H

RESULT

MONOCULAR HEAD

ALTERNATE CONSTRUCTION METHOD FOR MONOCULAR HEAD

Shortcut functions

In Exercise 2 we used the AutoLISP function DIST to determine the distance between two previously defined points, e.g. 'P9' and 'P10'. This could have been simplified with the AutoLISP 'shortcut' function DEE which gives the distance between two end-points and is used as an expression within the CAL command.

Another shortcut function is ILLE which gives the intersection of two lines defined by four end-points and is much more simple than using the ILL (END, END, END, END) function, also used in Exercise 2.

Mid-point function

A very useful short cut is the function MEE which gives the mid-point between two end-points. As an exercise in using this function, locate a circle in the middle of any of the monocular head inclined faces by firstly moving the UCS to the chosen face, followed by:

```
    COMMAND: CIRCLE
centre point: 'CAL
  expression: MEE
             : select two diagonals and complete the command
```

The result is shown in Figure 95.

Figure 95

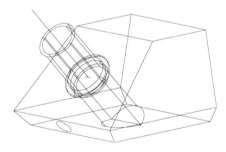

The above AutoLISP function offers an alternative method to the use of point filters or construction lines.

Sectional views

Most complex drawings benefit from a sectional view. In the case of assembly or subassembly drawings, the sectional view is almost a necessity. AutoCAD (Release 13) has two commands that help in this respect: SECTION and SLICE.

There is a little confusion in the naming of these commands, as the conventional sectional view associated with orthographic projections is created with the SLICE command, not the SECTION command.

Before created a section, join the eyepiece tube to the monocular head with the UNION command to create a composite solid:

> COMMAND: SAVE *(for use with the final project)*
> COMMAND: UNION
> *Prompt* Select objects: *select the eyepiece tube and the monocular head*

The resulting composite is the combined volume of both those objects.

Using the SECTION command

Create a new layer called SECTION and set the colour of the layer to red, making the layer SECTION current. The SECTION command uses the intersection of a plane and solid to create a region. Now, with reference to Figure 96,

> COMMAND: SECTION
> *Prompt* Select objects: *select the newly created composite*
> Section plane by Object/Zaxis/View.XY/YZ/ZX/
> <3points>: *press 'Enter'*
> First point on the plane: *select the mid-point of 'A'*
> Second point on the plane: *select the mid-point of 'B'*
> Third point on the plane: *select the mid-point of 'C'*

Figure 96

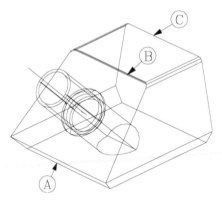

Using the MOVE command, move this composite region to convenient location above the monocular head. Notice that the section is a combination of both objects. Hence, and the SECTION command creates a region of the selected composite. Then using the UCS command and the 3POINT option, place the UCS 'xy' plane coplanar with the region.

Using the EXTRUDE command

The EXTRUDE command creates a solid primitive by extruding 2D objects along a specified path.

COMMAND: EXTRUDE
Prompt Select objects: *select the section (you cannot extrude crossing polylines – Rule 13)*

Path/<Height of extension>: 100
Extrusion taper angle<0>: 0

Shade the extrusion to confirm the result. Notice the direction of extrusion in the positive 'z' direction (see Figure 97). Try using a negative extrusion, noting the results. When complete, freeze this layer by returning to the MODEL layer.

Figure 97

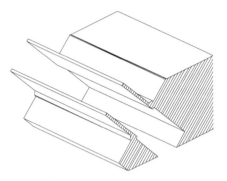

Copy the composite to show two identical objects side by side.

Using the SLICE command

SLICE is the command most people associate with the creation of sectional views.

COMMAND: SLICE
Prompt Select objects: *select the copied object (composite)*
(*Prompt as for SECTION*): *select the 3 mid-points in the same way as you selected points for the SECTION command*

Both sides/<Point of desired side of
         the plane>: *pick a point at the rear of the composite*

The result is shown in Figure 98.

Figure 98

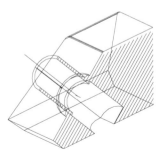

As you create your solids and regions, AutoCAD allows certain properties to be extracted from these objects for the benefit of designers wishing to perform scientific calculations, such as the centroid of the composite mass, the moment of inertia, radii of gyration and the principal moments about the centroid.

Using the MASSPROP command

The above mentioned properties of solids and regions are extracted using the MASSPROP command. For instance:

```
              COMMAND: MASSPROP
Prompt Select objects: select any one of the composites
       Write to file<N>: enter Y for Yes
              file name: enter a convenient name
```

When you enter file name, the extension 'MPR' will be automatically added to it. This file is created in a format that can be printed or imported for processing by spreadsheet or database software.

```
MASSPROP DISPLAY, TEXT SCREEN OR FILE

Mass:                   183420.8312
Volume:                 183420.8312
Bounding box:        X: -23.7873  --  89.7500
                     Y: 0.0000    --  73.7873
                     Z: -45.0000  --   0.0000
Centroid:            X: 48.8822
                     Y: 26.9013
                     Z: -21.3395
Moments of inertia:  X: 293451901.7382
                     Y: 671677480.6049
                     Z: 748089688.9083
Products of inertia: XY: 258155962.0098
                     YZ: -99206801.1507
                     ZX: -188448985.4518
Radii of gyration:   X: 39.9985
                     Y: 60.5140
                     Z: 63.8635
Principal moments and X-Y-Z directions about centroid:
                     I: 73262124.2187 along [0.9749 0.2190 0.0399]
                     J: 152494926.8592 along [-0.2224 0.9521 0.2098]
                     K: 178379196.0348 along [0.0079 -0.2134 0.9769]
```

As you will see from the report, many aspects of the composite are analysed. The accuracy and units used in the report can be controlled by different variables. Note that because AutoCAD uses a density of 1, mass and volume have the same value.

It is often good practice at this stage to allocate material to finished objects in preparation for rendering. Our completed composite should be made from 'ALUMINUM' (note the American spelling). We will make use of the MATLIB

command. This command imports and exports material to and from a library of
materials (see Figure 99). A new drawing contains only the default *GLOBE*
material. Select ALUMINUM in the displayed library list and import to the
materials list. Using the RMAT command (for Render MATerial), attach
ALUMINUM to the composite by highlighting ALUMINUM in the materials
list and choosing the ATTACH option. Then select the composite shown in
Figure 100.

Figure 99

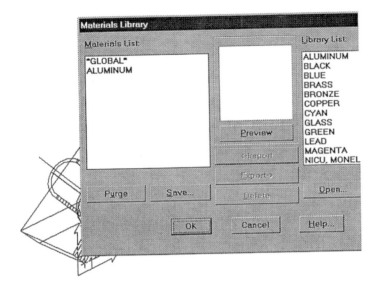

Whilst this is the end of the quick exercise in solid modelling, it is important
not to forget the inclusion of attributes at this stage. I differentiate these 'two
Ms' as M for Manufacturing and M for Management. Both are of equal
importance. Unfortunately, M for Management is neglected by many authors
and CAD users, even those planning nationally recognised curricula fail to stress
the importance of a common database containing manufacturing (vectors) and
management (attributes) information.

Figure 100

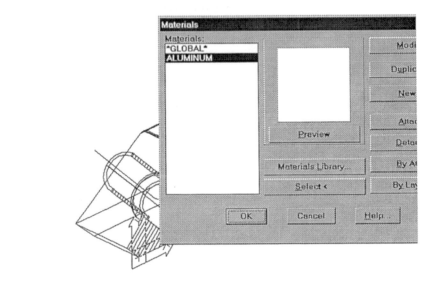

Rendering

From AutoCAD Release 13 onwards, the RENDER command gives the opportunity for a default rendering without any knowledge of the command and without the need to define such properties as material, lights, target, scene and so on, as was the case with previous software. The RENDER command default setting uses a virtual 'over the shoulder' distant light that is fixed for all rendered images. For the purpose of this initial part of the book, we will restrict our rendered views to the default settings as these give a satisfactory introduction to this technique and are simple to use.

Front face

When AutoCAD renders the face, it determines the front and back faces by the direction of the 'normal'. To understand the normal, draw an imaginary square constructed in an anticlockwise direction in the ' x,y' plane of this page; the normal to this imaginary face is a vector in the positive 'Z' axis towards you. (Use the right hand rule for confirmation.)

Back face

If you construct the imaginary face as above in a clockwise direction, the normal to this face will be perpendicular to the page but in the opposite direction. AutoCAD will interpret this as a back face.

To avoid problems with rendering, draw all faces consistently (anticlockwise). Do not mix clockwise with anticlockwise surfaces when constructing your models.

Rendered surfaces

To appreciate the possible effects of a rendered surface, observe a cylinder with good surface reflectivity (polished surface) using a single light source, noting the tonal and colour variations across the surface of the visible cylinder. The tonal variations are dependent upon such factors as material, surface texture, wavelength of light, absorption, reflectivity, angle of incidence and so on.

Practical example of rendering

Consider a cylinder as shown in Figure 101. The cylinder is constructed as a polygon for simplicity – the fewer the faces needed to describe an object, the faster the computing time. Illuminated by a single point source, the incident light rays are reflected by the 3D surfaces of the cylinder. All the surfaces are constructed in an anticlockwise direction resulting in the normals, shown as arrows, emerging from the front faces.

Optical theory

Note how the angle of incidence is equal to the angle of reflection, an optical principle we will incorporate into the 3D design project in Part Three. Note also how only one of the light rays shown in the figure reflects in the direction of the observer and that the back faces receive no illumination from this particular light source. These two types of face represent the two extremes of rendering and show why rendering back faces is not necessary when considering a simple rendered view.

Collimation

Consider the light source placed at infinity (think of the sun). The resultant incident rays would be parallel (collimated), consequently an increased number of reflected rays would be reflected in the direction of the observer parallel to the reflected ray shown in Figure 101. If, however, the surface texture were not smooth, then the reflected rays of light would be diffused or scattered in all directions, reducing considerably the number of rays reflected in the direction of observation, hence reducing the light intensity of the model (see Figure 102).

Figure 101

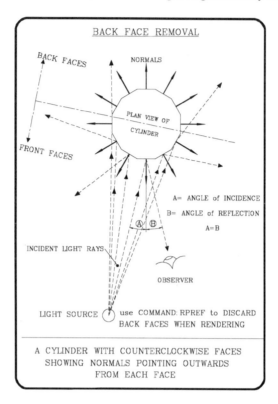

BACK FACE REMOVAL

BACK FACES

NORMALS

PLAN VIEW OF CYLINDER

FRONT FACES

A= ANGLE of INCIDENCE

B= ANGLE of REFLECTION

A=B

INCIDENT LIGHT RAYS

OBSERVER

LIGHT SOURCE   use COMMAND: RPREF to DISCARD BACK FACES WHEN RENDERING

A CYLINDER WITH COUNTERCLOCKWISE FACES SHOWING NORMALS POINTING OUTWARDS FROM EACH FACE

Light ray modification

When the material of the model or the model surface texture causes a modification to the phase relationship between two identical interfering beams

Figure 102

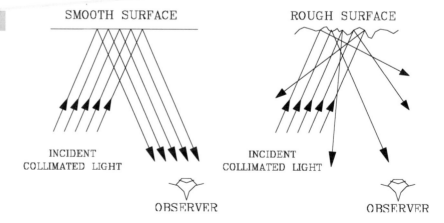

SMOOTH SURFACE

ROUGH SURFACE

INCIDENT COLLIMATED LIGHT

INCIDENT COLLIMATED LIGHT

OBSERVER

OBSERVER

of light so as to be out of phase by 180°, then the amplitude value for this condition is zero, also causing a loss of light intensity.

Cone of light

In Figure 101, the reflected rays are shown as a single line or ray of light for simplicity. In practice these reflected rays are the centre of a cone of light. It is the combination of these cones of light, being the result of variations in absorption or reflection, reaching the observer, that accounts for the tonal and colour variations of the object being observed.

With developments in software and hardware, the time taken to render a model is constantly being reduced; however, it is possible to reduce the rendering time even further by:

- preventing AutoCAD from reading the back faces,
- GOURAUD rendering (blends colour across a surface to simulate the smoother appearance),
- creating a rendered file.

These three techniques are described below.

Back face removal

To discard the back faces enter:

```
COMMAND: RPREF
Prompt Render preferences dialogue box
   selection: MORE OPTIONS
Render options dialogue box
   selection: DISCARD BACK FACES
```

GOURAUD rendering

Render time can also be saved by selecting GOURAUD under RENDER QUALITY in the 'Render Options' dialogue box as above. GOURAUD renderings are slightly lower in quality than PHONG renderings but are faster. This type of rendering smoothes out the multifaceted surfaces by calculating light intensity at each pixel to achieve a more realistic model, blending adjacent colours and surfaces to simulate smooth and non-faceted images.

File render

Using the RENDER command rendered images can be saved to a file for redisplay at a later date (or for transfer into other software or systems). This has the effect of reducing the time required to repeat the RENDER command for the same rendered image. Once the rendered image has been saved to file, it can be redisplayed instantaneously by using the REPLAY command.

Alternatively, render the image to the screen prior to saving the rendered image to a restricted file format as below, thus making the file available to the REPLAY command. The file formats are:

- TGA (Truvision Format)
- TIFF (Tagged Image Format)
- GIF (Compuserve Image Format)

One other advantage of rendering to a file is the ability to render the image at a higher resolution than that of your working system configuration, offering the option to display the saved image on an alternative system which has a higher resolution display.

There is an ever increasing list of file formats available from within the RENDER command, accessed as follows:

COMMAND: RENDER *(or use the 'teapot toolbar ') to display a dialogue box*
: *select* FILE *under* DESTINATION
: *select* MORE OPTIONS *under* Destination
: *select* FILE TYPE *under* File output configuration
: *select* RENDER SCENE *from the original dialogue box*
: *turn on* SMOOTH SHADING *under* Rendering options

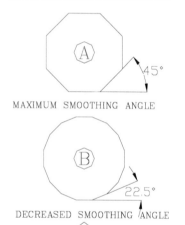

Figure 103

MAXIMUM SMOOTHING ANGLE

DECREASED SMOOTHING ANGLE

INCREASED SMOOTHING ANGLE

The three options are illustrated in Figure of 103. The maximum smoothing angle (part A of the figure) smoothes the edges between polygon faces, having a default setting of 45°. In part B the smoothing angle is decreased for improved smoothing. Part C shows how increasing the angle of smoothing above 45° produces polygon rendered images.

Name the file and destination from the rendering file dialogue box.

If, when rendering solid models such as a cylinder or the eyepiece tube, the models appear to have a polygon construction, try altering the following:

- the smoothing angle,
- the style of rendering,
- the system variable FACETRES value from the default setting of 0.5 to 1.0 or even more when necessary.

Different methods of working

It is time to consider the way in which we translate between different associated views on the screen. For simplicity our current mode of working has been restricted to a single screen viewport, changing from a 2D to a 3D view by the AutoCAD VIEW command (Rule 12).

TILEMODE

With the system variable TILEMODE set to 1, it is possible to split the screen into a series of different tiled viewports in various configurations. This enables a series of different associative views to be displayed on the screen at the same time, such as is required for orthographic projections, similar to the detailed drawing of the monocular head shown in Figure 15 at the beginning of Part One. This configuration was achieved by using the VPORTS command set to four viewports. For small screens this configuration can be restrictive for construction purposes. You can only operate in one viewport at a time; however, it is possible to select from within the command mode, objects from a different viewport from that of the command or currently active viewport.

To help you envisage the relationship between viewports and tile modes,

- Think of viewports as a series of screens within the screen.
- Think of TILEMODE1 as tiles in contact at their edges, such as in a kitchen or bathroom, with no tile spacing or overlapping.

Before we experience the VPORTS command (see Part Two), I wish to progress to a working method used by many CAD users involved with 3D designs when translating between 2D and 3D views.

Alternative method to VIEW/RESTORE

When the system variable TILEMODE is set to zero it is possible to overlap viewports, enabling full 2D screen construction with a small 3D viewport located at some convenient point on the screen within the 2D viewport.

Figure 104

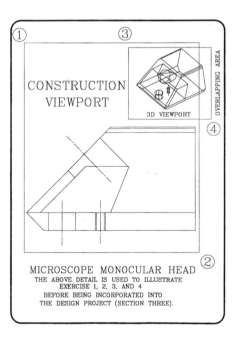

Figure 104 shows a different configuration for the construction of the monocular head from that of four independent viewports used in the original diagrams (Figure 15). The main area of the screen is used for the orthographic view, with a much smaller 3D viewport overlapping the construction viewport.

UCSFOLLOW

If the system variable UCSFOLLOW is set to 1 in the construction viewport and the UCSICON value is set to ORIGIN in the small viewport, then changes to the UCS location in the 3D viewport cause an automatic plan view (looking down the 'Z' axis) in the construction viewport.

This method of working offers a considerably larger screen construction area and is attractive to those CAD users using small screens. In order to change from one associated view to another for editing purposes in the construction viewport, simply change the location of the UCS in the 3D viewport.

To set the screen for this method of working enter:

```
COMMAND: TILEMODE
         : 0  (zero)
```

If any screen graphics exist when changing the TILE mode to zero, the screen is cleared. This presents problems to many students of AutoCAD who fear 'all is lost' and inhibits them from any further exploration of what is termed 'paper space'.

Paper space

To control the number of viewports and layout of paper space, enter the following:

```
        COMMAND: MVIEW for model view
    Prompt ON/OFF/Hideplot/Fit/2/3/4/Restore/<First
           point>: pick point '1' in Figure 104
    Other corner: pick point '2' (perseverance is rewarded by the return
                  of the original graphics)
        COMMAND: MVIEW
               : pick point '3'
               : pick point '4'
```

It is very important that point '4 ' is located outside the edge of the construction viewport boundary for future selection purposes as this viewport is made active by picking in the area of this viewport outside the area of the main viewport.

Now enter the MSPACE command. Notice the return of the UCSICON to the two viewports. Make the small viewport active by picking within this area of the 3D viewport and enter:

```
COMMAND: VIEW
       : R
       : 1 (see Rule 3)
COMMAND: UCSICON
       : OR
```

Check that the UCSFOLLOW variable is 0. Make the construction viewport active and enter:

```
COMMAND: UCSFOLLOW
       : 1
```

The above command causes automatic plan view changes to coincide with UCS changes to the 3D viewport.

Change the location of the UCS in the 3D viewport by firstly making the viewport active to confirm the automatic view changes to the construction viewport. This should offer you an alternative method of working and is worthy of serious consideration for those CAD users who find their current screen size somewhat restrictive for 3D design.

Editing viewports

If a location of the 3D viewport needs moving during the editing session, enter:

```
COMMAND: PSPACE for paper space
COMMAND: MOVE
```

Pick the outline of the viewport located outside the construction viewport and move to a new location. To change the size of the viewport, use GRIPS in paper space. The MSPACE command will then return you to the editing mode.

Completed drawings

When the drawing is complete, remove the tiled outline from the view by moving the outline to a frozen layer (CHPROP command) in paper space. To remove the small viewport from view, use the ERASE command or switch off the viewport, using the MVIEW command. Whilst there is considerably more to learn about paper space, I hope that you now have the confidence to test out this method of working by using it to complete the following tasks, forming your own judgment as to its value for your particular needs.

Tasks

1. Create a solid model of the microscope limb by using classic geometry primitives and Boolean operations to create three holes in the limb (Figure 105).

    Using edge primitives chamfer the top two edges 3 ¥ 45°.

    Note the location of the WCS. Save the drawings for future use.

Figure 105

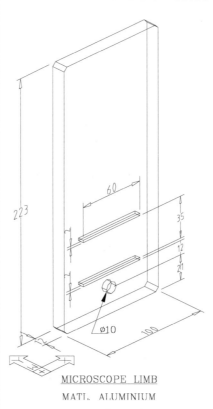

MICROSCOPE LIMB

MATL. ALUMINIUM

2. Create a solid model of a mild steel cam post in Figure 106 by using a swept primitive (REVOLVE). Use your own dimensions for the missing geometry details. Save the drawing for future use.

Figure 106

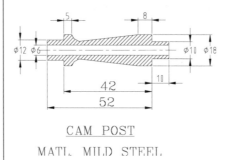

CAM POST

MATL. MILD STEEL.

3. Create a solid model of the aluminium cam wheel in Figure 107 using a swept primitive (EXTRUDE). The wheel's height is 10 mm. The axis of rotation is coplanar to the 'Y' axis in WCS.

Figure 107

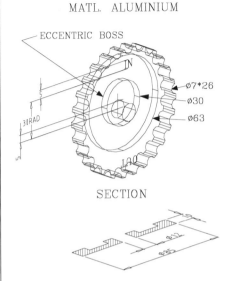

CAM WHEEL
MATL. ALUMINIUM

ECCENTRIC BOSS

ø7*26
ø30
ø63

SECTION

Hint:
(a) Rotate the UCS 90° about the 'X' axis.
(b) Draw the complete profile before using the EXTRUDE command.
(c) Give a thickness value to the text and subtract this value using a Boolean operation.
(d) To create the eccentric boss, extrude the 73 outside dia. and 30 inside dia. a distance of 5 mm.
(e) Subtract this eccentric boss and the cam wheel on the reverse side to the text, with its ' top dead centre' in line with the engraved text 'IN'.
(f) Save the further use.
(g) Render the subassembly similar to the view shown in Figure 108.

Figure 108

4. Parabolic curved reflectors (see Figure 109) are used in light paths when the light rays are to form a parallel beam (collimated light). Consider the problem of drawing a car headlight reflector requiring a parabolic curve. Choose any convenient dimension for this task. Figure 110 shows the resultant curves of a cone with four different cutting planes: circle, ellipse, parabola and hyperbola.

Figure 109

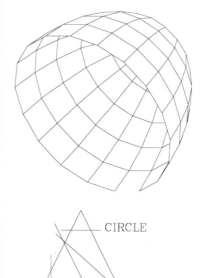

Figure 110

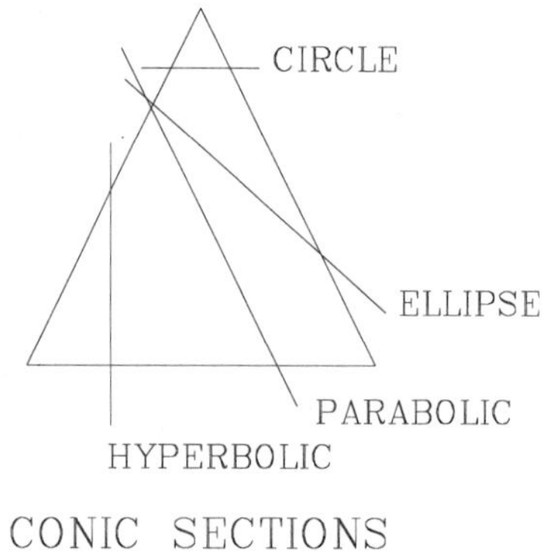

CIRCLE

ELLIPSE

PARABOLIC

HYPERBOLIC

CONIC SECTIONS

Hint:
(a) Rotate the UCS 90° about the 'X' axis.
(b) Construct a solid cone.
(c) Use the SECTION command to create a parabolic section.
(d) Explode the section and trim half of the parabolic curve.
(e) Revsurf half of this curve about the axis of revolution.
(f) Render the curve.
(g) Saved this parabolic reflector for future use.

Exercise 4
Lines in space and true length

On completion of this exercise the reader shall be able to:

■ Construct and visualise a line in space, and determine its length.
■ Use the ELEVATION command in conjunction with the THICKNESS command.
■ Use the AutoLISP function NOR to achieve a plan view normal to a 2D object.
■ Use lines in space to construct the surface development of a pyramid and a cylinder.
■ Apply the TRIM command to apparent intersections.
■ Polyedit a polyline using the FIT subcommand to create a smooth curve.
■ Use the DIVIDE command in a practical example.
■ PEDIT a line in space for TANGENT curve fitting.
■ Use the 3DARRAY command.
■ Use the transparent `CAL command to calculate an OFFSET value.
■ Determine vectorial viewports more precisely.
■ Determine an angle within the CAL command.

Students of geometry will recognise the value of 3D graphics and models as vital tools to the understanding of 'lines in space' and the constant need to refer to visual aids to convert the abstract into the concrete.

Certain 3D books are available in this respect. With the use of specially coloured glasses, jumbled 2D coloured lines are transformed into magical 3D images that appear to rise from the surface of the paper, making the books a most valuable visual aid for students of plane geometry.

A set of questions on lines in space was a regular feature of most awarding bodies in 'O' level geometry test papers, proving the downfall of many students. With computer 3D graphics, this is no longer a problem.

With the need to develop spatial concepts in GCSE design courses, the use of modelling is currently an essential requirement. However, with the introduction of computer graphics into the GCSE syllabuses, students are now presenting design assignments for assessment which have been produced entirely by advanced solid modelling techniques.

Lines in space

A 3D line in space is a problem in 'compound' angles (angles 'B' and 'C' in Figure 111). The length of the line when viewed in the direction of arrow 'A' is shortened relative to angle 'B'. The true length of the line is achieved when viewed normal to angle 'B' coplanar to angle 'C'. (See 3DL.LSP, *A Practical Guide to AutoCAD AutoLISP*).

Figure 111

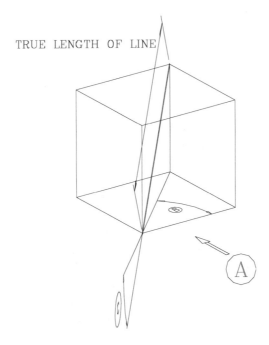

Whilst the solutions can be achieved by graphical means, solutions may also be achieved mathematically. Once more, this is no longer a problem with the aid of 3D computer graphics.

Let us reduce lines in space to a practical problem. A structural engineer requested a simple solution to the following problem. Figure 112 shows a roof structure with four different lines in space, 'A', 'B', 'C' and 'D'. These lines are

Figure 112

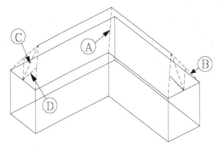

LINES IN SPACE A,B,C and D.

at a compound angle to the walls of the building. What is the length of these four lines?

Start a new drawing with suitable limits having a SNAP value of 5 and enter the following:

COMMAND: ELEV

Prompt New current elevation: *enter* 0 *(zero)*
New current thickness: 40

draw the ground plan to the dimensions shown in Figure 113.

Figure 113

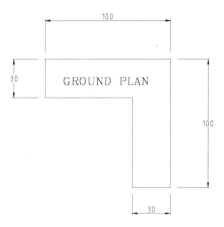

Now enter:

```
COMMAND: VPOINT
        : enter -1,-1,1
COMMAND: HIDE
```

Notice the resultant 3D faces are created as a pocket not a boss

```
COMMAND: VPOINT
        : enter 0,0,1
```

This is the same result as the PLAN command, looking down the positive 'Z' axis. (If in doubt, use the right hand rule.) Now, we use the ELEV command as an alternative to the UCS command used in Exercise 1 to move up and down the 'Z' axis:

```
COMMAND: ELEV
elevation: enter 65 i.e. 25 above the top of the wall
thickness: enter 0 (zero)
```

Now draw the roof apex as shown in Figure 114.

When complete, return the elevation and the thickness to zero. If you discover at a later stage of your drawing that you have forgotten to return the elevation and thickness to zero (something that often happens with this method of moving

Figure 114

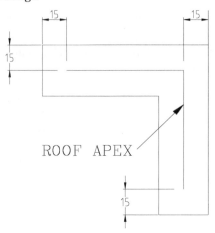

ROOF APEX

up and down the 'Z' axis), edit your drawing with the CHPROP and/or MOVE commands.

I don't wish to be drawn into recommending 'the best method' in computer graphics as there is often more than one solution to a particular problem. I am a firm believer that the best solution is the one that you are currently happy with at a particular stage of your development.

Now enter:

```
COMMAND: VPOINT
        : enter -1,-0.75,1
```

Complete the drawing (see Figure 115) by adding lines 'A', 'B', 'C' and 'D' (11 lines in total). Make sure you remember Rule 1: no free-hand sketching; use the end, intersection and mid-points to locate the lines accurately. Save the viewpoint.

Figure 115

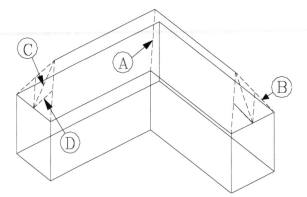

Quick plan view

In order to illustrate a quick plan view without moving the UCS, construct a circle on one of the roof inclined faces (Figure 116) by first moving the UCS to that particular face. (Remember CIRCLE is a '2D' command.) When complete, return to the WCS.

Figure 116

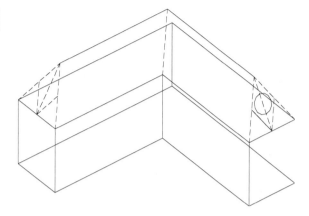

Consider a situation where you required a view looking normal or perpendicular to a circle, arc or polyline anywhere on the 3D model. At the command prompt enter:

```
COMMAND: VPOINT
          : `CAL
 expression: NOR
          : select the circle and observe the results
```

When complete, return to the previously saved viewpoint in preparation for the LIST command. This command displays database information of selected objects. The type of information depends upon the object selected. In our case, the length of material used in the roof structure ('true' length of line) is required. At the LIST command prompts, select each spar in turn, comparing your results with the values in Figure 117.

Figure 117

SPAR	LENGTH
A	32.7872
B	32.7872
C	29.1548
D	16.3936

Alternative method

Use the shortcut function DEE (distance between two end-points):

```
      COMMAND: CAL
   expression: DEE
            : pick ends of the line required
```

Surface development

Surface development of cones, cylinders and pyramids is often a problem of lines in space and true lengths of line. Consider the problem of a five-sided regular pyramid with a vertical height of 30 mm and a maximum length of each side 10 mm (Figure 118).

Figure 118

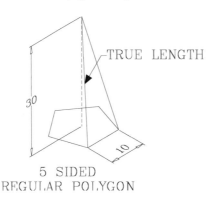

Open a new drawing with layers CONS and DEVT. Make layer CONS current. Enter:

```
                COMMAND: POLYGON
        Prompt Number of sides: 5
   Edge/<Centre of polygon>: enter E
      first end-point of edge: pick a convenient point on the
                               screen
   second end-point of edge: @10,0
                    COMMAND: ARC
                           : use the default 3POINT method
                           : use the OSNAP mode MID to select
                             'P1', 'P2' and 'P3'
```

Figure 119

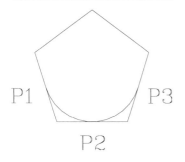

The result is shown in Figure 119. We are now able to construct a line in space using the arc and polygon as construction geometry. Change to layer DEVT (DEVelopmenT):

```
   COMMAND: VPOINT
          : enter -1,-1,1
```

Figure 120

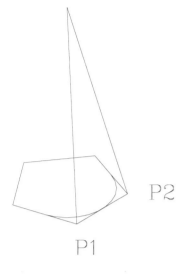

P2

P1

```
COMMAND: LINE
      from: .XY
        of: CEN
    CEN of: select the arc
need Z value: 30
        to: select 'P2'
        to: select 'P1'
        to: C for Close
```

The triangle represents the boundary of one of the sides of the pyramid (Figure 120). Before using the ARRAY command to rotate five sides about the apex of the triangle, change the UCS to the same plane as this inclined triangle by using the 3POINT option, and freeze the CONS layer.

Alternatively, use the CAL command to determine angle 'A' as follows:

```
        COMMAND: CAL
Prompt expression: ANG(END,END,END)
               : select the apex of the angle, then select fhe
                 opposite vertices
```

Surface development of pyramid

With reference to Figure 121, enter:

```
COMMAND: PLAN
       : accept the <Current UCS> option
COMMAND: DIM
       : use the ANGULAR subcommand to determine angle 'A'
```

Figure 121

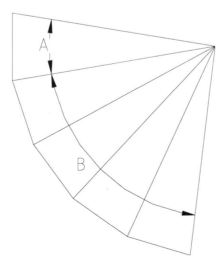

A

B

With the aid of the CAL command it is now possible to determine the angle to fill with the POLAR ARRAY command, i.e. angle B = 4 × Angle A.

Use the ARRAY command to complete the surface development of the pyramid. (See TRUEL.LSP in *A Practical Guide to AutoCAD AutoLISP* for a simple solution to this problem.)

When the surface to be developed is curved, such as that of a cylinder or a cone, a different approach is necessary. Use a series of lines or cutting planes within the area of intersection in the same way as the conventional draughting method to determine the true lengths.

The introduction of the object snap (OSNAP) mode, APPARENT INTERSECTION made this task simple. It enabled the intersection of two or more objects in 3D space to be detected even when they did not actually intersect.

Surface development of a cylinder (alternative approach)

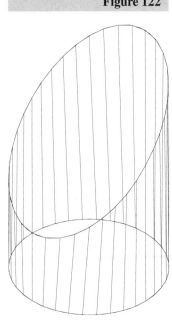

Figure 122

The procedure to draw the surface development of a right cylinder, cut at an angle as in Figure 122 (i.e. two pipes of equal diameter, brazed or welded to form a bend) is well covered in *A Practical Guide to AutoCAD AutoLISP*, Ref. CYL.LSP. As this is an exercise in lines in space, we will consider an alternative approach to the problem.

Open a new drawing with layers CONS and DEVT, making layers CONS current. In the WCS, move the UCS origin to the middle of the screen:

```
COMMAND: LINE
    from: -50,0
      to: @0,0,150
```

The stages in the following procedure are illustrated in Figures 123 to 132. Enter:

```
               COMMAND: ARRAY
Prompt Select objects: enter L for Last
Rectangular or Polar: enter P for Polar
         centre point: 0,0
       number of items: 12
         angle of fill: 360
               COMMAND: VPOINT
                     : -1, -0.8,1
                     : save this view as '1' (Figure 123)

               COMMAND: UCS
                     : X
                     : 90
               COMMAND: LINE
```

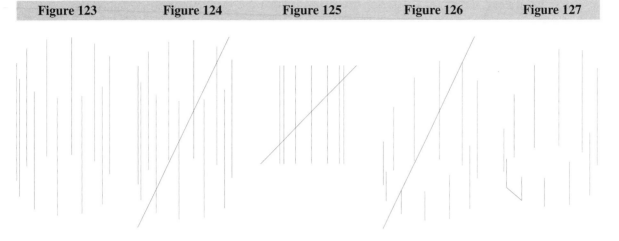

Figure 123   Figure 124   Figure 125   Figure 126   Figure 127

```
                          from: -80,0
                            to: 70,150  (Figure 124)

                       COMMAND: PLAN  (current UCS)
                       COMMAND: TRIM
        Prompt Select cutting edge: L  for Last
                   Select objects: APPINT  for APParent
                                   INTersection
                               of: F  use the Fence selection method
                                   to select all the extended lines
                                   (Figure 125). In the event of
                                   failure, check the projection mode

                       COMMAND: VIEW
                             : restore view '1' and erase the
                                   inclined line. Save the current
                                   UCS as '1', return to the WCS.
                                   Change to layer DEVT (Figure 126)

                       COMMAND: LINE
                          from: END
                       END of: select the end of a line
                            to: END
                       END of: select the end of adjacent line
                                   (Figure 127)

                       COMMAND: UCS
                             : use OB or E to rotate the 'X' axis in
                                   line with the last line by selecting
                                   this line (Figure 128)
```

Figure 128	Figure 129	Figure 130

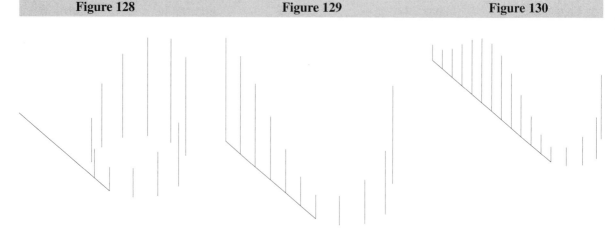

```
        Prompt Select objects: L
                            : R for Rectangular
               number of rows: 1
            number of columns: 6
     distance between columns: END
                      END of: select one end of the line
                          to: END
                      END of: select the other end of the line
```

Set the OSNAP to END mode and move six of the vertical lines to their new location (Figure 129).

Use the MIRROR command to extend the development to 13 vertical lines (Figure 130).

Before using the PLINE command to draw a line from the end of each vertical line (Figure 131), change the UCS, using the 3POINT method to locate the horizontal lines in the 'X' axis and the vertical lines in the 'Y' axis.

Make sure that all the required entities or objects are on layer DEVT before freezing layer CONS. (CHPROP). Then:

Figure 131	Figure 132

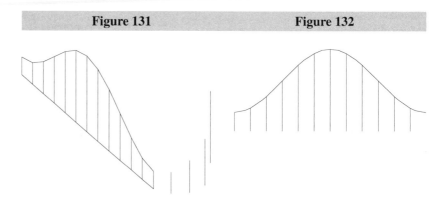

```
COMMAND: PEDIT
```
    : *select the polyline and fit the curve (Figure 132)*

Those readers who have the AutoLISP Macro CYL.LSP can load and run this macro, superimposing one curve on top of the other for direct comparison. This will help with your particular choice of method.

Construction errors

One source of error in the line construction method is the length of the horizontal line representing the circumference. This line was constructed from 12 chords, in the same way as the traditional draughting method, and as such will be slightly short (depending upon the number of vertical lines used in the construction).

For a precise method of construction, draw a horizontal line the length of the circumference of the cylinder, using the transparent `CAL command to determine the length of the line, followed by the DIVIDE command to divide this line into the required number of divisions before moving the vertical construction lines to their new location, as follows:

```
COMMAND: LINE
        from: select a convenient point
          to: `CAL
  expression: [@PI*100<0]  i.e. πD =
                CIRcumference
     COMMAND: DIVIDE
Prompt Select object: enter L for Last
<Number of segments>: 12
```

It is now possible to move the construction lines to the end-point of each line and to complete the surface development.

Remember the OSNAP setting. I find this similar to switching the car lights on when it is foggy, with every intention of switching off the lights at the end of the journey – somehow I always seem to forget. Remove the OSNAP setting (see Rule 3). Fortunately, modern car designers have incorporated an audible warning system for car drivers (no such luck for CAD users).

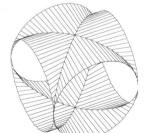

Figure 133

Intersecting cylinders

A similar problem involving lines in space is the construction of the intersection between two cylinders of equal diameter and at right angles to each other (Figure 133).

Consider a problem involving 50 mm diameter cylinders. Start a new drawing with the CONS layer current and the UCS origin in the middle of the screen. The stages in the following procedure are illustrated in Figures 134 to 139. At the command prompt enter:

Figure 134

```
COMMAND: LINE
Prompt from: 25,0
        to: 0,0 construction line in the 'x' direction
        to: 0,25 construction line in the 'y' direction
COMMAND: LINE
Prompt from: 0,25,25
        to: 25,0,0 This is the 'line in space' for future
                   editing
COMMAND: VPOINT
        : -0.5,-1,1
        : save this view as view '1' (Figure 134)
```

Figure 135

```
COMMAND: UCS
Prompt Rotate about: x
            angle: 90
                : save as FRONT
COMMAND: ARC
                : C
   centre point: 0,0
    start point: 25,0
    end point  : 0,25  (Figure 135)

COMMAND: UCS
Prompt Rotate about:  Y
            angle: -45  (Figure 136)
```

The next part of the procedure involves the tangent editing of polyline:

Figure 136

```
COMMAND: PEDIT
        : select the line in space and make into a polyline
        : select E for Edit
        : T for Tangent. This option attaches a tangent
          direction to the line at the displayed vertex, marked
          by the 'X' in Figure 136, for future editing
Angle degrees:  0 note the direction of the displayed arrow
        <N>: accept the default value for the next vertex
        : T
Angle degrees: 270 once more note the direction of the arrow
        : X
        : F for Fit. The curve passes through both vertices in
          the specified tangent direction
        : X
COMMAND: SURFTAB1
        : 16
```

Change to layer FACES in preparation for the construction of a 3D mesh.

Figure 137

COMMAND: RULESURF

Prompt `Select the first ruling curve:` *select the end of the arc, above the 'Y' axis*

`Select the second defining curve:` *select the same end of the polyline (Figure 137)*

COMMAND: UCS
  : *restore FRONT*
COMMAND: MIRROR
`Select objects:` *select the mesh, using the end of the construction line drawn in the 'x' direction as first and second points of the mirror line*
COMMAND: MIRROR
`Select objects:` *select both meshes, using 0,0 and 'F8' (ORTHO) for the mirror line (Figure 138)*

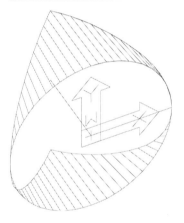

Figure 138

COMMAND: 3DARRAY
`Select objects:` *select the four meshes*

The meshes should be selected using the POLAR option with the end of the construction line originally drawn in the 'y' direction with 'F8' in the current 'Y' axis as the centre point of the array and second point on the axis of rotation, respectively. Finally, freeze the CONS layer and test the results with the HIDE or Shade command. The results are shown in Figure 139.

Figure 139

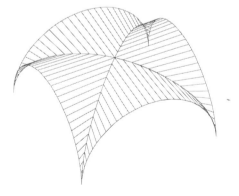

3D to the rescue

When two pieces of wood positioned at right angles to each other form a joint, the result is a 45° mitre or 'picture frame' joint. Many readers will have performed this task with the aid of a mitre block and tenon saw. Industrial manufacturing methods involve the use of a circular saw with the wood located against a fence positioned at 45° to the circular saw.

Figure 140

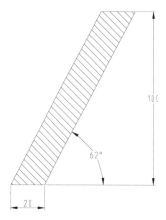

If mitres are to be produced from such sections with a short base, as shown in Figure 140, it becomes more practical to place one of the longer sides on the horizontal table against the fence. The result of this practice is to change both the 'fence angle' and the 'cutter angle' as the fence is no longer at 45° and the circular saw does not rotate about the horizontal axis (our old friend the 'compound angle').

3D problem solving

A local company manufacturing kitchen furniture experienced problems determining both the angles using a 'trial and error' solution. The following 3D computer graphics solution relieved the company of its 'guestimation' method, saving on time, scrap and operator stress.

There are two solutions to the problem: wire frame and solid modelling. For this exercise we will use a wire frame.

Figure 141   **Figure 142**

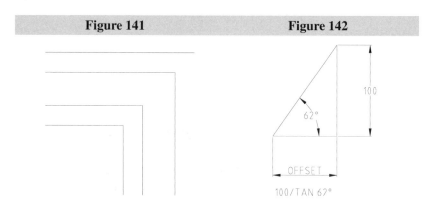

In order to determine the intersection lines in space, consider the top right-hand corner joint (think of a picture frame). Open a new drawing with layers CONS and INTER, making the CONS layer current. In the WCS, using the PLINE command, draw two lines at right angles to each other and offset this polyline 20 mm to represent part of the plan view of the base (Figure 141). To offset these two polylines to represent the top of the section, use the following:

```
COMMAND: OFFSET
         : `CAL
expression: +100/TANG(62)
```

Select both lines to offset, and move these two polylines up the positive 'Z' axis 100 mm using the MOVE command (Figure 142). Notice the use of the trigonometric ratio (tangent) within the transparent CAL command. TANG is a standard AutoLISP function. Next, enter:

```
COMMAND: VPOINT
         : -0.5,-1,1
```

Using the OSNAP in END mode complete the section and intersection lines as shown in Figure 143. The section lines are included for clarity, you don't have to include them. Remember, no free-hand sketching – Rule 1.

Figure 143

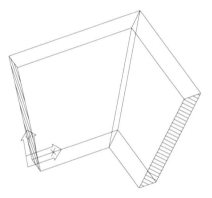

The view looks as though a perspective has been applied. This is not the case – it is because the side walls of the section incline inwards.

Fence angle determination

Move the UCS to the section as shown using the 3point option. In order to reduce the image from two sections to one, explode the four polylines:

```
                COMMAND: CHPROP
```
Prompt `Select objects:` *select the entire section containing the*
                                UCS icon, remembering to include the
                                four lines of the intersection
`Change what property:` LA *for Layer*

Figure 144

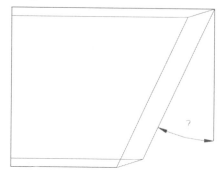

Select layer INTER, making this layer current, and freeze the layer CONS. Save the current UCS as BASE using the PLAN command to create the view as shown in Figure 144. Draw a vertical line from the apex of the intersection using 'F8' (ORTHO).

```
            COMMAND: CAL
  Prompt expresssion: ANG(END,END,END)
                   : select the apex of the angle, then select the two
                     opposite vertices (erase the vertical line)
```

The calculated angle represents the fence angle (Figure 145).

Figure 145

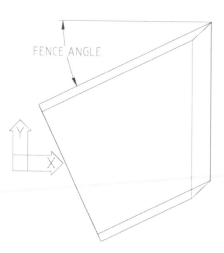

FENCE ANGLE

```
            COMMAND: ROTATE
  Prompt Select objects: select every object
             base point: use the apex of the intersection
         rotation angle: enter the value obtained for the CAL
                         command
```

(Note: The CAL command could have been used transparently within the Rotate command if desired.) This now represents the position of the material on the machine table when the section is located against the fence. The circular saw needs to be at an angle to the table in order to cut the intersection plane.

Cutter angle determination

Use the 3point option to locate the UCS in the intersection plane, use objects snaps such as MID, END and PER, respectively, to locate the UCS. Draw a line from (0,0,0) to any given length using 'F8' (ORTHO), as shown in Figure 146. Restore the saved UCS (BASE), then enter:

Figure 146

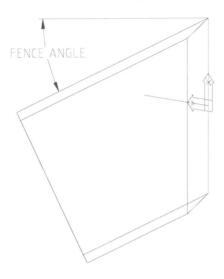

```
COMMAND: UCS
        : X
        : 90
```

Draw a line from the end of the last line, as shown in Figure 147, using the CAL command as above to determine the cutter angle.

Figure 147

Tasks

1. Refer back to the structural engineering problem at the start of this exercise.
    (a) Determine the length of a spar constructed from the mid-point of line 'B' to the perpendicular of the wall beam.
    (b) Determine the total area requiring roof tiles.

2. A box having a sectional dimension of 130×55 mm is required to contain a rod 155 mm in length (neglect the diameter of the rod). What is the minimum depth of box required? (Solutions by graphics.)

3. Construct the surface development of a truncated pyramid combining the methods used in the two exercises in the text (to develop a pyramid and a truncated cylinder).

4. Construct a vaulted roof using the same technique as the one we used in the intersecting cylinders problem, with dimensions of your choice.

5. The cutter problem described in the text involved two sections of material at right angles to each other. Determine the fence angle and cutter angle when the two pieces are $120°$ to each other (included angle) using exactly the same section as in the exercise.

Exercise 5
Customised solutions to 3D design

On completion of this exercise the reader shall be able to:

- Create a polygon mesh by specifying the coordinates of each vertex (3DMESH command).
- Use a script file to simplify certain AutoCAD commands.
- Create a polyface mesh by using the PFACE command.
- Understand the value of AutoLISP programs.
- Automate external data reading for graphical construction.
- Give a brief description of an AutoLISP program and determine the contents of the variables used in the program.
- Describe the value of subroutines.
- Define parametric geometry.
- State the value of 'menu picking' for standardising parametric designs.
- Recognise different types of menu layout with their contents.
- Automate data collection in support of the design process by external writing to a file.
- Describe AutoCAD database reading.

AutoCAD is designed in such a way as to enable customisation of many of its major features, offering the possibility to expand and shape AutoCAD according to the user's particular needs.

Any system that simplifies the 3D computer design process is worthy of serious consideration, especially when it can be customised to meet specific industrial and commercial requirements. Script files and AutoLISP files are most beneficial in this respect.

This quick look at customised solutions will be limited to the use of script files, AutoLISP files and menu files. However, there are many more ways in which you can customise AutoCAD to the benefit of 3D design.

Complex 3D design lends itself naturally to some form of automated customisation of a parametric nature. Any commercial activity that can group its designs into family or similar graphical constructions can benefit from customisation.

Script files

The script file is used for automating repetitive tasks or for tasks of a complex nature that may need editing. A script file is an ASCII text file containing AutoCAD commands that are processed in the same way as a batch file when you run the script. Script files have no decision-making ability and cannot pause for interactive input.

Consider the tedious process of specifying vertex points within the 3DMESH command, only to find that an input error requires the entire sequence of vertex points to be re-entered at the keyboard. This is only one problem that can be solved by the use of a script file: there are more problems than most CAD users appreciate that can be solved by the use of a script file, hence its underutilisation.

The 3DMESH command is used to create a surface model constructed from a series of planar facets such as a 3D topographical model of a mountainous terrain or even the facets of our monocular head. It is best used in conjunction with script files (or an AutoLISP routine).

The density of the mesh is governed by the specified matrix of 'M' and 'N' vertices, very similar to an irregular surface grid constructed from rows and columns in the 'x' and 'y' directions (Figure 148).

Figure 148

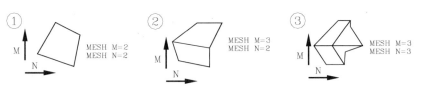

The intersection of each line represents the different vertex points and need to be specified in a particular order. Defining vertices begins with vertex (0,0) followed by the coordinate points ('N') for each vertex in the first row of 'M', continuing with vertices in row 'M + 1', followed by row 'M + 2' and so on. For example, part 2 of Figure 148 would be defined as follows:

```
          COMMAND: 3DMESH
    Prompt MESH M size: 3
          MESH N size: 2
Row 'M1' Vertex (0,0): needs the coordinate value
         Vertex (0,1): needs the coordinate value
Row 'M2' Vertex (1,0): needs the coordinate value
         Vertex (1,1): needs the coordinate value
Row 'M3' Vertex (2,0): needs the coordinate value
         Vertex (2,1): needs the coordinate value
```

In Exercise 1, reference was made to the AutoLISP file MONO.LSP (see Appendix A) that automatically created the monocular head from a series of keyboard input values for length, width and so on, in response to screen prompts.

As an exercise in the use of script files, let us construct the monocular head using the same dimensions as the previous three exercises involving the monocular head. I have deliberately used tedious coordinate dimensions to illustrate the benefits of a script file for, if like me, you are prone to making keyboard errors then editing the script file is not a problem.

Figure 149

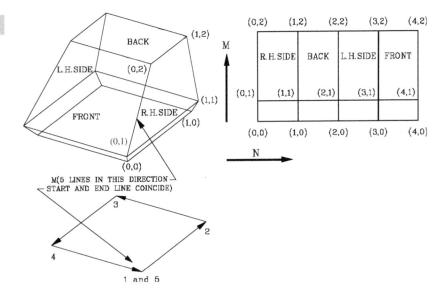

To simplify the 'M/N' mesh diagram, consider the four faces, FRONT, R.H. SIDE, BACK and L.H. SIDE, as a surface development of rectangles (Figure 149 – ignore for the benefit of the diagram the value of the coordinates).

Script file for monocular head

Use your preferred text editor such as Edit (DOS) or Notepad (Windows) to create the following file A:MONO.SCR (making sure to use '.SCR' as the extension):

```
MONO.SCR

3DMESH
5
3
110.1352,125.9689,0
99.8852,120.0511,10.25
149.8852,130.0511,60.25
199.8852,125.9689,0
199.8852,120.0511,10.25
199.8852,130.0511,60.25
199.8852,204.1333,0
199.8852,210.0511,10.25
199.8852,200.0511,60.25
```

```
110.1352,204.1333,0
99.8852,210.0511,10.25
149.8852,200.0511,60.25
110.1352,125.9689,0
99.8852,120.0511,10.25
149.8852,130.0511,60.25
```

Notice that the last three lines of coordinates are a repeat of the first three coordinate points $(0,0) = (4,0)$, $(0,1) = (4,1)$ and $(0,2) = (4,2)$ giving a total of 15 different coordinate points, i.e. 5('M') × 3('N').

COMMAND: SCRIPT
Prompt Script name: A:MONO

Use the HIDE or SHADE command with a convenient viewpoint noting the absence of a 3D face on the top of the monocular head. The PFACE command is a better solution to this type of problem.

Using the PFACE command

The PFACE command creates a 3D polyface mesh, vertex by vertex, and is similar to the 3DFACE command. You define a polyface mesh by specifying each vertex, preferably in some form of geometrical order such as 1 to 5 in Figure 149. Once every vertex coordinate point has been entered, pressing 'Enter' on a blank line causes AutoCAD to prompt for the vertices to be assigned to each face, beginning with face '1'. When all the vertices for face '1' have been entered, pressing 'Enter' on a blank line causes AutoCAD to prompt for the vertices of face '2' and so on (see Figure 150).

```
            COMMAND: PFACE
    Prompt VERTEX 1: specify a point
           VERTEX 2: specify a point
           VERTEX 3: specify a point
           VERTEX 4: specify a point
           VERTEX 5: specify a point
           VERTEX 6: press 'Enter'
  FACE 1, VERTEX 1: 1
  FACE 1, VERTEX 2: 2
  FACE 1, VERTEX 3: 3
  FACE 1, VERTEX 4: press 'Enter'
  FACE 2, VERTEX 1: 2
  FACE 2, VERTEX 3: 4
  FACE 2, VERTEX 4: 5
  FACE 2, VERTEX 5: press 'Enter'
  FACE 3, VERTEX 1: press 'Enter'
```

Figure 150

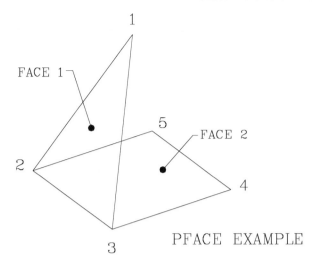

Using a text editor such as Notepad (Windows), edit the A:MONO.SCR file as shown in the program and save as A:MONO2.SCR. Remember to enter the blank lines as shown, not forgetting the two blank lines at the end of the program. AutoCAD accepts a blank line or a space in the script file program as an 'Enter' key input to terminate a command or subcommand.

```
MONO2.SCR

PFACE
110.1352,125.9689,0
99.8852,120.0511,10.25
149.8852,130.0511,60.25
199.8852,125.9689,0
199.8852,120.0511,10.25
199.8852,130.0511,60.25
199.8852,204.1333,0
199.8852,210.0511,10.25
199.8852,200.0511,60.25
110.1352,204.1333,0
99.8852,210.0511,10.25
149.8852,200.0511,60.25

1
2
5
4

4
5
8
7
```

```
7
8
11
10

10
11
2
1

2
3
6
5

5
8
9
6

8
9
12
11

11
2
3
12

12
3
6
9
```

The first part of the program defines the twelve different points or vertices involved in the construction of the monocular head – simply remove the last three rows of figures from the A:MONO.SCR file.

The surfaces of the monocular head are divided into nine individual groups (including the top of the head), each individual face containing four vertex points.

The second part of the program contains the nine individual faces (groups of four digits) separated by a blank line.

Now enter:

```
COMMAND: SCRIPT
       : A:MONO2
```

Hide or shade the drawing to confirm the results, using a convenient viewpoint.

AutoLISP programs

You can write your own AutoLISP programs or use third-party shareware programs. AutoLISP is not difficult to learn but you must become familiar with the language. AutoLISP programs are particularly suited to solid modelling as they are designed to automate repetitive activities. Parametric programs are of great value when constructing solid or surface models. All designers should be encouraged to identify family parts or objects that are of a parametric or repetitive nature for potential programming when constructing 3D models.

Rule 15
When constructing solid models, keep alert to the potential for automatic creation by customisation.

Who, for example, wishes to construct countersunk or counterbore holes, when all that is necessary is to load and run an AutoLISP program that prompts you for the variables prior to constructing the object automatically. You can have your most commonly used programs loaded automatically whenever you enter the drawing editor if you so wish.

AutoLISP programs are particularly beneficial to companies when the program relates directly to the specific needs of that company. You do not have to limit your horizons to simple 'nuts and bolts': many very sophisticated programs created by 'in-house designers' are replacing the more tedious and time-consuming methods of constructing 3D models.

I have to admit my long-standing enthusiasm for engineering design does not extend to the more mundane aspects of detail draughting, in particular the implementation of BS 4500(A) *Limits and Fits*. I am sure that I am not alone in this respect.

Nevertheless, the subject is of great importance to the satisfactory functioning of a vast range of everyday components and assemblies. Furthermore, if not conducted satisfactorily it can lead to expensive design failures. It is important to bear in mind that most design failures are due to the lack of attention to detail and not the design concept.

We should therefore look to automate, as far as possible, such processes. In fact, any form of data collection, be it from reading, tables, catalogues, manuals or any other form of literature, in the process of constructing computer graphics, should be performed automatically. All that is necessary is the construction of a database file in such a way as to be directly accessible by an AutoLISP program, all the different grouped data being associated with a unique tag.

Let the computer extract the data when required, eliminating error in the collection of data (providing the correct tag is used), offering an instant update in the event of any editing of the database file, reducing designer fatigue and freeing the designer for more creative and rewarding activities.

The process may appear somewhat complicated at first, but it really is simple and should be used more often to accommodate in-house family grouping of graphics.

Consider as an exercise the construction of 3 boxes with data collected from an external database (Figure 151). I have deliberately simplified the exercise. In practice the number of variables (length, width, height) and objects (boxes '1', '2' and '3') in the database would be much larger and the graphics more complex. These boxes could in fact be: tolerances, bearings, beams – in fact any parametric geometrical construction that can be grouped into a family. Try this exercise and see what you think.

Figure 151

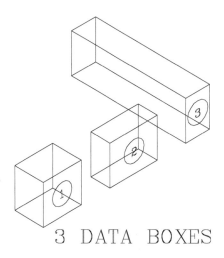

3 DATA BOXES

Database reading

Using an ASCII text editor create the following database file. Leave a blank line at the top of the file. Use comma delimited format (CDF) for your data file. There should be no spaces at either the front or the end of each line. Do not place a comma after the last entity in each line of data. Do not include the line number in your file.

```
Name of file:  A:BOXES.DAT
Line no. 1
Line no. 2     **1
Line no. 3     40,30,100
Line no. 4     **2
Line no. 5     50,20,30
Line no. 6     **3
Line no. 7     25,120,20
```

The two asterisks '**' are placed before the data group number so as to create a unique 'tag' for that set of data. You do not have to use the same tag, but be consistent with the following AutoLISP file. The rows of data represent the values for length ('LE'), width ('WI') and height ('HT'), separated by commas.

With the aid of this AutoLISP file it is possible to open the database file (BOXES.DAT), locate a particular record of data by means of the unique tag and to assign this record to a variable (DATA) for further use (just as you would assign PI to the value 3.142). A flow chart of the procedure is set out in Figure 152.

Using the text editor Notepad (Windows) or a similar type of editor, create the following AutoLISP file. Those readers with a Windows type operating system will be able to toggle back and forth between Notepad and AutoCAD by pressing the 'Alt' and 'Tab' keys simultaneously.

Figure 152

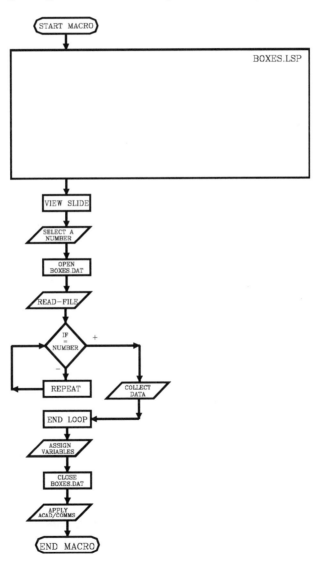

Name the file A:BOXES.LSP. (Make sure that all AutoLISP files have the extension '.LSP'.)

Notice that each of the lines in the program between the first opening parenthesis and the last closing parenthesis (the function) is indented. The actual number of spaces indented is not important. The purpose is to show the structure of the program and to help check the program in the event of an error message when loading.

```
BOXES.LSP

(DEFUN C:BOXES ()
(GRAPHSCR)
(SETQ CODE (GETINT "\n\tPLEASE ENTER THE REQUIRED CODE NUMBER ")
      NUMBER (STRCAT "**" (ITOA CODE))
      BD (OPEN "A:BOXES.DAT" "r")
      FIND (READ-LINE BD)
)
 (WHILE FIND
  (SETQ FIND (READ-LINE BD))
   (IF (= FIND NUMBER)
    (SETQ DATA (READ-LINE BD) FIND NIL)
   )
 )
(CLOSE BD)
; (STRTOLST)
; (DRWBOX)
)
```

Try to copy the BOXES.LSP program with care, noting spaces, parentheses and quotation marks as required. An explanation of the program is given below.

- Line 1 – Defines the name of the function (user defined function). The 'C' indicates a new AutoCAD command to be created called BOXES. (I try to use the same function and file name whenever possible.) The function starts with a left-hand parenthesis and ends with a right-hand parenthesis on line 17.
- Line 2 – Flicks from the text screen to the graph screen if it is necessary.
- Line 3 – Think of the function SETQ (set quotant) as LET, hence LET CODE is equal to the input value. The variable named CODE is then assigned to the input value, in this case '1', '2' or '3'. Whenever a function starts with the letters GET, the program pauses for a user input, hence the need for a screen prompt ('...'). The '\n' code, prints the prompt on a new line. The '\t' code indents the prompt one indent to the right.

    You can simplify programming by making multiple assignments with the SETQ function. I have used a new line in each case to clarify the program (this is not essential).

    The SETQ function begins with an opening parenthesis on line 3 and ends with a closing parenthesis on line 7, thus balancing the number of left- and right-hand parentheses within the function.

- Line 4 – The two asterisks are placed in front of the code value and assigned the variable name number, hence if CODE = 2 then NUMBER = **2
- Line 5 – The database file called BOXES.DAT is opened for reading. Note that the 'r' at the end of the line must be in lower case.
- Line 6 – The first line of this data file is then read, i.e. the blank line at the top of the file.
- Line 7 to 12 – The loop starts at line 7 and ends at line 12. It searches the data file until an identical match is found (between the requested number and a line in the data file – see line 10). Once this line is located in the data file, line 11 of the AutoLISP program reads the next line in the database file, assigning the record or line of data to the variable 'DATA'. Hence, using 'CODE = 2' as an example, 'DATA' = 50,20,30. At the same time the variable 'FIND' is set to NIL, thus closing the WHILE loop. Be careful not to enter a zero instead of NIL. This would have the effect of 'locking-up' the program as the WHILE loop would be set to infinity and would never close.
- Line 13 – Once the program has assigned the record or line of data to the variable 'DATA', all that is required is to close the WHILE loop and
- Line 14 – Closes the file BOXES.DAT (BD).
- Lines 15 to 16 – These are sub-routines to be used later. Because the lines begin with a semi-colon, AutoCAD ignores them as being comments, ignoring everything to the right of the semi-colon. (The same as the REM statement in basic for those with long enough memories).We will remove the semi-colons when the program is completed satisfactorily.

Testing the program

At the command prompt enter:

```
COMMAND: (LOAD "A:BOXES")
  Prompt C: BOXES
```

This prompt indicates success. If an error message appears, return to the AutoLISP program, checking for accuracy of typing, make any necessary corrections, save the file and reload it in AutoCAD as above.

If you still have problems loading the file, try to detect the line of program causing the problem by entering the following at the command prompt.

```
COMMAND: !CODE
```

If this prompts a value other than NIL continue

```
COMMAND: !NUMBER
```

Continue entering the variable names in the order of the program until you detect the prompt NIL, this being the offending line.

Run the new BOXES command by entering at the command prompt:

```
COMMAND: BOXES
```

Enter a value between 1 and 3 (this being the database tag) when prompted from the screen. The resultant list of values is now assigned to the variable 'DATA' and can be recalled for use at any time by entering:

```
COMMAND: !DATA
```

Run the new BOXES command once more, changing the value of the tag (between 1 and 3) and noting the new value for 'DATA'.

The data extracted from the file BOXES.DAT is in the form of a string; any further usage in this format is limited. We need to convert the string to a list of three entities. Each one of the three entities is then allocated variables 'LE' for length, 'WI' for width and 'HT' for height. Once these AutoLISP variables have been allocated a value it becomes a simple matter of using these values within an AutoLISP macro to create the graphics.

Building the data string into a list

In order to convert the string to a list extend the program as shown in version 2 of BOXES.LSP.

```
BOXES.LSP version 2
(DEFUN C:BOXES ()
(GRAPHSCR)
(SETQ CODE (GETINT "\n\tPLEASE ENTER THE REQUIRED CODE NUMBER ")
      NUMBER (STRCAT "**" (ITOA CODE))
      BD (OPEN "A:BOXES.DAT" "r")
      FIND (READ-LINE BD)
)
  (WHILE FIND
   (SETQ FIND (READ-LINE BD))
    (IF (= FIND NUMBER)
     (SETQ DATA (READ-LINE BD) FIND NIL)
    )
  )
(CLOSE BD)
(STRTOLST)
;(DRWBOX)
)
(DEFUN STRTOLST ()   ;STRing TO a LiST
(IF DATA
 (PROGN
  (SETQ SLENGTH (STRLEN DATA)
        COUNT 1 CHAR 1)
   (WHILE (< COUNT SLENGTH)
    (IF (/= "," (SUBSTR DATA COUNT 1))
     (SETQ CHAR (1+ CHAR))
          (SETQ NUM (ATOF (SUBSTR DATA (1+ (- COUNT CHAR)) CHAR))
           DATALST (APPEND DATALST (LIST NUM)) CHAR 1)
    )
    (SETQ COUNT (1+ COUNT))
```

```
        )
     (SETQ NUM (ATOF (SUBSTR DATA (1+ (- COUNT CHAR)))))
    )
   )
  )
```

You will need to reload the program (LOAD "A:BOXES") before testing with:

```
COMMAND: (STRTOLST)
```

In the event of an error '*CANCEL*' will appear on the screen. Once the new function loads successfully, remove the semi-colon from the start of line 15, i.e. (STRTOLST).

In order to extract part of the string, the above program uses the STRLEN function to find its length and the SUBSTR function to extract the parts of the string separated by commas. The number of characters (CHAR) in each individual string is counted within the loop searching for the commas. Finally, the individual strings are returned as a real number by the function ATOF prior to the creation of a list with no commas or quotation marks.

This part of the program may appear a little complicated to those new to programming. However, the good news is that once created as a subroutine as above (STRTOLST) it becomes available for further use in any program we desire at any time (providing it has been loaded).

Load and run the edited AutoLISP macro BOXES.LSP. Remember to reload the program if further editing is found necessary.

Testing the list

To check the activities of the program enter:

```
COMMAND: !DATALST  and note the resultant list
```

If at this stage you continue to run the program, the APPEND function extends the list of values in increments of three. You will need to empty the datalist ('DATALST') before continuing with:

```
COMMAND: (SETQ DATALST NIL)
```

As a final check on the type of data used in the program, enter:

```
COMMAND: (TYPE DATA)
              and
         (TYPE DATALST)  noting the results
```

Assigning list contents to variables (parsing)

To name the three different parts of the datalist we need to assign the variables 'LE', 'WI' and 'HT' to the above list with the function MAPCAR. Once the variable values have been established they can be used to create the desired graphics.

Extend the file BOXES.LSP as shown in version 3 of BOXES.LSP.

```
BOXES.LSP version 3

(DEFUN C:BOXES ()
 (GRAPHSCR)
 (SETQ CODE (GETINT "\n\tPLEASE ENTER THE REQUIRED CODE NUMBER ")
       NUMBER (STRCAT "**" (ITOA CODE))
       BD (OPEN "A:BOXES.DAT" "r")
       FIND (READ-LINE BD)
 )
  (WHILE FIND
   (SETQ FIND (READ-LINE BD))
    (IF (= FIND NUMBER)
     (SETQ DATA (READ-LINE BD) FIND NIL)
    )
  )
 (CLOSE BD)
 (STRTOLST)
 (DRWBOX)
)
(DEFUN STRTOLST ()   ;STRing TO a LiST
 (IF DATA
  (PROGN
   (SETQ SLENGTH (STRLEN DATA)
         COUNT 1 CHAR 1)
    (WHILE (< COUNT SLENGTH)
     (IF (/= "," (SUBSTR DATA COUNT 1))
      (SETQ CHAR (1+ CHAR))
           (SETQ NUM (ATOF (SUBSTR DATA (1+ (- COUNT CHAR)) CHAR))
            DATALST (APPEND DATALST (LIST NUM)) CHAR 1)
     )
     (SETQ COUNT (1+ COUNT))
    )
     (SETQ NUM (ATOF (SUBSTR DATA (1+ (- COUNT CHAR)))))))
   )
  )
 )
(DEFUN DRWBOX ()   ;DRaW BOX
 (MAPCAR 'SET '(LE WI HT) DATALST)
 (SETQ P1 (GETPOINT "\nPLEASE PICK THE CORNER OF THE BOX "))
 (COMMAND "BOX" P1 "L" LE WI HT)
 (SETQ DATALST NIL)
)
```

Load and test the program or subroutine as before by entering

```
COMMAND: (DRWBOX)
```

When satisfied with the program, remove the semi-colon from the start of line 16.

Using the program

Now for the exciting bit! Load and run the final version of BOXES.LSP, sit back and enjoy the results of your endeavours. When complete, test for the values of the variables 'LE', 'WI' and 'HT' in the same manner as we tested for the 'DATA' value and the 'DATALST' values previously.

In the case of more complicated graphics, with a greater number of objects to select from, we need a system to remind us of the value of each CODE. There are a number of different ways to achieve this, one of the easiest solutions is to create a 'slide' file to help the user select the appropriate code.

Using a SLIDE file

Create a slide file as shown in Figure 153 using the MSLIDE command with the name BOXES.SLD. It is often a good idea to save this slide as a drawing: editing of a slide file is not possible. I find 'sods law' usually applies when you don't save the drawing, i.e. you discover the need to edit the slide file.

Figure 153

3 DATA BOXES

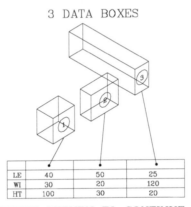

LE	40	50	25
WI	30	20	120
HT	100	30	20

PRESS RETURN TO CONTINUE

When the slide file is complete, add the following line to the BOXES.LSP file after (GRAPHSCR):

```
(COMMAND "VSLIDE" "BOXES" PAUSE "REDRAW")
```

The pause lets the user view the slide file without imposing a time delay causing the program to continue only when the 'Enter' key is pressed. Remember that the above exercise used a series of different boxes as its family group. In practice, the graphics would be more complex, the permutations greater, with a much larger database.

For the more ambitious reader, why not extend this exercise by creating the PURLIN database as shown in *A Practical Guide to AutoCAD AutoLISP*. You can use the same subroutine for changing a string to a list (STRTOLST) as above.

When considering the type of graphics suitable for database extraction as above, if the resultant graphics are parametric objects, entirely proportional in the 'X' scale and the 'Y' scale, then WBLOCKs are a better solution in conjunction with AutoLISP and screen menus (a subject I will deal with next). Database reading is best suited to those objects whose scale factors are not proportional in the 'X' axis, 'Y' axis or 'Z' axis (such as the construction of a purlin section) and to those objects resulting from complex graphics and/or a large number of values read from tables of figures, not forgetting those mundane tasks associated with detail draughting.

The above exercise has been devised to demonstrate the simplicity of linking graphics with an external data file when vectors are the only consideration. If, however, numerous attributes are to be linked with the graphics via an external database management system, AutoCAD uses SQL to communicate with the DBMS, a description being beyond the scope of this publication.

Simple command customisation

I find the most commonly used subcommand of the PEDIT command is the option 'J' for Join, particularly when using a polyline to create a 3D mesh (EDGESURF).

Try the following shortcut:

```
LIP.LSP  ;  lines into polylines

(DEFUN C:LIP ()
(GRAPHSCR)
(SETQ SS (SSGET))
   (COMMAND "PEDIT" SS "Y" "J" SS "" "X")
)
```

SSGET prompts the user to 'select objects'.

Once the AutoLISP macro is loaded (it could be loaded automatically if added to the ACAD.LSP file), enter the new command LIP, select the objects as prompted from the screen by window or crossing to form a single polyline of the selected objects.

Menu customisation

Menu customisation is particularly useful for those application-specific tasks performed on a regular basis. You can improve productivity and efficiency by modifying the existing ACAD.MNU file or by creating your own 'MNU' file. Certain organisations have developed specific menu files to suit different tasks or contracts (remember Rule 15).

Over the years AutoCAD has increased the number of files associated with the menu file; these files vary according to the operating system in use. The two main files being the menu template file (.MNU) and the compiled menu file (.MNX). As this is only a 'quick look' at customisation of menus, we can ignore the remaining files for the moment.

There are five different menu areas available for customisation, the screen menu area being the most common choice for customisation. However, an increasing number of CAD users operating with Windows are customising the screen toolbar section. For this exercise we will have a look at screen menu customisation.

As mentioned previously, when family shapes are proportional in every respect, then use a WBLOCK inserted from a customised menu such as a rectangle (for simplicity) representing a door, with the 'X' scale and the 'Y' scale values obtained by the AutoLISP GETREAL function.

AutoLISP variables and functions can be used from within the menu as well as the standard AutoCAD commands. When you select an item from the menu, it is as if you had entered the command or function directly from the keyboard.

AutoLISP as a menu driver

A menu driver can be used to facilitate easy picking of the desired combination of parameters. There are three basic reasons to use a menu driver to drive a custom parametric 3D design program.

- **Nominal identity** – A menu driver can be set up for the user to pick an object from a list of names. For example, beams can be grouped by shape (as we will see later). They can then be subgrouped by breadth, depth, thickness and length in such a way as to restrict the number of permutations (avoiding an infinite range of sizes).
- **Early set-up 'all at once'** – Setting up parameters of a figure each time it is drawn usually requires looking up the dimensions in some form of table. A designer who is involved in looking up and entering all the parameters during the drawing process is doing intermittent clerical work.

  Setting up a list of parameters for a large group of parametric objects can be achieved with the aid of a computer file, available for automatic reading at any time (such as our last exercise).
- **Automatic drawing** – A program that is designed to work from a table of values can also combine the nominal SELECT function to start the parametric drawing of a 3D object automatically once the selection has been made.

Standardising parametric design

To illustrate the principle involved, I've simplified a problem experienced by an engineering company manufacturing its own beam sections from sheet metal as part of the fabricated structure of all its products.

I have limited the standard sectional variations to three for simplicity. The designers had to construct the beams of their choice repeatedly and were allowed to use an infinite range of parametric sizes. All the different beams were constructed using AutoCAD in the conventional manner and were an integral part of every design.

Practical problem

The request was for a solution offering automatic construction of the chosen standard shaped 3D beam, to restricted parameters with lengths of integer values, located at specific insertion points, achieved by 'picking' only.

In Figures 154 to 156 and their associated AutoLISP programs, 'P1' represents the chosen insertion point of the different sections. Variables 'B', 'D' and 'T' appear in the programs as values previously defined within the menu structure.

Solution to the problem

Using a text editor, create the three different AutoLISP programs C1, C2 and C3.LSP and save to drive A. Take care when entering the program to differentiate between 'P1' and PI, and between 'O' (for Origin) and 0 (Zero). Figure 154 shows C1.DWG.LSP, Figure 155 C2.DWG.LSP and Figure 156 C3.DWG.LSP.

Figure 154

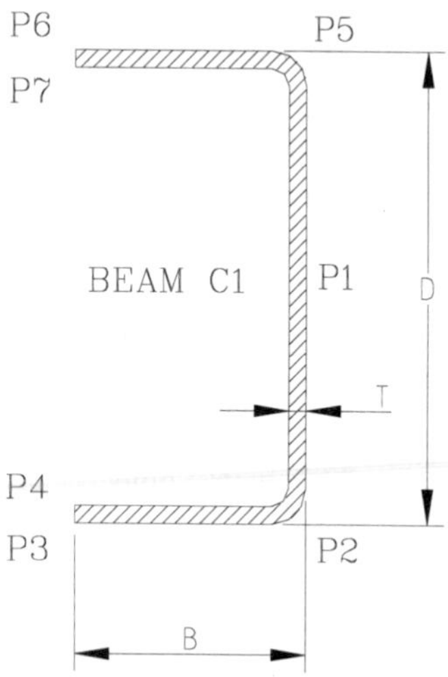

```
C1 .LSP

(DEFUN C:C1 ()
 (GRAPHSCR)
  (SETQ P1 (GETPOINT "\n\tPLEASE PICK THE INSERT POINT "))
  (COMMAND "UCS" "O" P1)
   (SETQ P1 (LIST 0 0) P2 (LIST 0 (/ (- D) 2))
          P3 (POLAR P2 PI B) P4 (POLAR P3 (/ PI 2) T)
          P5 (LIST 0 (/ D 2)) P6 (POLAR P5 PI B)
          P7 (POLAR P6 (* (/ PI 2) 3) T)
   )
   (COMMAND "PLINE" P3 "W" "0" "0" P2 P5 P6 ""
            "FILLET" "R" (* 2 T) "FILLET" "P" P1
            "OFFSET" T P1 P4 ""
            "LINE" P3 P4 "" "LINE" P6 P7 ""
            "PEDIT" P6 "J" "F" P6 P3 "" "" "")
     (COMMAND "EXTRUDE" P6 "" LENGTH ""
            "UCS" "P")
 )
```

Figure 155

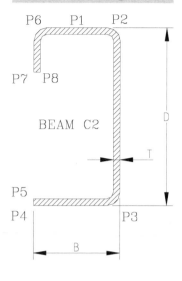

P6   P1   P2

P7   P8

BEAM C2

T

D

P5

P4   P3

B

C2.LSP

```
(DEFUN C:C2 ()
 (GRAPHSCR)
  (SETQ P1 (GETPOINT "\n\tPLEASE PICK THE INSERT POINT "))
  (COMMAND "UCS" "O" P1)
   (SETQ P1 (LIST 0 0) P2 (POLAR P1 0 (/ B 2))
         P3 (POLAR P2 (* (/ PI 2) 3) D)
         P4 (POLAR P3 PI B) P5 (POLAR P4 (/ PI 2) T)
         P6 (POLAR P2 PI B) P7 (POLAR P6 (* (/ PI 2) 3)(/ D 4))
         P8 (POLAR P7 0 T)
   )
   (COMMAND "PLINE" P7 "W" "0" "0" P6 P2 P3 P4 ""
         "FILLET" "R" (* 2 T) "FILLET" "P" P1
         "OFFSET" T P1 P8 ""
         "LINE" P7 P8 "" "LINE" P4 P5 ""
         "PEDIT" P7 "J" "F" P7 P8 P5 P4 "" "" "")
     (COMMAND "EXTRUDE" P6 "" LENGTH ""
         "UCS" "P")
)
```

Figure 156

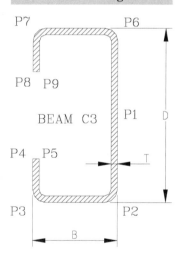

P7   P6

P8   P9

BEAM C3   P1   D

P4   P5   T

P3   P2

B

C3.LSP

```
(DEFUN C:C3 ()
 (GRAPHSCR)
  (SETQ P1 (GETPOINT "\n\tPLEASE PICK THE INSERT POINT "))
  (COMMAND "UCS" "O" P1)
   (SETQ P1 (LIST 0 0) P2 (LIST 0 (/ (- D) 2))
         P3 (POLAR P2 PI B) P4 (POLAR P3 (/ PI 2)(/ D 4))
         P5 (POLAR P4 0 T) P6 (LIST 0 (/ D 2))
         P7 (POLAR P6 PI B) P8 (POLAR P7 (* (/ PI 2) 3)(/ D 4))
         P9 (POLAR P8 0 T)
   )
   (COMMAND "PLINE" P4 "W" "0" "0" P3 P2 P6 P7 P8 ""
         "FILLET" "R" (* 2 T) "FILLET" "P" P1
         "OFFSET" T P1 P5 ""
         "LINE" P4 P5 "" "LINE" P8 P9 ""
         "PEDIT" P8 "J" "F" P8 P9 P5 P4 "" "" "")
     (COMMAND "EXTRUDE" P1 "" LENGTH ""
         "UCS" "P")
)
```

Notice in the above AutoLISP programs how the structure can be divided into two parts, having selected the insertion point:

- **Part 1** – The definition of all the required points (or variables) to construct the graphics, i.e. 'P1', 'P2', 'P3' and so on, by creating a 2D list or by specifying a distance from a given point at an angle in radians, i.e. polar, a given point, at an angle, a set distance. Note the difference in the order of these entities, they are different from the normal AutoCAD polar coordinate '@ DISTANCE<ANGLE' when the angle is in degrees.

■ **Part 2** – The use of the defined variables within standard AutoCAD commands. Don't try to load and run these new functions (C1, C2 and C3) at this stage as they are dependent upon certain predefined variable values ('B', 'D', 'T' and 'LENGTH') to complete the function.

The pre-defined variables are to be selected or picked from a screen menu. It is possible to edit the standard ACAD.MNU file to include this requirement; however, I would strongly recommend the use of a separate menu for development purposes until the new menu has been successfully tested.

Menu layouts

There are a number of different ways to lay out menus – single page or multi-page menus. Multi-page menus can be flat, tree, sequential or random. For this example, I will use a sequential menu layout.

The sequential menu is used for applications that follow a predefined hierarchical order such as the selection of the four different beam parameters, progressing from one page to the next when each menu condition has been satisfied, with the final condition returning the user to the start-point of a new selection (Figure 157).

Constructing a menu file

Using a text editor create the menu file A:SILO.MNU. This file consists of AutoCAD commands, AutoLISP functions and variables, and a group of special character codes used by the AutoCAD menu and command interpreter.

```
SILO.MNU

***SCREEN
**S
[AutoCAD]^C^C^P$S=X $S=S (SETQ T-MENU 0) ^P$P1=POP1

[BEAMS]$S=X $S=BREADTH
```

```
**BREADTH 3
[BREADTH]
[ 50 ]^C^C^P(SETQ B 50);$S=DEPTH
[ 75 ]^C^C^P(SETQ B 75);$S=DEPTH
[ 100 ]^C^C^P(SETQ B 100);$S=DEPTH
[ 150 ]^C^C^P(SETQ B 150);$S=DEPTH
```

```
[ 200 ]^C^C^P(SETQ B 200);$S=DEPTH
[ 300 ]^C^C^P(SETQ B 300);$S=DEPTH


**DEPTH 3
[DEPTH]
[ 75 ]^C^C(SETQ D 75);$S=THICKNESS
[ 100 ]^C^C(SETQ D 100);$S=THICKNESS
[ 150 ]^C^C(SETQ D 150);$S=THICKNESS
[ 200 ]^C^C(SETQ D 200);$S=THICKNESS
[ 300 ]^C^C(SETQ D 300);$S=THICKNESS
[ 400 ]^C^C(SETQ D 400);$S=THICKNESS


**THICKNESS
[THICKN-S]
[ 1.5 ]^C^C(SETQ T 1.5);$S=LENGTH ^P(SETQ LENGTH (GETINT))
[ 2.0 ]^C^C(SETQ T 2);$S=LENGTH ^P(SETQ LENGTH (GETINT))
[ 2.5 ]^C^C(SETQ T 2.5);$S=LENGTH ^P(SETQ LENGTH (GETINT))
[ 3.0 ]^C^C(SETQ T 3);$S=LENGTH ^P(SETQ LENGTH (GETINT))
[ 3.5 ]^C^C(SETQ T 3.5);$S=LENGTH ^P(SETQ LENGTH (GETINT))


**LENGTH
[LENGTH]
[1]1D^H
[2]2D^H
[3]3D^H
[4]4D^H
[5]5D^H
[6]6D^H
[7]7D^H
[8]8D^H
[9]9D^H
[0]0D^H


[ OK ];$S=BEAMS


**BEAMS 3
[ C1 ]^C^C(IF(NOT C1)(LOAD "A:C1"));C1;$S=SCREEN
[ C2 ]^C^C(IF(NOT C2)(LOAD "A:C2"));C2;$S=SCREEN
[ C3 ]^C^C(IF(NOT C3)(LOAD "A:C3"));C3;$S=SCREEN


[ VIEW ]^C^CVSLIDE;A:SILO;
[DEL-VIEW]^C^CREDRAW;
```

Labelling menu commands

Look at the menu items, the first special character you encounter is a pair of square brackets '[ ]' . These characters control what is displayed on each of the screen pages by entering a label between square brackets such as '[BEAMS]'. This will display 'BEAMS' on the screen.

The square brackets signify labels to the menu interpreter. The characters that follow the right-hand bracket ']' make up the macro itself. Only eight

Figure 157

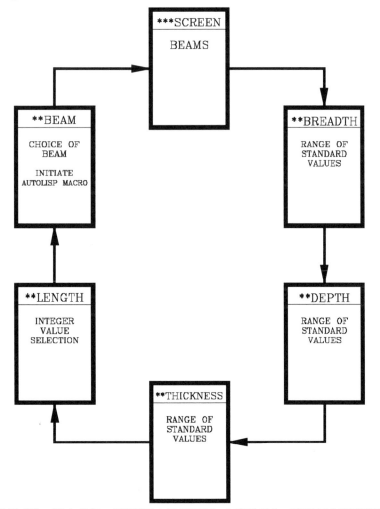

MULTI—PAGE HIERARCHY MENU STRUCTURE

characters display on the screen menu label. If a lengthy label is used for documentation purposes, only the first eight characters of the documentation are displayed on the screen. Hence, make your labels short and descriptive. Blank menu items can be achieved by empty square brackets as well as blank lines in the menu structure. Make sure that there are ten blank lines at the end of the first page of the SILO.MNU. This is used to remove from the screen display any items visible from the previous menu page when one screen page is superimposed upon another.

Menu file sections

Menu file sections are identified by a special label, as we are using the screen menu section. Note that the start of the menu indicates this with '***' on line 1.

Menu sections can be very large and run into a number of pages. Submenus are smaller groups of menu items that can be called or made visible from within the main file section or from within another submenu. For instance, '**S' is a submenu of the '***SCREEN' section. Note the '$S = BREADTH' after the '[BEAM]' label. This instructs the processor to search for the submenu '**BREADTH' and to display to the screen all items between the label '[BREADTH]' and the end of the section, i.e. '[300]' and so on.

Special characters in menus

There are over 20 different characters available for use with menu macros. As this is only a quick look at customising 3D design, I will restrict the explanation to those used in the SILO.MNU program (see *AutoCAD Customization Guide* for further reference).

Most command macros start with two or three '^C's. In a menu the 'Ctrl+C' keystroke combination is a special code that cancels any previous or current AutoCAD command. I am sure that you have all entered a command not realising that you have not yet cleared the previous command loop (especially dimensioning). This is the same problem.

The special character '^P' ('Ctrl+P') is used to control the menu items displayed on the screen by toggling the MENUECHO function on and off. This is particularly useful when you do not wish to have the AutoLISP functions displayed on the screen as the macro is in operation.

A semi-colon ';' is the special character that represents a press of the 'Enter' key from the keyboard. When a menu item is selected, if there are no special codes at the end of the line, AutoCAD places a blank after it before processing the command sequence, thus terminating the command. In the case of the AutoLISP GETINT function (see end of lines in **THICKNESS submenu), this function pauses for an input value terminating in a space or 'Enter' key-press, hence the need for the special character '^H' ('Ctrl +H') in the **LENGTH submenu. When a value for thickness is picked, the SETQ function assigns this value to the variable 'T', displays the **LENGTH submenu and pauses for input, assigning the value to the variable named 'LENGTH' when the 'Enter' key is pressed. The ** LENGTH submenu enables you to select the numbers one at a time (displayed in the prompt area of the screen) to build up the integer value (i.e. 17946, etc.). Each time a number is selected the '^H' character issues a backspace, deleting, in our case, the letter 'D' for delete (it could be any character of your choice) thus avoiding the processor terminating the function with the entry of a space, and allowing the function (GETINT) to continue selection numbers. When the integer is complete, select the 'OK' label – note the use of the semi-colon to terminate the function.

Finally, when all the parameters have been 'picked' the **BEAMS submenu is displayed for you to select the type of beam section. I have included the AutoCAD commands to enable the use of a slide file called A:SILO. Make a slide file (MSLIDE command) of the different sections to help the user select the appropriate beam. Once one of C1, C2 or C3 is selected, the processor checks to see if the AutoLISP routines have been loaded (IF and NOT functions), doing so if this is not the case, prior to running the AutoLISP programs we created at the start of the exercise.

Leave ten blank lines at the end of the **BEAMS submenu to avoid part of the previous page (**LENGTH) being diplayed on the screen below the '[DEL-VIEW]' label.

Testing the menu file

Before running the program, make sure that the screen menu is active by selecting this option from the OPTIONS–PREFERENCES pull-down menu (Release 13 onwards).

```
COMMAND : MENU
         : A:SILO select .MNU This menu will be automatically
           compiled. Page 1 of the submenu **S should now be visible
           on the screen
```

If you need to edit the program, select the .MNU file, not the .MNC file when reloading the menu with:

```
COMMAND : MENU
         : A:SILO
```

Once the menu has been tested satisfactorily, the compiled file .MNC can be selected. You may then wish to make this customised menu part of your standard ACAD.MNU file.

Using the customised menu

Now for rigor mortis in your left hand. 'Pick' the label 'BEAMS' at the top of the screen menu, completing the entire graphics from a series of screen 'picks'. If for some reason an error occurs, try to detect the point in the menu causing the termination of the program by entering at the command prompt !B, !D, !T, !LENGTH and so on (one at a time) until a NIL value is returned, this being the offending section of the program.

When the drawing is complete, change the viewpoint (–1,–1,1 and so on) to confirm the results. Remember to locate the current UCS in the required plane before using the BEAMS menu.

A picture is worth a thousand words; at least that is how the saying goes. This is the reason for using a slide file to aid the menu selection of objects. A much more enhanced selection process would be to create an icon menu from individual AutoCAD slides which are stored in a slide library.

In the above menu (SILO.MNU) we used the VSLIDE command followed by REDRAW (selected from the BEAMS submenu) before selecting the chosen beam. This process can be speeded up and automated into one command by means of an icon menu. (See later exercise for the solution to this process.)

File linking

In a previous exercise we used AutoCAD to read data from an external file (BOXES.DAT) to provide information for an AutoLISP routine. In the case of many objects created in a drawing, there is a need to collect and store relevant management information automatically as the drawing is being created. This aspect of 3D computer graphics is much neglected resulting in underutilisation of existing technology.

Writing to a file

Using our SILO.MNU as an example of automatic writing to an external file, let us incorporate the facility to write a material cutting list to an external file with the same name as the current drawing but with the extension '.MAT'. This file can then be imported into the production software for processing without the need to refer to a drawing, making for a much more accurate and efficient use of management information.

First, edit C1.LSP.

```
C1.LSP

(DEFUN C:C1 ()
 (GRAPHSCR)
 (SETQ P1 (GETPOINT "\n\tPLEASE PICK THE INSERT POINT "))
 (COMMAND "UCS" "O" P1)
  (SETQ P1 (LIST 0 0) P2 (LIST 0 (/ (- D) 2))
        P3 (POLAR P2 PI B) P4 (POLAR P3 (/ PI 2) T)
        P5 (LIST 0 (/ D 2)) P6 (POLAR P5 PI B)
        P7 (POLAR P6 (* (/ PI 2) 3) T)
  )
 (COMMAND "PLINE" P3 "W" "0" "0" P2 P5 P6 ""
          "FILLET" "R" (* 2 T) "FILLET" "P" P1
          "OFFSET" T P1 P4 ""
          "LINE" P3 P4 "" "LINE" P6 P7 ""
          "PEDIT" P6 "J" "F" P6 P3 "" "" "")
   (COMMAND "EXTRUDE" P6 "" LENGTH ""
        "UCS" "P")
        (SETQ M (GETSTRING "\nPLEASE ENTER THE MATERIAL ")
        SM (STRCAT "MATERIAL= " M)
        WIDTH (+(-(* 2 B)T)(- D T))
        DNAME (GETVAR "DWGNAME")
        MFILE (STRCAT DNAME ".MAT")
        SW (STRCAT "CUTTING SIZE= "(RTOS WIDTH 2 2) "*")
        SW2 (STRCAT SW (RTOS LENGTH 2 2))
        OFILE (OPEN MFILE "w")) ;lower case "w"
```

```
(WRITE-LINE "MATERIAL CUTTING LIST" OFILE)
(WRITE-LINE SM OFILE)
(WRITE-LINE SW2 OFILE)
(CLOSE OFILE)
          )
```

Reload C1.LSP and test for the existence of a new file by picking 'BEAM' from the screen menu. When complete, use a text editor (or DOS command) to view the contents of your file having an extension '.MAT' placed in your working directory.

```
MATERIAL CUTTING LIST
MATERIAL= MILD-STEEL
CUTTING SIZE= 172*137
```

This technology can be extended to collect unlimited management information in an external file. Most CAD users recognise the need for 'vectorial' reading of a drawing for manufacturing purposes, automating the process (as required) by translating this information via a standard protocol such as DXF and IGES files directly to the machine tool software but fail to make the connection between the drawing and the need to read the drawing to collect management information.

Reading the AutoCAD database

Customisation offers a company considerable benefits and comes in many different guises. In Exercise 2 we started using AutoLISP; in Exercise 4 we worked on roof true lengths. This exercise involved the construction of beams and the automatic calculation of management information. I therefore wish to conclude this quick introduction to 3D design by combining these experiences to customise roof truss design.

Man has always needed a roof for shelter. Considerable design development has taken place over time with respect to the materials used, the technology involved and the geometrical construction. The pitch angle of house design has varied from the sharp angle required to shed water quickly from a thatched roof to the present pitch angle of between 22.5° and 37.5°. (See *A Practical Guide to AutoCAD Geometry* by Bousfield for the derivation of the 22.5° roof angle.)

The different types of roof trusses include fink truss, fan truss, double 'W' shape, Pratt 4 and many others, all forming different family groups, all inviting the CAD user to customise the solution.

Automated roof design

In this example I wish to use the fink truss design to illustrate part of a requested solution by a construction engineer wishing to automate the graphics process, including the display in Figure 158 of the total length of material used in the roof construction.

Figure 158

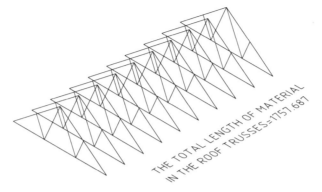

Open a new drawing and create a special layer called ROOF. The AutoLISP program ROOF.LSP requests input values for the truss span, number of trusses and the spacing between each truss, before constructing a 3D view of the roof design on its own layer, displaying the total length of material used in the construction by reading the AutoCAD database and searching for 'ENTITY (or OBJECT) = "LINE" ' on layer ROOF prior to adding together the total lengths of each line.

ROOF.LSP

```
(DEFUN C:ROOF ()   ; FINK truss roof design
(GRAPHSCR)
 (SETQ LA (GETVAR "CLAYER"))
  (IF (= LA "ROOF")()(COMMAND "LAYER" "S" "ROOF" ""))
(PROMPT "\nPLEASE PICK THE BOTTOM CORNER OF THE ROOF ")
(COMMAND "UCS" "O" PAUSE)
 (SETQ P0 (LIST 0 0 0)
       S (GETREAL "\nPLEASE ENTER THE ROOF SPAN ")
       NU (GETINT "\nPLEASE ENTER THE NUMBER OF TRUSSES ")
       SP (GETREAL "\nENTER THE DISTANCE BETWEEN EACH TRUSS ")
       ANG (/ (* 37.5 PI) 180)
       P1 (LIST (/ S 2) 0 (* (/ S 2)(/ (SIN ANG)(COS ANG))))
       P2 (LIST (/ S 2) 0 0)
       P3 (LIST (/ S 3) 0 0) LENGTH 0)
(COMMAND "LINE" P0 P1 "" "LINE" "MID" P1 P3 P1 "" "LINE" P0 P2 ""
         "MIRROR" "C" P0 P1 "" P1 (LIST (CAR P1) 10 0) ""
         "ARRAY" "C" P0 (LIST (+ (CAR P0) S)(CADR P1)) ""
         "R" NU 1 SP)
(SETQ E (ENTNEXT))
 (WHILE E
  (SETQ ENTTY (CDR (ASSOC 0 (ENTGET E)))
        LAYNM (CDR (ASSOC 8 (ENTGET E))))
   (IF (AND
        (= ENTTY "LINE")(= LAYNM "ROOF"))
        (PROGN
          (SETQ ST (CDR (ASSOC 10 (ENTGET E)))
               END (CDR (ASSOC 11 (ENTGET E)))
               LEN (DISTANCE ST END)
               LENGTH (+ LEN LENGTH))
```

```
                 )
              )
          (SETQ E (ENTNEXT E))
        )  ; while loop
      (COMMAND "UCS" "P" "VPOINT" "1,-1,1" "ZOOM" "E")
      (PRINC "\nTHE TOTAL LENGTH OF MATERIAL IN THE ROOF TRUSSES= ")
      (PRINC (RTOS LENGTH 2 3))
      (PRINC)
    )
```

Remember to include the last closing parenthesis in your program.

Make sure that the prompt area of the screen has at least two visible lines for the PRINC statement to be visible.

Testing and using the program

At the command prompt enter:

```
COMMAND: (LOAD"A:ROOF")
  Prompt C: ROOF
```

Indicating a satisfactory loading of the program with the creation of a new AutoCAD command, ROOF. Run the program, responding to the screen prompts, and sit back. Let the computer take the strain.

In concluding this quick introduction to 3D design, a major emphasis has been the construction of graphics with only a brief mention of management information such as the exercise in writing to an external file. It would be remiss of me to exclude any reference to the use of attributes. This is a very important aspect of computer graphics not covered in this introduction. Remember that vectors are only part of the information required in the communication of 3D objects.

Tasks

Tasks 1–5 relate to the beam construction exercise in the text.

1. Edit C2.LSP and C3.LSP for automatic external writing of a material cutting list using the subroutine (MAT) and altering the line in the program containing the calculation for width, i.e. '(SETQ WIDTH (+ etc.'.

2. Include the HATCH command in any of the AutoLISP macros C1, C2 or C3.LSP to hatch the section of the beam.

3. Modify the insertion point ('P1') of any of the AutoLISP macros C1, C2 or C3.LSP.

4. Extend the AutoLISP macro chosen in task 3 to write to an external file the volume of material used in the selection of the beams in preparation for cost/unit volume calculation.

5. (For the more ambitious readers.) Extend the AutoLISP program to automatically include a group of holes required for assembly purposes.

6. Complete Figure 159 by running the AutoLISP macro ROOF.LSP using a span of 125 with 35 spacing between 8 bays of trusses. Add the columns, purlins and cross-bracing with a short wall as shown.

Figure 159

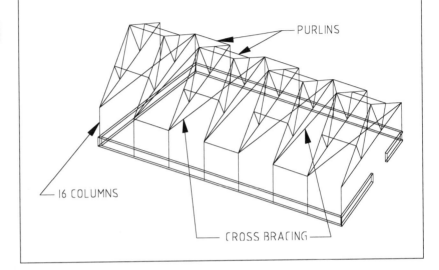

PURLINS

16 COLUMNS

CROSS BRACING

Summary of the basic rules of 3D design

Rule 1	Free-hand sketching

No free-hand sketching. Always construct objects in the required 2D plane by looking directly down the positive 'Z' axis unless objects already exist to aid the *exact* location in a 3D view.

Rule 2	Layers

Make full use of the LAYER facility when building a 3D model. Always use a special layer for construction purposes.

Rule 3	OSNAP override

Make sure that there is no overriding OBJECT SNAP mode active when selecting objects from the screen. (It is advisable for beginners of 3D design to restrict the use of the OSNAP command as they frequently forget to set the OSNAP command to 'NONE' on completion, causing problems for further object selection from the screen.)

Rule 4	UCS–VIEW save

Remember as you build up a 3D model to save by number useful views and by name UCSs.

Rule 5	Rectangle start

A useful starting point when constructing a 3D model is to create a wire frame box (part of the model or a 'crate') with the 'x,y' plane in the WCS on a construction layer. This is a helpful visual aid when moving the UCS about the model in terms of some concrete object.

Rule 6	Point filters

Use point filters if any one or more of the required 'x,y,z' coordinates already exist in the 3D model.

Rule 7	RULESURF

When selecting objects or edges of the ruled surface, if one of the two boundaries is closed, then the other boundary or edge must also be closed.

Rule 8	Same space objects

Avoid, where possible, two or more objects occupying the same space when using composites to build a 3D model.

Rule 9	Computer calculations

Let the computer perform any necessary calculations. There is no justification for resorting to pencil and paper or hand-held calculators to perform mathematical tasks.

Rule 10	Hidden text

When attaching text to a 3D object, give the text a 'Z' value (thickness) otherwise the text will not hide.

Rule 11	WBLOCK UCS

When creating a WBLOCK of a 3D object for later insertion into a drawing, make sure that the current UCS 'Z' axis is normal to the required 2D plane.

Rule 12	3D view

If the screen size restricts you to a single 2D viewport for the construction of 3D models, always create a 3D view such as VPOINT –1,–1,1 for constant reference, using the view restore and undo commands.

Rule 13	Swept profiles

Avoid using intersecting profiles (figure-of-eight) to create swept solids.

Rule 14	Swept primitives

When building a solid model, keep the number of solid primitives as small as possible. Use swept primitives where possible if further editing is not anticipated.

Rule 15	Customisation

When constructing solid models, keep alert to the potential for automatic creation by customisation.

Part Two
Exercises in surface/solid modelling

Contents

Part Two links the two other parts by a series of progressively arranged practical exercises, integrating the rules and commands of Part One with practical examples designed to develop the competences necessary for the 3D surface/ solid modelling project in Part Three.

Objectives

On completion of Part Two the reader shall be able to:

- Apply ELEVATION and THICKNESS commands to the solution of design problems.
- Create viewports in model and paper space for associative orthographic projections by graphical manipulation.
- Use the DVIEW command to view a 3D model from various points in space.
- Apply perspective projections to a 3D model.
- Use clipping planes to create a cut-away section.
- Use the UCSFOLLOW system variable to automate the plan view.
- Apply all the basic surface and solid primitives.
- Use and describe the system variables SURFTAB1 and SURFTAB2 for the control of surface mesh density.
- Use the PEDIT command to edit a mesh vertex to a predetermined point.
- Use the EXPLODE command to convert a polygon mesh to individual 3D faces and to create holes in a polygon mesh.
- Apply Boolean operations to regions and solids.
- Incorporate parametric variables into a script file.
- Convert 3D points between different coordinate systems.
- Understand the properties of conics.

Exercise 1
Office desk design

Thickness, elevation and solid(s)

One of the quickest methods of providing a 3D model is by using the commands THICKNESS, ELEVATION and SOLID (do not consider the SOLID command as that which is used when solid modelling).

The THICKNESS command

Figure 160

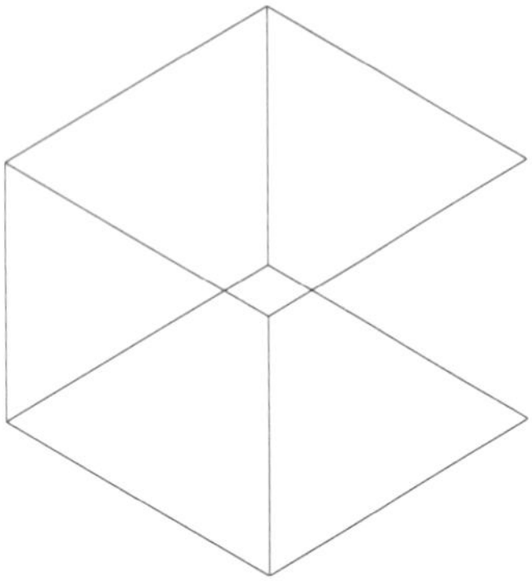

If an entity such as a line, circle or ellipse, is given 'thickness' then the entity will possess depth in the 'z' plane. This is best demonstrated with an example. Do not confuse the AutoCAD command THICKNESS with line width.

Set thickness to 60 by entering:

```
                    COMMAND: THICKNESS
Prompt new value for thickness: 60
```

Draw a square using the LINE command of 60 × 60. From the pull-down menu VIEW, select presets South West to view your drawing. It should look like Figure 160. Save this view as SW, as follows:

```
            COMMAND: VIEW
                Prompt: enter S for Save
    view name to save: SW
            COMMAND: HIDE
```

Figure 161

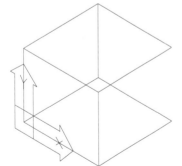

This will remove hidden lines. You will notice the box has sides, but no top or bottom.

An alternative method is to draw the square in 2D and use DDCHPROP command to change the thickness by means of the dialogue box (DDMODIFY).

There is a disadvantage to both these methods of constructing 3D faces in that no holes or apertures can be produced in the faces for such items as windows or doors. They would only appear as lines on the surfaces.

Limitations of the THICKNESS command

Place the UCS on the side of the box as shown in Figure 161 and draw a circle on the side with a thickness of –60. You can draw the circle in your 3D view.

Note the results, using the HIDE command for confirmation. Where is the hole? There isn't one as such, only a cylinder with a circle on the face (Figures 162 and 163).

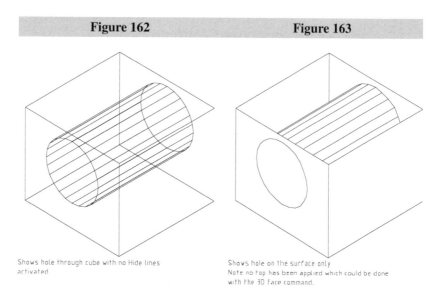

| **Figure 162** | **Figure 163** |

Shows hole through cube with no Hide lines activated

Shows hole on the surface only
Note no top has been applied which could be done with the 3D face command.

Place the UCS on the side of the cube by the 3POINT method.

```
COMMAND: UCS
        : 3 for Three Point
```

Place the origin at bottom left, positive in 'X' to the right bottom corner and positive in 'Y' top left. If the icon does not appear on the cube as shown use:

```
COMMAND: UCSICON
        : OR for Origin
```

Using the FILLET and THICKNESS commands

An object with thickness can be filleted as shown in Figure 164.
    Use your existing cube and consider this as a 3D object. Enter:

```
COMMAND: FILLET use a radius of 10
```

Activate the FILLET command and pick the edges of the box at positions 'P1' and 'P2' as shown in Figure 164. Fillet all the remaining corners to produce the shape shown in Figure 165.

Figure 164   **Figure 165**

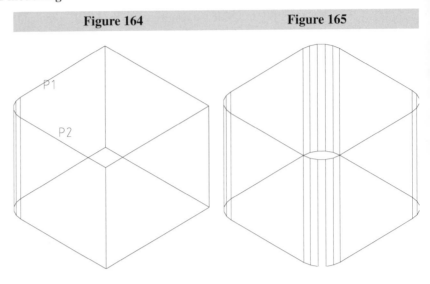

The ELEVATION command

Elevation is the intersection point of the 'X', 'Y' and 'Z' axes and can be moved in the 'Z' axis relative to its current location in a positive or negative direction. At the command prompt enter:

COMMAND: ELEVATION
Prompt new value for elevation <0.00>: 50 *and press*
'Enter'

Any entities now drawn will be located 50 units above the original plane (Figure 166). This command is useful for such items as table tops or kitchen worktops.

Figure 166

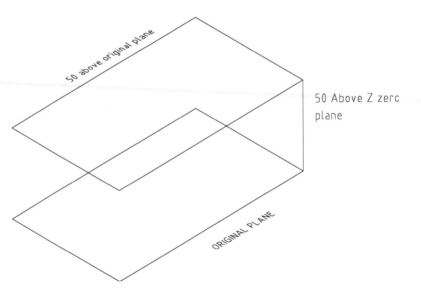

Note: If object snap (OSNAP) is used to select entities, the ELEVATION command will be overridden.

The SOLID command

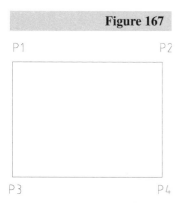

Figure 167

P1   P2

P3   P4

The SOLID command creates solid filled polygons which, unlike entities with thickness, cannot be seen through when using the HIDE command. The combination of thickness with solid could be used to produce a table top, i.e. set elevation at 700 and use solid command with a thickness of 20. This would produce a solid top of 20 thickness above the original plane of 700, resulting in six faces. These faces appear filled when viewed normal to the face (FILLMODE=1).

The SOLID command must be used by picking in the order of 'P1', 'P2', 'P3', 'P4' (see Figure 167) otherwise a bow tie effect will be produced (see Part One). The FILL command controls the filling of the solid when viewed down the 'Z' axis.

COMMAND: FILL
Prompt ON/OFF< >: OFF

Figure 167 shows a view with FILL off.

Exercise 1: Office desk

When drawing in 3D you may find it difficult to visualise the objects when viewed in 2D on the screen.

Start with a wire frame box of the required outer dimensions for quick realism (see Rule 1). For this exercise set new drawing limits of 0.000,0.000 bottom left and 2500.000, 2000.000 top right. Do not forget to zoom all, to regenerate the screen drawing area.

All dimensions for this exercise are in millimetres. A plan of the desk that we are going to construct is shown in Figure 168. Start by creating several layers and giving them colours of your choice:

CON
SIDE1
SIDE2
TOP
DRAW1
DRAW2
BLOTTER

Set a new grid spacing of 50. Set the layer CON current and remain in the WCS. Draw a rectangle of 1250 × 650. At the command prompt enter:

Figure 168

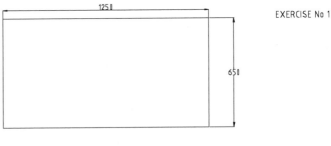

EXERCISE No 1

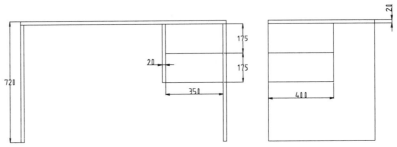

DESK
3D DESIGN

```
COMMAND: COPY
Select objects: select the rectangle with
                a window
basepoint of displacement: @0,0,0
second basepoint of displacement: @0,0,700
```

Draw in vertical lines from the corners using OSNAP INT (Figure 169) and set a view of south-west from the presets. Save this view as 'SW'.

Change the layer to TOP and use the SOLID command with a thickness of 20 as follows:

```
COMMAND: THICKNESS
new value for thickness <0.000>: 20
```

Figure 169

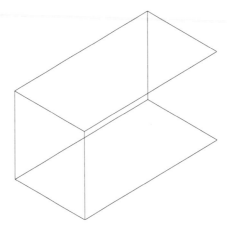

```
COMMAND: SOLID
```
                    (*Note:* FILLMODE *must be set to On*)
Prompt `first point:` *pick 'P1'*
        `second point:` *pick 'P2'*
         `third point:` *pick 'P4'*
        `fourth point:` *pick 'P3'*

Remember you must *not* pick around the rectangle in order otherwise a bow tie effect will result. The desk should now have a solid top (Figure 170).

Perform the command HIDE. You should not see through the top. Then enter the SHADE command. It will fill in the colour of the layer TOP.

Figure 170

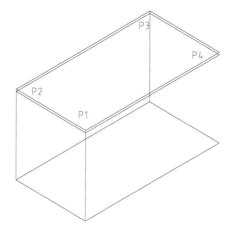

Drawing the sides

To draw in the sides set layer SIDE1 current. At the command prompt enter:

```
COMMAND: THICKNESS
new value for thickness: <700>
```

Figure 171

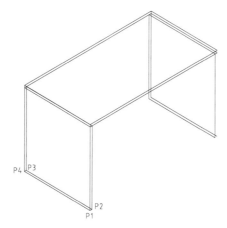

```
COMMAND: LINE
from point: starting at the bottom left at 'P1', pick the intersection
            point
  to point: @20,0 ('P2')
          : @0.650 ('P3')
          : @-20,0 ('P4')
          : C
```

This should have produced one end of the desk. This end can be copied to create the other end (Figure 171). Use object snaps for accuracy.

Constructing the drawers

The same procedure can be used to construct the two drawers. Draw separately and position when completed.

Change the thickness to zero. Set the layer CON current and draw a rectangle 350 × 400, representing the plan of the drawer front (turn off other layers), at a convenient location on the screen.

Copy this rectangle up 175 in the 'Z' axis to produce the top limit of the drawer. Draw in the vertical lines to complete the wire frame.

Place the UCS on the front of the drawer using the 3POINT option. Change the layer to DRAW1 and set thickness to –20. Perform the SOLID command and complete the drawer front with OBJECT SNAP mode set to INT. The result is shown in Figure 172.

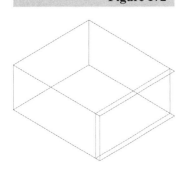

Place the UCS on one side using the same 3POINT method. Set the thickness to –15 and use the SOLID command to draw the side of the drawer.

Copy the drawer side to create the second side (Figure 173).

Place the UCS on the rear of the drawer and once again use the SOLID command to draw the back of the drawer.

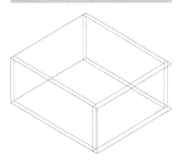

Task
Draw in the base of the drawer 5 thick.

Now move the drawer into the correct position in the desk using OSNAP (Figure 174). Copy the first drawer to complete the drawing.

Figure 174

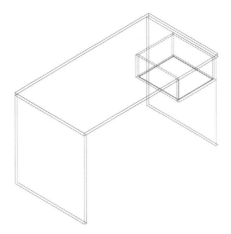

1. Design a method of supporting the drawers, including a handle for both drawers.

2. Place a blotter 5 mm thick on the desktop.

3. It is someone's birthday so why not celebrate? To do this you must provide a bottle and glass(es). Use your goblet constructed in Part One (Exercise 2), and scale to suit. Your finished desk should look something like Figure 175. (Note how the VPOINT command gives only parallel projection views.)

Figure 175

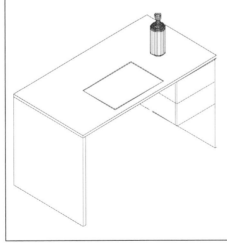

Exercise 2
3DMAN: surface modelling

In Exercise Two of Part One, we explored the 3D command. This exercise gives the opportunity to apply the following range of 3D subcommands or options:

PYRAMID	DISH	CONE
SPHERE	MESH	WEDGE
TORUS	DOME	BOX

Use these subcommands in conjunction with UCS control and simple mesh editing to create the 3D model drawing of a man, shown in Figure 176.

Figure 176

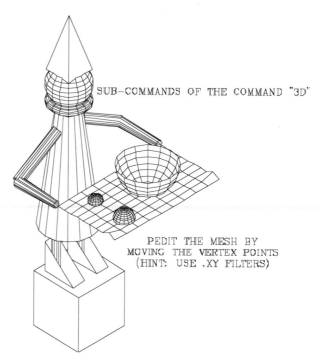

SUB-COMMANDS OF THE COMMAND "3D"

PEDIT THE MESH BY
MOVING THE VERTEX POINTS
(HINT: USE .XY FILTERS)

Construct the drawing using your own dimensions, moving the UCS into the desired 'x,y' plane for each subcommand. Note the modification to the surface of the tray (polygon mesh).

This exercise offers a first look at polygon mesh editing.

Experimentation

When the initial drawing is complete, prior to experimenting with mesh editing, it is a good idea to make use of the UNDO command:

```
COMMAND: UNDO
```
Prompt `Auto/Control/BEgin/End/Mark/`
  `Back/<Number>:` M *for Mark*

This places a mark in the undo information.

When experimentation is complete, if the current progress is not required, enter:

```
Command: UNDO
```
Prompt `<Number>:` B *for Back*

This restores the drawing to the condition prior to experimentation.

Mesh editing

There are three basic editing methods for a 3D polygon mesh:

1. The use of a SCRIPT (or AutoLISP) file to generate a 3D mesh (see page 102).
2. Editing with GRIPS.
3. Using the PEDIT command (see Exercise 11 on car design).

Editing with GRIPS

When grips are active, small squares (pickboxes) appear at the geometrical points of the selected objects. These points can be edited by 'dragging' with the mouse rather than entering commands. This is a very simple method of editing but there is need for caution: 'Break Rule 1 at your peril'.

Tasks

Try the following two exercises. Start from a 3D viewpoint, with the GRIPS system variable set to 1:

1. (a) Select the cone, pyramid, wedge, or whatever. Note how the grips offer geometrical point editing.
   (b) Modify the location of these points by dragging to change the shape of an object. Take care when selecting points to note the current UCS.

(c) Change the viewpoint to view the object from different directions to establish the true location of the edited points.

2. (d) Move the UCS into the 'x,y' plane of the tray.
   (e) Select or 'pick' the tray to display the pickboxes at the mesh vertex point 'HOT'.
   (f) Modify the location of the selected point as follows (no free-hand sketching):

   Method 1
   COMMAND: *(Prompt when GRIPS are 'hot')*
      : B *for Basepoint*
      : @
      : @ 0,0,10

   Method 2
   COMMAND:
      : B
      : 0,0,0
      : 0,0,10

   (g) Change the viewpoint to view the object from different directions, thus confirming the accuracy of this method of mesh editing (modified vertex points in the positive 'z' direction).

If the 'x,y' plane of the polygon mesh is parallel to the current UCS 'x,y' plane, there is no need to move the UCS to that of the object when relative (@) coordinates are used to relocate the vertex points.

See the exercise on mesh editing (Exercise 11, car design) for the use of the PEDIT command for vertex editing from within a command.

Exercise 3
Garage design

In the previous two exercises we constructed vertical faces or walls by means of the THICKNESS or SOLID command. This exercise demonstrates the benefit and ease of solid modelling compared with surface modelling vertical walls.

Creating the walls

Set appropriate limits for the plan of the garage (Figure 177).

Draw the plan of the walls and polyedit into two polylines, one entity for the inner wall and one entity for the outer wall.

Create a view from VIEW presets, pick 'south-west' and save this view as 'SW'. Extrude the walls to a height of 2800 (see page 68 for help). The resulting extrusion at this stage is a solid with no inside.

The solid with HIDE is shown in Figure 178.

Figure 177

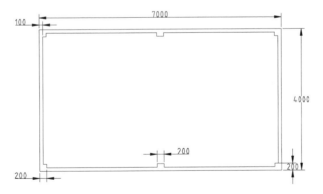

Creating a composite region

In order to create the garage walls use the Boolean operation SUBTRACT (see page 35) following the prompts at the command line. Figure 179 shows the result of the SUBTRACT command.

Because the walls of the garage have been constructed as a solid and not by means of the THICKNESS command as used when constructing the desk sides (in Exercise 1), it is possible to create a hole in the wall for such items as doors and windows.

Figure 178	Figure 179

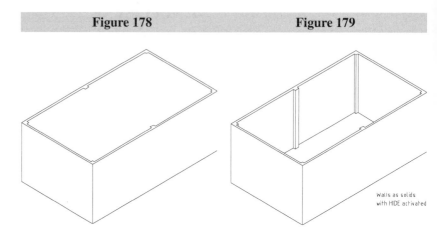

Walls as solids
with HIDE activated

Creating the front door

Place the UCS at the outer bottom left-hand corner of the garage front wall. Create the view shown in Figure 180 (door shown) as follows.

Draw a rectangle using the PLINE command to the dimensions given in the figure as follows:

```
        COMMAND: PLINE
Prompt From point: 1000,-10
              : @0,2010
              : @-2000,0
              : C
```

Figure 180

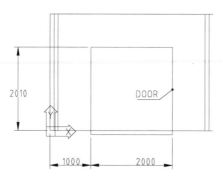

Restore the saved view 'SW' and extrude the rectangle (door) by –200 in the 'z' plane as shown in Figure 181. Use the Boolean operand to subtract this rectangle from the main garage.

Figure 181

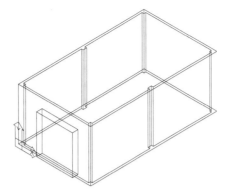

As we have seen in Part One, there are a number of different methods available for the construction of solid models. For example, the same result could have been achieved by using the BOX command to create the hole in the wall.

Recall Rule 8: 'Avoid where possible objects occupying the same space when creating composites.' It is good practice when subtracting one object from another as above, to avoid occupation of the same space by overlapping the edges of the solid to be subtracted. If problems are experienced with the above process, check Rule 8. If all goes well, the drawing of the garage with the aperture for the door should appear as in Figure 182. Use the HIDE command to check the process.

Figure 182

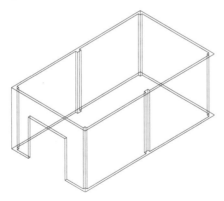

Creating the side door

Position the UCS on the side of the garage, changing the view to the side elevation as shown in Figure 183 by using the PLAN command.

Select an appropriate technique for the construction of the side door to the dimensions shown.

Use the Boolean operation SUBTRACT to create the door opening.

Figure 184 shows the completed view of the four walls.

Task
Design and add apertures for windows in the door side and rear.

Figure 183

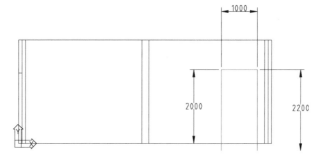

Figure 184

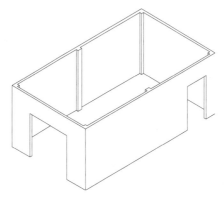

Adding the roof

Roof truss

For help, see Exercise 5 in Part One. Figure 185 shows details of the required roof truss construction. Draw the first truss using a thickness of –40.

Figure 185

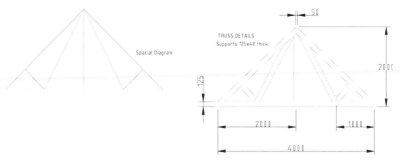

Locating the trusses

Move the first truss into position on the top of the wall at the garage door end (Figure 186). Use OSNAPs for location.

Difficulty may be experienced when trying to pick end-points and/or intersections on the solid wall. How could we avoid this problem? Time to reflect upon Rules 2, 3 and 5.

Figure 186

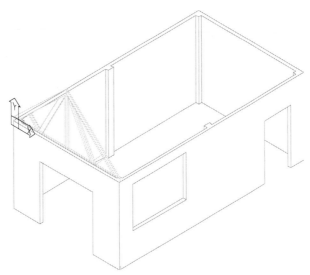

Arraying the trusses

To construct the roof, the single truss can be arrayed using the ARRAY 2D or 3D command. Position the UCS appropriate to your command.

Hint: As you move around a 3D model it is necessary to locate the UCS in a series of different positions. It is good practice to save the UCS with a name you can associate with in order that it can be restored at a future time (remember Rule 8).

Use the RECTANGULAR ARRAY subcommand with a distance between the columns of 7000/7 (even though this is a simple calculation – see Rule 9). The last truss will need to be adjusted to bring it back in line with the wall. Figure 187 shows the roof trusses in position.

Figure 187

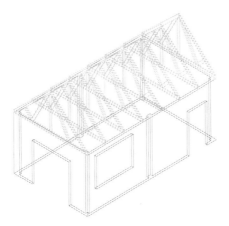

Add the roof spar to fasten the trusses together by drawing a rectangle as a polyline on the end of the first roof truss and extrude 7000.

Create a 3D face for the roof felt or alternatively use the SOLID command with a thickness of 3. (This is not shown on Figure 187 for clarity.)

To make life easier, remember Rule 5 and create a wire frame of the garage on a construction layer (Figure 188) and use this for the accurate positioning of entities.

Figure 188   **Figure 189**

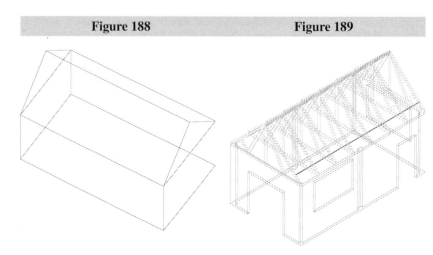

Draw the section of the tile lat 25 × 20, at a distance of 370 along the roof truss and extrude the length of the garage. Figure 189 shows the first tile lat in position 370 mm along the roof truss.

The roof tiles should now be added. Draw the tile to the dimensions specified in Figure 190 for a concrete single lap tile and save as a block or WBLOCK for insertion. The UCS should be placed in the appropriate position for correct insertion at an angle to lay on the tile lats (see Rule 11).

Figure 190

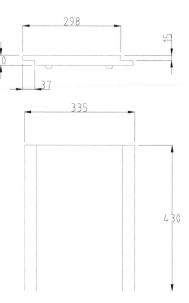

Before the first tile can be inserted as a block in the correct position the fascia board should be created with a section of 25×150 at the end of the roof truss as shown in Figure 191.

Extrude the fascia board the length of the garage.

Insert the first tile to sit on the tile lat and the fascia (Figure 192). Use the ARRAY command to array the tile the length of the garage to complete the first row of tiles (Figure 193).

Figure 191   **Figure 192**

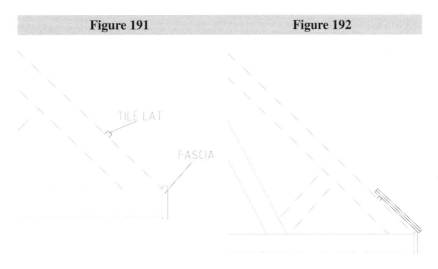

TILE LAT

FASCIA

Figure 193

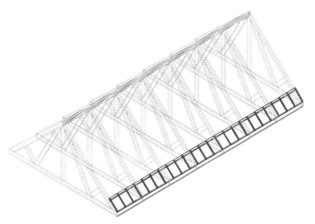

Tasks

1. Complete the roof tiling using a tile head lap of 75 mm. (You will need to consider the UCS position.)

2. Add the guttering by drawing the section and extruding.

3. Add ridge tiles to the apex of the roof.

4. Design and add doors to the garage.

Garage design: alternative method of construction

When constructing the garage walls we subtracted one solid from another to create a composite solid. Notice how the cross-section of the walls in the 'x,y' plane is consistent at all times. Now revisit Rule 14 (swept primitives).

Had it been possible to form a joint in one of the corners to create a continuous loop of the section outline, a better solution would have been to create a region of the cross-section (in the 'x,y' plane) and to extrude this region to the height of the garage wall (only use swept primitives if editing of the section is not anticipated). See the next exercise for this type of solution.

Path extrusion

When the cross-section of objects similar to the garage walls are consistent in the 'x,z' or 'y,z' plane, a different approach is necessary. The following example has a consistent cross-section in the 'x,z' plane and can be created as recommended above, extruding the section (region) along a path as opposed to a height.

Paths can be lines, circles, arcs, elliptical arcs, polylines or splines. The path should not lie on the same plane as the cross-section or profile, nor should there be areas of high curvature in the path. If one end-point of the path is not in the plane of the profile, AutoCAD moves the path to the centre of the profile.

The path must be an open polyline, restricted to the 'x,y' plane. If the plan of the walls or the path is drawn as a closed polyline such as the original garage plan, an error prompt would appear when attempting to extrude a section along this path.

For the cross-section of the walls to retain its positional relationship with the path, locate the section or profile at the end-point of the path (vertex point).

Holes in in the swept primitive for windows or doors can be created by subtracting classic geometrical primitives or other swept primitives from the original solid model to create a composite solid.

On completion of the EXTRUDE command, AutoCAD deletes or retains the original object depending upon the system variable value for DELOBJ:

DELOBJ = 1   Objects are retained (default value)
DELOBJ = 0   Objects are deleted

Tasks

Use the same basic dimensions as that of the garage for the room shown in Figure 194.

1. Create a region of the 'x,y' plane cross-section, including:
   (a) Outer wall projections
   (b) Skirting board
   (c) Dado rail
   (d) Cornice

2. Create the extrusion path in contact with the region (as shown in Figure 194).

3. Produce a swept primitive of the walls.

Figure 194

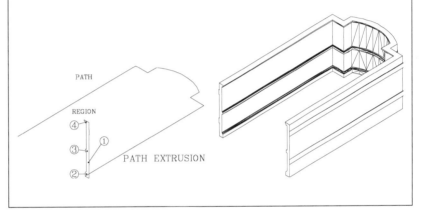

A satisfactory outcome to this task will be good preparation for the construction of the microscope fabricated limb, in Part Three.

Exercise 4
Vice body design

The previous exercise demonstrated certain limitations of surface modelling, in particular the geometric shapes available with such commands. This exercise employs a more complex profile in the generation of a solid model, developing competences encountered in Part One.

Creating the profile

Set appropriate limits for the vice body.

Side elevation

Orientate the UCS in 'X' through 90°. This can be done by icon selection from the UCS toolbar (Figure 195).

Figure 195	Figure 196

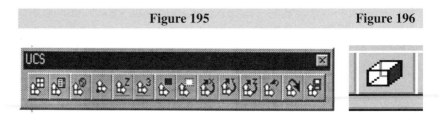

Using the graphics icon (Figure 196) to view the vice body from the side, select from the VIEW toolbar.

Use the PLINE command to draw the profile as shown in Figure 197 starting at 'P1' and working clockwise.

If you use the LINE and ARC commands you must polyedit (PEDIT) to produce a closed single entity.

From the SOLIDS toolbar select the extrude icon as follows:

```
                    COMMAND: EXTRUDE
          Prompt Select objects: pick the profile
Path/<Height of extrusion>: -86
```

Figure 197

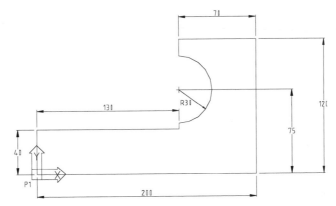

AutoCAD extrudes objects along the positive 'Z' axis of the object's coordinate system. At the prompt:

```
extrusion taper angle <0>:  press 'Enter'
```

Extrusion taper angles are from –90° to +90°. Positive angles taper inwards from the selected object, negative values taper outwards from the selected object.

Plan view

Position the UCS on the top surface using the graphics icon (Figure 198). Draw the elongated slot in position on the top surface and extrude by –50. (**Note**: The slot must be a polyline closed entity.)

Figure 198

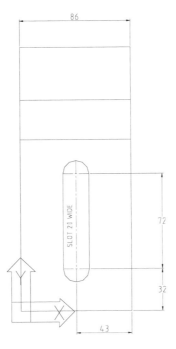

Figure 199

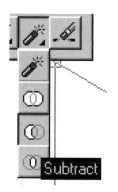

A Boolean operation can be used to subtract the volume of the slot from the main body. Select the 'Subtract' icon which lies under the 'Explode' icon in the flyout of the MODIFY toolbar. The icon is shown selected in Figure 199.

Alternatively, use the keyboard to enter the SUBTRACT command and follow the screen prompts as follows:

```
COMMAND: SUBTRACT
Select objects: select the main body and press 'Enter'
             : select the elongated slot and press 'Enter'
```

Select the 3D view South West using the icon method from the VIEW toolbar (see Figure 200) and save this view as 'SW' (Figure 201).

```
COMMAND: VIEW
Prompt ?/Delete/Restore/Save/Window: S for Save
                                   : SW for South West
```

Figure 200

The 3D view with HIDE is shown in Figure 202.

Figure 201	**Figure 202**

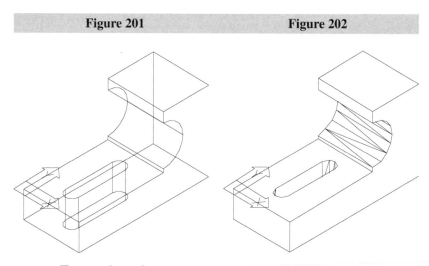

Front elevation

Locate the UCS on the model front as shown in Figure 203.

Use the graphics icon to produce the front view. Save this view as 'FRONT'.

To draw the tenon groove in the base of the vice, construct a rectangle using the PLINE command and extrude the full length of the model as follows:

```
COMMAND: PLINE
Prompt from point: 18,2
       to point: @0,10
              : @50,0
              : @0,-10
              : C
```

Figure 203   Figure 204

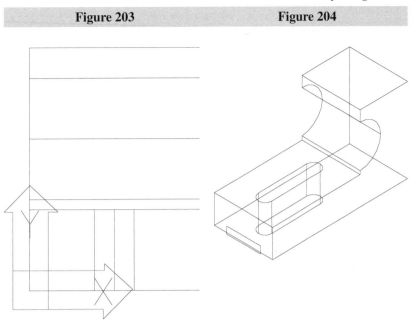

The rectangle drawn as a polyline can now be extruded the full length of the model, –220 (Figure 205).

Figure 205

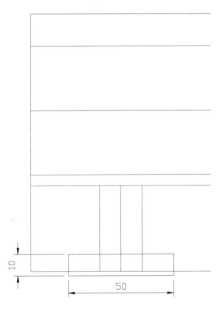

Subtract, as before, the rectangular extrusion from the main body of the vice (Figure 206) and hide, shade and render the solid model to display the view shown in Figure 207.

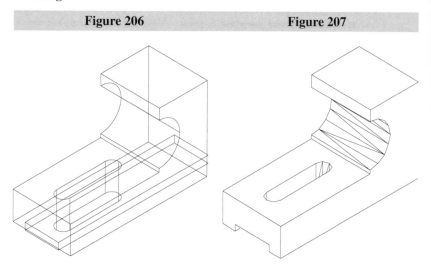

Figure 206   **Figure 207**

Filleting solids (edge primitives)

With the FILLET command it is possible to add rounds and fillets to selected objects by firstly specifying the fillet radius value prior to selecting the edges (in the same way as 2D fillets are specified).

If you select the three adjacent edges that converge at a vertex to form a corner, AutoCAD creates a vertex blend, like part of a sphere. It is also possible to select a CHAIN of edges for filleting with a single pick.

Filleting edges without exiting the command

With reference to Figure 208, at the command prompt enter:

```
                COMMAND: FILLET
 Prompt current fillet radius = (A value)
      <Select first object>: select edge 'A'
    Enter radius <Current>: 6
 Chain/Radius/<Select edge>: R for Radius
    Enter radius <Current>: 4
```

Figure 208

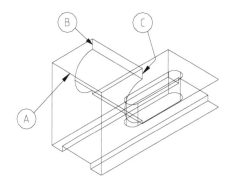

```
Chain/Radius/<Select edge>:
```
select edges 'B' and 'C'
```
Chain/Radius/<Select edge>:
```
press 'Enter'

Filleting a chain of edges

We are going to fillet the chain of edges indicated in Figure 209.

```
                    COMMAND: FILLET
```
Prompt `current fillet radius = 4`
```
        <Select first object>:
```
select edge 'D'
```
      Enter radius <Current>: 6
```
```
Chain/Radius/<Select edge>:
```
`C` *for Chain*
```
Chain/Radius/<Select edge>:
```
select edge 'D' once more. All the tangential edges are highlighted to form a chain
```
Chain/Radius/<Select edge>:
```
press 'Enter'

Note that nine edges have been filleted (five lines and four corners) within the chain (Figure 210).

Similar results can be achieved when editing solids with the CHAMFER command.

Figure 209	Figure 210

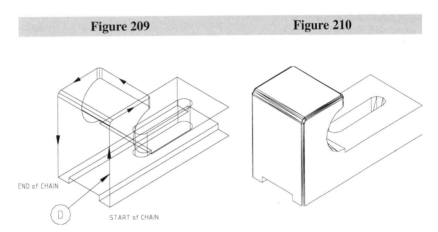

Exercise 5
Model space, paper space and viewports

In Part One (page 76) we considered two different ways in which to translate between different associated views on the screen. To complete the section on different methods of working, we need to look at the subject of 'multiple views' in more detail.

When drawing in the conventional manner using the drawing board and a pencil, the first consideration is the size of the object to be drawn and hence the size of the piece of paper required. When drawing using a CAD system the last thing we need to consider is the size of the paper required for the plot. The size of paper only becomes a concern when the drawing is completed. This does not of course mean that the limits are disregarded in CAD, as all items are drawn 'real size'. Scaling can take place from the 'Plot' dialogue box settings to achieve the desired results, but must never be used to scale an object to fit the size of paper.

Rule 16
Never sacrifice the integrity of the database. Always enter object data at a scale of one-to-one. (If you need to enlarge part of a view for clarity, consider using viewports with TILEMODE=0.)

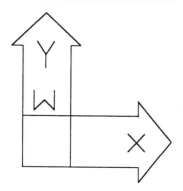

Figure 211

Model space

Model space is where you create the basic drawing or model. When applying 3D drafting and design techniques, all drawing is carried out in what is known as 'model space'. When in model space the normal icon is displayed (Figure 211). All the basic 3D commands can be used to create a model.

Multiple viewports

When working in model space it is possible to split the working screen into several areas called 'viewports' where the model can be viewed from different points in space in each port. Any work carried out on the model in one viewport is automatically updated in the remaining viewports. When you work in tiled viewports you are in model space.

The easiest way to set up multiple viewports is by means of standard view icons (see Figure 212).

When the VPORTS command is invoked, a series of subcommands enables the standard screen configuration to be created (1, 2, 3 or 4 viewports). For instance:

```
COMMAND: VPORTS
Prompt Save/Restore/Delete/Join/SIngle/?/2/
    <3>/4: enter an option
```

The JOIN subcommand enables two existing adjacent viewports to be combined into one larger viewport.

The 'Viewport' dialogue box

The 'Tiled Viewport' dialogue box is selected via VIEW–Tiled Viewport–Layout of the pull-down menu. It is shown in Figure 212.

Figure 212

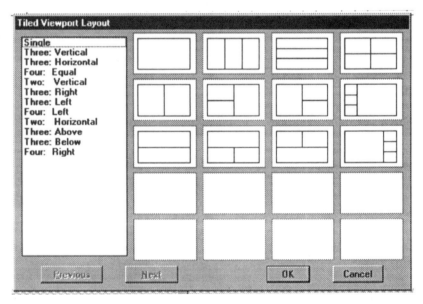

By combining different configurations with the DIVIDE and JOIN subcommands you can create all the basic screen configurations required for 3D design and orthographic projections (including auxillary views).

The problems occur when you wish to take a plot of the model with several views, as only the active viewport will plot when working in model space.

When a 3D model has been created you may wish to produce fully dimensioned orthographic views. This is where paper space is invaluable.

When considering multiple model space viewports it is important to ask the question: 'Why do I need multiple views to create the model?' (as this inevitably leads to reduction in the screen size working area).

We have previously considered two other ways in which we translate between different associated views on the screen.

> **Rule 17**
>
> If you are using a relatively small screen for the production of orthographic projections from a 3D model, do not be tempted into multiple viewports earlier than is necessary.

To incorporate multiple viewports into a prototype set-up is, in my view (no pun intended), a mistake.

Paper space

Figure 213

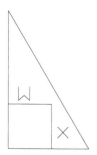

The concept of paper space is best understood by considering a number of pictures such as are drawn and painted by primary school pupils and then put together on one large background sheet as a collage. You can move the pictures around on the background but you cannot alter the actual pictures themselves.

To enter paper space, type TILEMODE at the command prompt as follows:

```
        COMMAND: TILEMODE
Prompt New value for tilemode<1>: 0
```

The paper space icon will be displayed as shown in Figure 213. The screen will also be cleared as explained on page 78.

The blank screen now represents the 'paper' on which you wish to arrange the pictures.

The MVIEW command

The MVIEW command enables you to create 'floating' viewports with similar multiple view configurations to that of the VPORTS command.

- TILEMODE=1 Use VPORTS to create tiled viewports
- TILEMODE=0 Use MVIEW to create floating viewports

Consideration should be given to any border requirements before implementing the MVIEW command. This enables you to draw objects and add title blocks and annotation directly into the paper space view without it being repeated in each individual viewport.

Floating viewports

When you create floating viewports using the MVSETUP command, additional configurations are available including a standard third angle projection configuration and the facility to 'rectangular array' a viewport by specifying the number of rows and columns in the required configuration.

Suitable layout

Because the MVIEW command creates floating viewports offering the ability to move, stretch, copy and so on (GRIPS), it is possible to start a drawing with limited viewports, adding further viewports by editing the existing one as the drawing progresses.

With paper space you are not restricted to the plotting of a single model space view, as is the case with tiled viewports.

All model editing is conducted in models space (MSPACE–PSPACE toggle) with adequate screen prompts in the event of default.

View control

Individual control of views is achieved by the ability to freeze or turn off layers independently within a viewport without affecting the remaining viewports – a technique most satisfying when dimensioning and annotating individual viewports. The GLOBAL FREEZE facility is used to remove from view (when plotting) the paper space viewport boundaries.

Aligning views

You can arrange the objects of your drawing by aligning the view in one particular floating viewport with the view in another viewport as follows. From the

VIEW MENU
FLOATING VIEWPORT
MVSETUP
Enter 'A' for Align

You are then able to align

- Horizontally a point in one viewport with a basepoint in another viewport.
- Vertically a point in one viewport with a basepoint in another viewport.
- Angled points in one viewport relative to another by specifying a distance and an angle. This is particularly suited to auxillary views.

Practical application: VICE BODY

In order to carry out this exercise, load the vice body drawing (previous exercise) from file.

Create a viewport layer

A new layer should be created to display the viewport outline. The new layer could be called anything you wish but we will choose PSVPORTS and give it colour, magenta. Make this layer current.

Creating a layer for the viewports will allow the boundaries of the ports to be turned off for plotting purposes, as will be described later.

Creating viewports in paper space

Figure 214

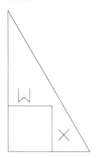

Ensure the drawing is displayed in WCS as a plan view with TILEMODE set to 1. To move into paper space set TILEMODE to 0 as follows:

```
COMMAND: TILEMODE
Prompt New value for tilemode<1>: 0
```

The paper space icon (Figure 214) will be displayed and the drawing will disappear from the screen. The limits should now be set in paper space. This would normally be determined by the intended paper size, say A3 (420, 297), regardless of model space limits.

From the VIEW pull-down menu select FLOATING MODEL SPACE, or at the command line enter the following:

```
COMMAND: MVIEW
Prompt ON/OFF/Hideplot/Fit/2/3/4/Restore/<First
          point>: 4 for four viewports
Fit/<First point>: 5,5
       Second point: 415,292
```

Figure 215

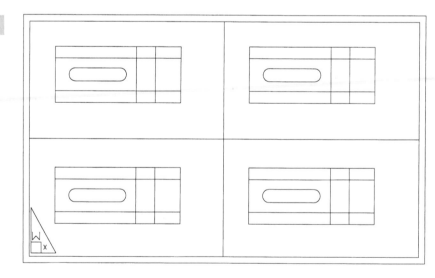

Note: If the title block is required, allowance will need to be made for its insertion.

The view of the vice body drawing will now appear as a plan view in each of the four viewports (Figure 215).

You can toggle between model space and paper space from the button at the bottom of the AutoCAD screen or by typing PSPACE or MSPACE on the command line.

Creating viewports

Change back into model space using the MSPACE command. (Note the return of the world coordinate system in each port.)

The four views of the model which are displayed in model space can now be set up in each viewport with the VPOINT command.

Left-clicking with the mouse button will make the respective port active, in preparation for the VPOINT command as follows.

To make the top left viewport active:

```
COMMAND: VPOINT
Prompt Rotate/<View point><0.0000,0.0000,
1.0000>: 0,-1,0
```

The viewpoints for the other three ports are:

Top right: –1,0,0
Bottom left: 0,0,1
Bottom right: –1,-1,1

Figure 216

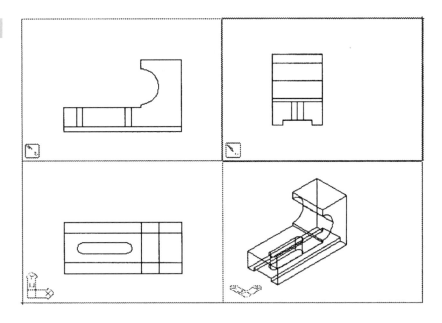

The views may appear too large for the viewports and must therefore be reduced. In each viewport enter:

COMMAND: Z *for zoom*
Respond: 8XP *for 0.8 paper space*

The views should now appear as shown in Figure 216.

It can be seen from the figure that the top-right view is not in line with the top-left view as required in orthographic projection. (See later notes on orthographic projection in this exercise). In paper space move the required views by selecting the tiled outline, aligning the views with the aid of the graphics cursor. A more precise alignment method will be considered later in this exercise.

Plotting the orthographic projection

Make sure you are still in paper space. At the command line type in:

COMMAND: MVIEW
Prompt ON/OFF/Hideplot/Fit/2/3/4/Restore/<First
                    point>: *enter* H *for Hideplot*
Prompt ON/OFF: ON
Prompt Select objects: *select the four tile outlines, not the model*

Some CAD users prefer to leave the creation of a special layer for the viewport outline until this stage of the drawing, that is:

1. Create a new layer.
2. Use the CHPROP command to move the paper space viewport outlines to another layer.
3. Freeze the new layer.

Freezing different layers in each viewport is particularly relevant when you begin to enter dimensions or comments to individual views. Without the ability to freeze individual views these dimensions or comments would appear in each viewport. The command VPLAYER sets the visibility within the individual layers, offering the opportunity to make one or more viewports visible whilst making the remaining viewports invisible. Alternatively, you can select the icon from the PROPERTIES toolbar located in the layer section, looking like the standard thaw/freezer symbol inside a rectangular tile, to freeze or thaw individual layers. Freeze off the layer PSVPORTS and make layer 0 current.

Use the normal plot routine with hide lines active. Ensure the DISPSILH command is set to 0.

Figure 217 shows the 3D view with all the hidden lines still visible. When plotted, hidden lines will be removed, as shown in Figure 218.

Figure 217

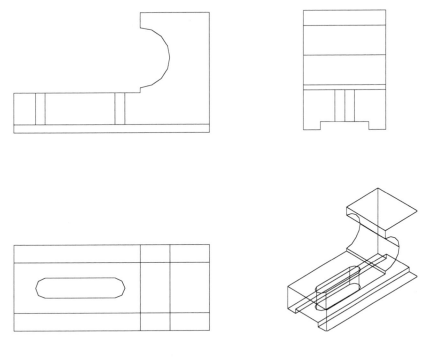

Figure 218

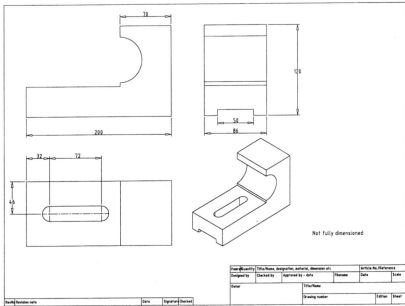

Orthographic projection

Paper space is an open invitation for 'orthographic projection' and for the 'dimensioning' of views. This section addresses some of the problems this brings to 3D CAD.

The ease with which AutoCAD model/paper space presents orthographic views, bypassing the traditional drawing board approach for the 2D convention of communicating 3D objects, presents new problems.

Model/paper space is an ideal vehicle for all forms of orthographic projection. However, its simplicity is leading to the neglect of basic projection principles not encountered when taught by the more traditional methods.

Coupled with the steady decline in both geometry and orthographic competences achieved in secondary education, it is therefore not surprising to find many students of 3D design benefiting from further studies in orthographic projection.

Orthographic projection is a 2D conventional representation of a 3D object (parallel projection) without perspective.

If straight parallel lines ('projectors') are taken from points of an object to another plane, this plane being normal to the parallel lines, the result is 'orthographic projection' (see Figure 219).

Figure 219   FIRST ANGLE ORTHOGRAPHIC PROJECTION

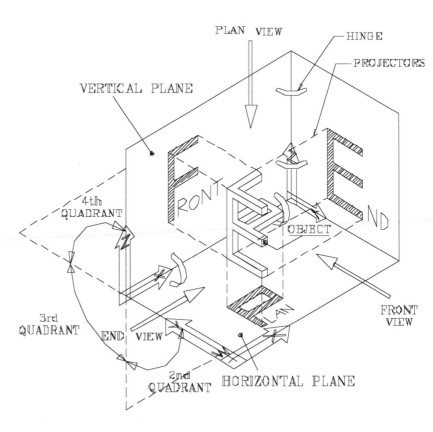

OBJECT SUSPENDED IN THE 1st QUADRANT

Principal planes

The two principal planes used in orthographic projection are horizontal and vertical. If these two planes intersect at the mid-point to form a cross, the object can be suspended in any one of four quadrants formed by the cross, resulting in the possibility of four different types of projection. The first and third quadrant or angle have become the two standard forms of projection (English and American, respectively).

The planes of projection do not have to be horizontal or vertical if views are required at angles other than 90° to the object. These views are referred to as auxiliary views.

First angle projection

Imagine the object in Figure 219 suspended in space between the horizontal and vertical planes in the first quadrant. By adding another vertical plane, it becomes possible to describe the object in terms of projection in the following right-angle planes:

1. x,y (PLAN)
2. x,z (FRONT)
3. y,z (END)

The three arrows in Figure 219 represent the direction of view or the 'line of sight' for the three basic orthographic views: 'front' elevation 'end' or side elevation, and 'plan'. Notice how the plan view results from looking down the 'Z' axis: this is consistent with the PLAN command used by AutoCAD to define a view.

If the 'x,y' plane (plan) and the 'y,z' plane (end) are rotated into the 'x,y' plane (front), like a sheet of drawing paper, the resultant views represent the convention for the 'first angle projection', all the three views aligned with each other. Think of paper space as the ability to move all these views relative to one another in the 'x,y' plane.

Third angle projection

It is only necessary to learn one projection, as the other projection is the complete opposite configuration of views. Third angle projection is the more logical and preferred type of projection, being the most commonly used projection in industry and the only projection specified in most modern GCSE syllabuses.

The CREATE subcommand of the MVSETUP command offers the option for 'standard engineering' viewports, resulting in third angle projection (Figure 220).

When laying out a third angle projection drawing, the view seen from the top of an object is placed on top of the object; a view seen from the left-hand side of an object is placed on the left-hand side of the object, and so on, resulting

Figure 220

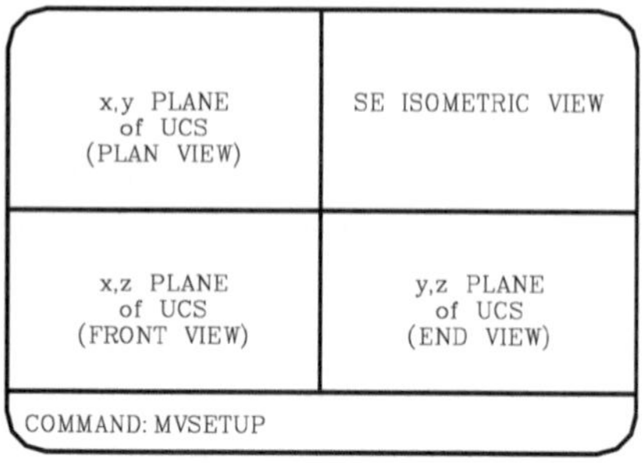

"STANDARD ENGINEERING" VIEWPORTS

in a more logical approach to the construction or reading of orthographic projection drawings.

Number of views

The above could falsely lead us into thinking that orthographic projection is about three views, namely front elevation, end elevation and plan. Remember that orthographic projection is only a language for the communication of vectors (and attributes): you would find it somewhat restrictive if sentences were limited to three words.

Ask the question: 'Does the minimum number of views adequately communicate the object?' If the answer is yes, leave well alone. It is not helpful to give more or duplicated information. I'm sure that most readers could adequately communicate their intentions at certain times with just one word (or perhaps two). Likewise, there are those occasions when one or two views are quite adequate for the communication of 3D objects.

Rules of projection

This is not a comprehensive set of rules on orthographic projection. The object of the six rules is to highlight the most common faults found on CAD drawings.

1. **Don't mix projections** – See the microscope assembly drawing (Figure 268) at the start of Part Three. This drawing contains mixed projection and was drawn to illustrate a typical projection fault seen on CAD drawings. If this view configuration is required, then one of the orthographic views should display a comment, indicating the direction of view (usually by means of an arrow).

2. **Associate views must be aligned in the viewports** – Use the subcommand ALIGN from the MVSETUP command for angled, horizontal and vertical alignment. (See the monocular head drawing, Figure 15 in Part One, for an example of the three above alignments.)

3. **Restrict views to a minimum** – It is not helpful to include more views than is necessary, simply because it is easy to achieve using a CAD system. Remember this is a communication, not a 'pretty picture'.
4. **Always include centre lines** – Centre lines are part of the object's geometry in terms of symmetry and, as such, are just as important as a line, arc or whatever.
5. **Enlarge with zoomed viewports** – When part of an object is to be enlarged for clarity of detail, consider the zoomed viewport instead of 'copy' and 'scale'. A zoomed object does not scale the drawing database.
6. **Restrict hidden lines** – Make full use of the MVIEW command to hide lines in certain viewpoints. It is not necessary to show hidden lines in every viewport.

Viewport alignment

When using viewports in paper space to create orthographic views, the view alignment between different views is not automatic and in many cases requires a degree of view adjustment. There are occasions when graphical cursor alignment of different views is not appropriate; a more accurate solution to the alignment of views is to use the MVSETUP command when TILEMODE is off.

With the MVSETUP command you can align one floating viewport with another viewport in relation to horizontal, vertical or angled elements of the drawing by panning the views in a specified direction. The process involves selecting a basepoint in the reference viewport (this viewport being active), prior to the selection of an alignment point in the viewport to be panned, as follows. First, with reference to Figure 221, horizontal panning:

```
COMMAND: MVSETUP
Prompt Align/Create/Scale viewports/Options/Title
    block/Undo: A for Align
Angled/Horizontal/Vertical alignment/Rotate view
        Undo: H for Horizontal
   basepoint: select point '1'
other point: select point '2' and note the results
```

Figure 221

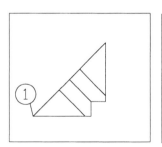
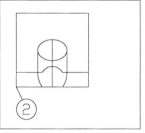

Figure 222 illustrates vertical panning:

```
COMMAND: MVSETUP
        : A
        : V for Vertical
        : select point '1'
        : select point '2' and note the results
```

Figure 222

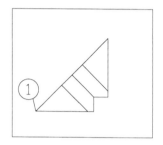 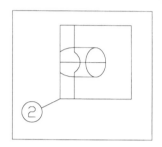

Finally, Figure 223 illustrates angled panning:

```
               COMMAND: MVSETUP
                      : A
                      : A for Angled
             basepoint: select point '1'
           other point: select point '2'
   distance from basepoint: select points '2' and '3'
      angle from basepoint: select points '1' and '3' and note
                            the results
```

Figure 223

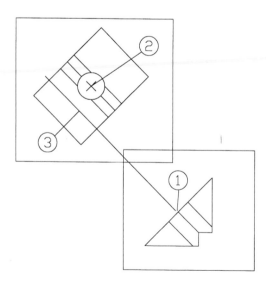

Dimensioning

Experience is the greatest teacher of dimensioning. With experience you learn where to look on a drawing for certain information. I seem to have spent most of my working life telling people to 'dimension the view that shows the shape'.

AutoCAD removes the need to exercise certain rules of dimensioning with the ability to preset dimensioning styles prior to use.

Most students of AutoCAD 3D design have previously experienced a 2D graphics course such as the City and Guilds 4351–01 course. Whilst this course tests for the ability to apply the DIMENSION command, it is not sufficient to prevent an increasing number of dimensioning errors appearing in the CAD drawings of this new generation of graphic communicators.

Rules of dimensioning

The following restricted rules on dimensioning are based upon common mistakes found on CAD drawings.

1. **Dimension the view that shows the shape** – See Figure 224. The implication of this rule is that the number of dimensions is not evenly balanced or shared between each view, and that sectional views usually attract the most dimensions. A sectional view without dimensions needs justifying.
2. **Group relative information on the same view** – Consider a number of tapped holes about a pitch circle diameter (PCD). Relative information includes PCD, coordinate location of PCD centre point, information relating to the thread (M6 × 1.5, etc.), depth of thread and number of holes about the PCD (usually equispaced). In order to obtain this information, the reader of the drawing should not have to collect information from a series of different views.
3. **Avoid non practical/geometrical dimensions** – (a) Avoid dimensions that cannot be measured (or which need advanced metrology equipment to do so); (b) if the maintenance of the dimension causes variations in its geometrical location, it is most likely in the wrong place.
4. **Extension lines almost touch the subject** – (DIMEXO system variable controls the separation.) When dimensioning, snap onto the end-points of objects (even if this means crossing the object outline) in order to avoid the error.
5. **Do not overdimension** – If the removal of a dimension does not restrict the ability to measure or manufacture the components, then the drawing is overdimensioned. When further dimensions (such as the overall length of a component) are added, beyond those that are necessary, place the additional dimensions inside brackets (see example 6 of Figure 224), indicating that this dimension is for 'information only' and not as part of its construction.

6. **Make full use of datums** – The ability to manufacture components accurately is directly related to the method of dimensioning and the use of datums. 'Dimensioning dictates the methods of manufacture.'

The datum face, edge or centre line should be as large as possible. The manufacture of the datum should be operation number one. Continuous dimensioning (DIMCONTINUE) or 'stringing dimensions in a line' can be the cause of accumulative errors. Note also the need to place smaller dimensions inside the larger dimensions, i.e. nearer to the outline of the drawing (smallest dimensions first).

Figure 224

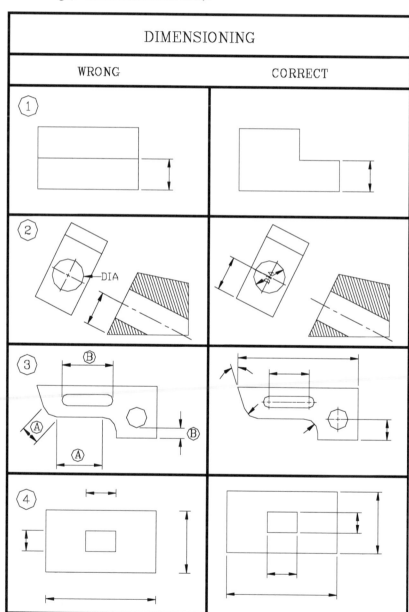

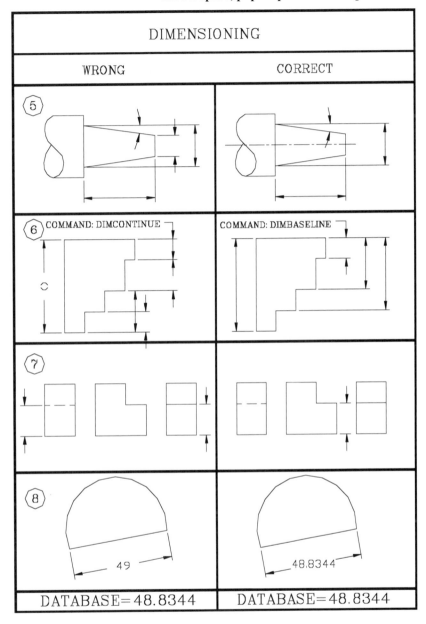

DIMENSIONING

WRONG	CORRECT

⑤

⑥ COMMAND: DIMCONTINUE | COMMAND: DIMBASELINE

⑦

⑧ 49 | 48.8344

| DATABASE=48.8344 | DATABASE=48.8344 |

7. **Repetitive dimensioning** – Do not repeat the same dimension on different views. This practice can lead to errors when modifications are made to a drawing at a later date.
8. **Do not override the database dimension** – The dimension shown on a drawing should be the same as the dimension held in the drawing database. When using the DIM command directly from the keyboard, or by certain editing facilities, it is possible to override the dimension displayed in the

prompt area of the screen. This is bad practice and can lead to errors if the drawing database is integrated with other technologies.

Take care with the UNITS command setting for the number of digits to the right of the decimal point as this can mask errors when dimensioning.

The above rules on dimensioning and projections are far from complete, but should help reduce the more common mistakes found on CAD drawings.

Exercise 6
3D views: parallel and perspective

3D AutoCAD drawing can be viewed from any point in space (model space). Consider the following four basic methods.

The first is the 'vectorial method'. Part One defined the point in space shown in Figure 225 by means of the VPOINT command, restricting the process to vectorial methods (i.e. −1, −1, 0.5).

Figure 225	Figure 226

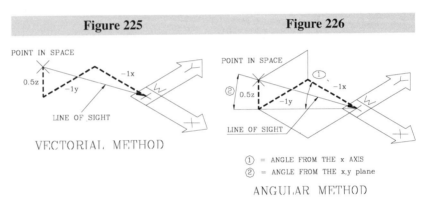

If a line is drawn from any point in space to the UCS origin, this line represents the 'line of sight'. By pressing 'Enter' at the first command prompt (VPOINT), a compass and axis tripod is displayed to help define the line of sight. This method is less frequently used since the arrival of the DDVPOINT command – the second method.

The DDVPOINT command offers an 'angular' solution to the line of sight as opposed to a vectorial solution. The command displays a dialogue box that offers the choice of the line of sight relative to the WCS or the current UCS.

Two image tiles are displayed in the dialogue box for the selection of angles '1' and '2' (see Figure 226) by clicking inside the sector of the image files or by entering the values into the two edit boxes.

Thirdly, a more restrictive set of 3D views can be selected from predefined line of sight, using graphics icons from a pull-down menu or toolbars (windows). This 'graphical' method is well suited for the standard orthographic views in first and third angle projection. Toolbars can be obtained directly from the keyboard (as well as from the pull-down menu) as follows:

```
                                  COMMAND: TOOLBAR
              Prompt Toolbar name (or all): VIEW
```

For a list of all toolbars available, use the TBCONFIG command.

All the above commands create 3D views in parallel projection. The need to apply perspective to a 3D view brings us to the fourth method, that of 'dynamic view'. However, before considering the DVIEW command, a little insight into the rules of perspective would be helpful when using perspective commands.

Perspective projection

As the distance between the subject being viewed and the eyepoint increases or decreases, so the size of the subject is decreased or increased, respectively, causing graphical changes such as the modification to parallel line in relation to the lines of sight.

Restricting our considerations to horizontal parallel lines for estimated perspective views, observe the following effects of perspective.

Figure 227

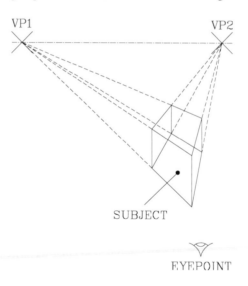

Figure 227 shows four parallel edges of the subject converging to the vanishing point 'VP1' and four parallel edges of the subject converging to the vanishing points 'VP2'. Note that the vanishing point 'VP1' and 'VP2' are horizontal, having also the same 'z' values as that of the eyepoint. Note also the position of the eyepoint (or camera) in relation to the two vanishing points.

It is this initial estimation of the line of sight that is so helpful when using the DVIEW command.

When a close-up view of the subject is required (inside the cube), as shown in Figure 228, a single vanishing point can be considered.

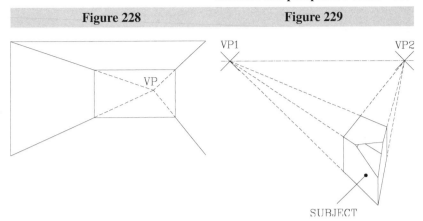

Figure 228   Figure 229

When estimating the line of sight from a given clipping view (or cutting plane) as shown in Figure 229, it is important to remember that the clipping plane is always perpendicular (90°) to the line of sight. Note the angular lines on the side faces. The greater the angle of these lines, the greater the angle of the line of sight in relation to the 'x,y' plane, i.e. the difference in 'z' values between the target point and the eyepoint or camera. If the line of sight were horizontal, the clipping plane lines on the two side faces would be vertical.

Whilst the above represents a very simplified view of what is graphically a much more complex subject, it should be sufficient to enable satisfactory lines of sight to be estimated within the DVIEW command.

Putting CAD into perspective

Dynamic methods

Perspective, colour-rendered images are a considerable advance in graphical communications compared with previous methods of presentation. The DVIEW command offers both parallel projection and perspective views with far more control over the 3D view than is possible with the VPOINT command.

The secret to successful dynamic views is no more complex than the ability to estimate an imaginary line of sight between two points, the target point and the eyepoint ('camera').

Line of sight

When determining a dynamic view, consider an imaginary line drawn from the eyepoint ('camera') to the target point. Those readers familiar with the use of a camera, will be used to setting the focal length of the camera lens to that of the subject: the subject becomes the target point, the camera optical axis being the line of sight. (Ignore reflex camera.)

The DVIEW command displays the target point at the centre of the screen.

End-points

Defining the end-points of the line of sight is the datum for any dynamic view and, like all datum, should be 'operation number one' when setting up a dynamic view. Whilst this can be achieved directly from the screen by cursor movements, I have yet to be convinced of a more suitable method than the following for students of 3D AutoCAD when defining the line of sight within the DVIEW command.

Using any suitable 3D drawing, create a plan view of the object (WCS) with adequate screen space to locate the eyepoint (see Figure 230). Enter the following:

Figure 230

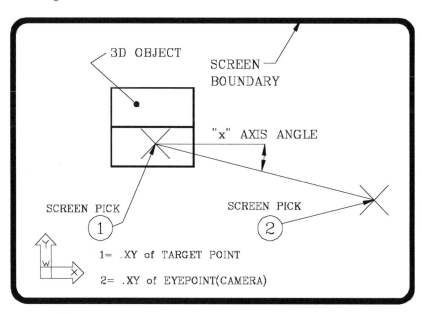

ESTIMATE THE "z" VALUES FOR 1 AND 2

z2−z1/DIST 1 to 2=TAN α

α = ANGLE FROM THE x,y PLANE

COMMAND: DVIEW

Prompt Select objects: *select objects from the screen*

Restrict the selection to a minimum for quick dynamic previews. This helps when dragging or updating images.

Alternatively, use the AutoCAD temporary display of a house by pressing the 'Enter' key (or create your own standard dynamic view and store as a WBLOCK called DVIEWBLOCK.

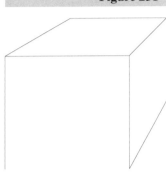

Figure 231

Prompt `POints <Exit>` *etc.:* *enter* PO *for Points*
　　`enter target point<>:` `.XY` *using point filters enables you to screen-pick points in the 'x,y' plane (WCS)*
　　　　`needs Z values:` *estimate the height of the target point above the 'x,y' plane*
　`enter camera point<>:` `.XY` *once more screen-pick the location of the point*
　　　　`needs Z value:` *estimate the height of the eyepoint (camera) above the 'x,y' plane*

This sets the line of sight for parallel projection. If a perspective view is required, enter D (for Distance). This moves the eyepoint along the line of sight a specified distance from the target point and turns on perspective viewing, displaying a special perspective icon (see Figure 231). (Turn off perspective viewing with the OFF subcommand.) Then:

Prompt `CAmera` *etc.:* *enter* CA *for Camera. Only slight adjustments to the line of sight may now be necessary*
　　Prompt `Zoom` *etc.:* *zoom and/or pan as required*
　　　　`<eXit>:` *enter* X *for Exit*

When viewing large objects such that the camera and target are located inside the object, the resultant view appears to locate the camera outside the object (prior to the DISTANCE subcommand). This is because it is the line of sight angle that has been interpreted from the points input, not from the distance from the target to the eyepoint (camera).

If perspective is ON when the subcommand POINTS is performed, then both the line of sight angle and the target to eyepoint (camera) are set.

If the points are specified in parallel projection, the eyepoint can be moved along the line of sight to the inside of the object by means of the DISTANCE subcommand.

■ **Zoom** – If perspective is off, the ZOOM subcommand option (under DVIEW) performs the equivalent of zoom centre. If perspective is on, the ZOOM subcommand option adjusts the camera lens focal length. The default lens value is 50 mm, similar to a 35 mm camera 50 mm lens. Increasing the lens length simulates the telephoto lens; decreasing the lens length simulates a wide-angle lens.

■ **TWist** – This option of the dynamic view command rotates the view about the line of sight.

■ **CLip** – The CLIP subcommand option (under DVIEW) produces cutting planes perpendicular to the line of sight giving the option to eliminate details above or below the clipping plane.

Parallel projection: clipping plane exercise

This exercise examines the relationship between the line of sight, the clipping plane and the system variable WORLDVIEW.

Set the following system variables:

COMMAND: SETVAR
Prompt Variable name? <>: ISOLINES
new value for variable <>:24
COMMAND: SETVAR
: DISPSILH
: 1

In the WCS use the CYLINDER command to construct a solid cylinder to the dimensions shown in Figure 232. The base of the cylinder will be located in the WCS 'x,y' plane.

Figure 232

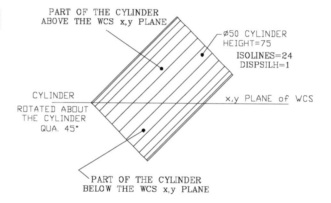

PART OF THE CYLINDER
ABOVE THE WCS x,y PLANE

Ø50 CYLINDER
HEIGHT=75

ISOLINES=24
DISPSILH=1

CYLINDER
ROTATED ABOUT
THE CYLINDER
QUA. 45°

x,y PLANE of WCS

PART OF THE CYLINDER
BELOW THE WCS x,y PLANE

DVIEW CLIPPING PLANE EXERCISE

Rotate the UCS 90° about the 'X' axis and rotate the cylinder 45° about the lower quadrant as shown in the figure. This will place part of the cylinder below the WCS 'x,y' plane.

At the command prompt enter:

COMMAND: DVIEW
Prompt Select objects: *select the cylinder*
CAmera/TArget/Distance/POints/PAn/Zoom/TWist/
   CLip/Hide/Off/Undo/<eXit>: *enter PO for Points*
enter target point <Current>: 0,0,0
enter target point <Current>: 0,0,10

This will create the line of sight normal to the WCS 'x,y' plane, i.e. down the 'Z' axis. The target point (0,0,0) will be in the centre of the screen, hence the need to zoom and pan as required.

Prompt line < >: *enter* CL *for Clip*
     Back/Front/<off>: *enter* F
distance from target: 0 *(zero)*

A positive distance places the clipping plane parallel and above the WCS 'x,y' plane (normal to the line of sight). A negative distance places the clipping plane parallel and below the WCS 'x,y' plane.

The resultant dynamic view (Figure 233) shows the clipping plane at the origin point of the WCS, normal to the 'Z' axis (the WCS 'x,y' plane).

<eXit>: *enter* X *and save the view*

Figure 233

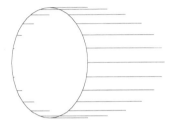

```
DVIEW "CLip" with FRONT off
NORMAL TO THE "LINE OF SIGHT"
TARGET DISTANCE=0 (WCS x,y PLANE)
```

Warning

You may be tempted to define the cylinder clipping plane by locating the UCS in the desired 'x,y' plane when the cylinder is erect, prior to executing the DVIEW command, defining the end-points of the line of sight as above. This causes problems due to the UCS reverting to the WCS during the points specification.

WORLDVIEW is the system variable that controls whether or not the current UCS changes to WCS during the DVIEW or VPOINT command. As a general rule, it is better to have:

■ WORLDVIEW = 1 as the default setting. This causes the current UCS to revert to WCS during the DVIEW or VPOINT commands.
■ WORLDVIEW = 0 causes the current UCS to remain unchanged.

Tasks

DVIEW tasks

1. (a) Alter the system variable to enable the 'x,y' clipping plane to be specified on an erect cylinder (via the UCS command).
   (b) Repeat the exercise without rotating the cylinder.

2. Reproduce the views shown in Figure 234, estimating:
   (a) the line of sight

(b) the clipping plane

(c) the lens value

3. With a non-document mode text editor, create the following AutoLISP file.

```
name file: PERSOFF.LSP
(DEFUN C: PEROFF ()
(COMMAND "DVIEW" "" "OFF" "")
)
```

Using a drawing from (2) above, load the file as follows:

```
COMMAND: (LOAD 'PERSOFF')
   Prompt: C:PERSOFF
COMMAND: PERSOFF  Resulting in a shortcut for switching off
                 perspective
```

Note: For ease of keyboard entry, customised commands should be as brief as possible. Try reducing the number of letters in this new command.

Perspective tasks

The following tasks refer to Figure 234.

4. Estimate the eyepoint and line of sight in Figure 234(a).

5. Estimate the eyepoint and line of sight in Figure 234(b).

Figure 234(a)	**Figure 234(b)**

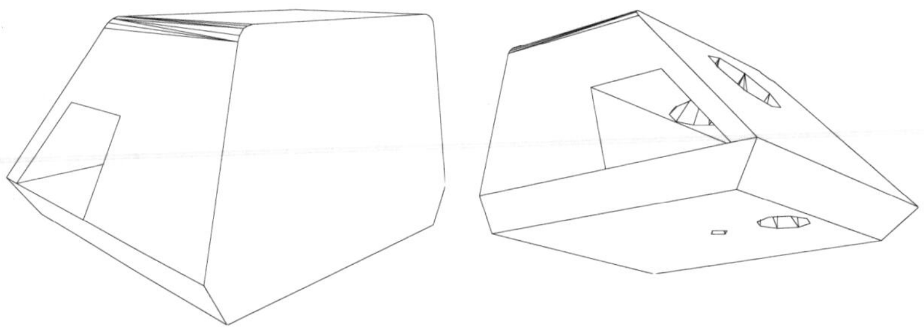

6. Change the FACETRES value, estimate the line of sight and location of the clipping plane in Figure 234(c).

7. Using a new clipping plane, estimate the lens value (zoom) in Figure 234(d).

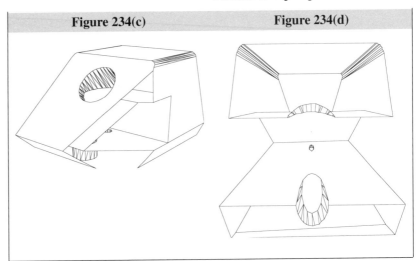

Figure 234(c)   **Figure 234(d)**

Exercise 7
Point translation (3D views)

It is important to remember that the UCS and views are not connected (see Rule 11). To change from one view to another does *not* alter the location of the UCS. If, for example, you use a screen icon to change from a front view to a side view, the UCS remains unaltered. However, within the VPOINT and DVIEW commands there is a temporary transparent UCS change (WORLDVIEW = 1). This causes a change to the value of any points used within these commands and is the subject of this exercise.

Calculating points

By entering a formula on the command line using the CAL command, it is possible to make use of object snap modes as well as variables in an expression to convert point values between UCS and WCS.

AutoCAD snap modes

Whenever the command CAL evaluates a snap mode, it prompts the user to select an object, returning the 'x,y,z' coordinates of the selected points.

Converting points

There are two different methods of point translation considered in this exercise:

- A CAL expression – U2W(P1) converts UCS 2 WCS of point 'P1' – W2U(P1) converts WCS 2 UCS of point 'P1'
- TRANS – An AutoLISP function for the translation from one system to another.

In Figure 235, point 'P1' is related to the WCS by:

1 unit movement in 'X' axis
2 units movement in 'Y' axis
3 units movement in 'Z' axis

in other words (1.0, 2.0, 3.0).

If the WCS is now rotated 90° anticlockwise about the 'Z' axis, as shown in part 2 of Figure 235, the 'W' is removed from the icon as it is no longer in the WCS but in a new UCS.

Figure 235

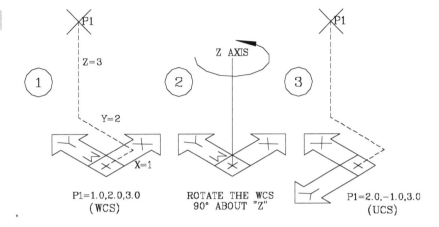

This new UCS has different 'X,Y' axes in relation to point 'P1', hence the relationship of 'P1' to the UCS is:

2 units movement in 'X' axis
−1 unit movement in 'Y' axis
3 units movement in 'Z' axis

in other words (2.0, −1.0, 3.0).

Coordinate system transformation

Set the following system variables:

PDMODE = 3
WORLDVIEW = 1
ISOLINES = 24
DISPSILH = 1

In WCS, create a solid wedge using the CUBE subcommand and change to VPOINT 1,1,1 (Figure 236).

Place the UCS on the inclined plane using the 3POINT option. It is from this UCS location that two points are to be specified along the line of sight. Locate a cylinder at the centre of the inclined face using point filters (Rule 6) to the dimensions shown in Figure 236. At the command prompt enter:

```
COMMAND: (SETQ P1 (CAL "[0,0,25]+CEN"))
         : pick the base of the cylinder (note the value).

COMMAND: (SETQ P2 (CAL "QUA"))
         : select the top quadrant of the cylinder (note also the value).
```

Figure 236

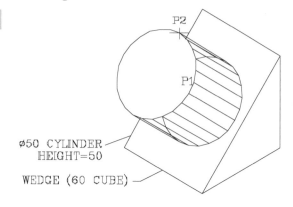

ø50 CYLINDER
HEIGHT=50

WEDGE (60 CUBE)

PRACTICAL EXAMPLE of POINT TRANSLATION

Point translation is performed next. Either of two methods could be used (method A is my preference):

Method A

COMMAND: (SETQ P1 (CAL "U2W(P1)"))
          : *note the value*

COMMAND: (SETQ P2 (CAL "U2W(P2)"))
          : *note also the changed value*

Method B

COMMAND: (SETQ CS_ FROM 1)
          CODE 1 = FROM UCS *where* CS *stands for coordinate
          system*

COMMAND: (SETQ CS_ TO 0)
          CODE 0 = TO WCS

COMMAND: (SETQ P1 (TRANS P1 CS_FROM CS_TO 0))
          : *translate 'P1' from UCS to WCS (note value). Zero indicates
          'P1' as a point*

COMMAND: (SETQ P2 (TRANS P2 CS_FROM CS_TO 0))
          : *translate 'P2' from UCS to WCS (note value)*

In order to place the clipping plane normal to points 'P1/P2', enter:

COMMAND: DVIEW
          : *select both cylinder and wedge*
Prompt <>: PO
Target<>: !P1
Camera<>: !P2
Prompt<>: CL

```
: F
: 0 (zero)
: X
```

Figure 237

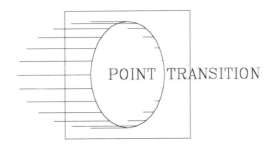

```
CLIPPING  PLANE  NORMAL  TO  POINTS  P1/P2
      POINTS  DEFINED  IN  UCS
CLIPPING  PLANE  CONSTRUCTED  IN  WCS
```

The resultant view shows the line of sight 'P2/P1' with the clipping plane through point 'P1', normal to the line of sight (Figure 237).

In order to confirm the results, change the UCS to WCS as follows:

```
COMMAND: UCS
        : press 'Enter' twice (this gives WCS)

COMMAND: POINT
        : !P1

COMMAND: POINT
        : !P2
```

The displayed points, entered in WCS, should coincide with the chosen points defined in the UCS.

Exercise 8
Parametric design using a script file

The object of this exercise is to create a spiral cable section (think of a telephone cable) suitable for inclusion in the design project of Part Three.

There are a number of different solutions to the creation of a spiral: AutoLISP macro, polyline editing with smoothing (PLINE–SPLINESEGS–SPLINEFRAME) and the SPLINE command. The individual points required to create the spiral can be entered directly from the keyboard (or 'filter picking') or from a predefined file such as as AutoLISP macro or a script file.

Solid spiral

To create a solid spiral the EXTRUDE command would be ideal – simply extrude a region (cross-section) along a path (spiral). However, AutoCAD currently rejects a spline created by editing a 3D polyline (3DPOLY command) or by using the SPLINE command as a suitable path for extrusion, hence the need to create a surface model of the spiral.

Surface model spiral

The EDGESURF command is used to create the spiral surface mesh (see Figure 238) using two arcs and two spiral splines. The splines are constructed from the two spiral splines. The splines are constructed from two script files, one for the parametric variables and one for the generation of the graphics (this could be one long file if you so wish). Changing a parametric variable such as the spiral radii involves the editing of a single entity in the parametric file in order to create the modified spiral, saving considerably the time necessary for design changes and operator fatigue.

Script files

In Part One, Exercise 5, we used a script file to define the vertex points of a 3D mesh (monocular head). The script file was used to read a sequence of coordinate

Figure 238

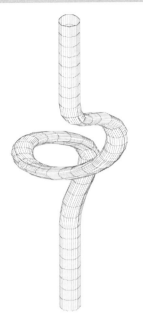

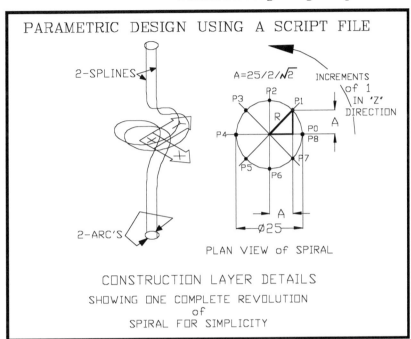

PARAMETRIC DESIGN USING A SCRIPT FILE

2-SPLINES

$A = 25/2/\sqrt{2}$ INCREMENTS of 1 IN 'Z' DIRECTION

2-ARC'S

PLAN VIEW of SPIRAL

CONSTRUCTION LAYER DETAILS

SHOWING ONE COMPLETE REVOLUTION
of
SPIRAL FOR SIMPLICITY

points within a command. Script files are often used to automate a sequence of commands, reading from a text file with an extension of 'SCR'. It is also possible to invoke a script file when starting-up AutoCAD (very useful when setting a 3D design drawing environment).

If the 'set-up' script file was called '3D' and the required file was called 'SAM', then enter ACAD SAM 3D when starting up AutoCAD. This creates a new drawing called 'SAM' and proceeds to issue the sequence of set-up commands read from the script file '3D'.

Demonstration or marketing displays can also be run from a script file using a sequence of timed views of different slides (MSLIDE–VSLIDE–DELAY–RSCRIPT). Another useful application of script files is to store particular plot settings in a series of standard plotting scripts, avoiding the need to remember particular settings – simply invoke the required script file when a particular PLOT configuration is required.

Comments

Script files can contain information or helpful comments in the same way as an AutoLISP file. Any line that begins with a semi-colon (;) is considered a comment and is ignored by AutoCAD when processing the script file. It is good practice to include comments in script files, particularly if other people are to use the file.

Warning: A blank space in a script file acts as an 'Enter' key input or command/subcommand terminator. Take care with the use of blank spaces in your script files.

Parametric variables

Because it is possible to incorporate AutoLISP variables within a script file, the script file becomes an ideal vehicle for the construction of complex graphics comprising a series of parametric variables.

Path construction

The length of the script file is dependent upon the number of coils required in the cable. Figure 238 shows the construction points for one revolution, 'P0' to 'P8'; these 'x,y' points are repeated for each coil. When creating the CABLE.SCR file (parametric file), repeat the first eight points (times the number of coils) by using the text editor facility. It then becomes a simple matter to edit the 'z' values of the coordinate points in increments of 1. For simplicity, only one revolution of the spiral coil is shown in the figure.

Create an ASCII text file of CABLE.SCR and CABLE2.SCR.

CABLE.SCR (parametric file)	CABLE2.SCR (graphic file)
cal	SPLINE
r=25/2	0,0,-40
cal	0,0,-30
a=r/sqrt(2)	0,0,-10
cal	!P0
p0=[r,0,0]	!P1
cal	!P2
p1=[a,a,1]	!P3
cal	!P4
p2=[0,r,2]	!P5
cal	!P6
p3=[-a,a,3]	!P7
cal	!P8
p4=[-r,0,4]	0,0,10
cal	0,0,20
p5=[-a,-a,5]	0,0,30
cal	0,0,40
p6=[0,-r,6]	
cal	
p7=[a,-a,7]	
cal	
P8=[R,0,8]	

There are no blank lines at the end of the CABLE.SCR file. However, in order to terminate the SPLINE command in CABLE2.SCR, it is necessary to include three lines at the end of the file containing a single space in each of the three lines. This accepts the default start and end tangents of the spline and terminates the command loop.

When the files are complete, enter the following:

```
            COMMAND: UCS
                  : 0  select a convenient point on the screen
            COMMAND: SCRIPT
   Prompt Script file: CABLE
            COMMAND: SCRIPT
   Prompt Script file <>: CABLE2  this creates the graphic. If the
                                  command does not terminate, check the
                                  use of spaces in the CABLE2.SCR file
```

An alternative method to the above would be to use the SPLINE command directly, having previously constructed the plan view of the spiral (as shown in Figure 238), using point filters ('.x,y') to select the intersection points ('P0' to 'P8') from the diagram, adding the 'z' values as prompted from the screen. (Beware of input errors.)

SPLINEDIT

Errors can be edited with the SPLINEDIT command. It becomes very useful to be able to refine and move the vertex points of a spline curve from within the SPLINEDIT command. My preference is the use of a script file, as this enables:

- Easy editing
- Use of parametric variables
- Simple command changes.

Tasks

To test the above three claims for script file use, try the following.

1. Change the parametric variable 'R' in the CABLE.SCR file and regenerate the graphics.

2. Change the command SPLINE to 3DPOLY (remember the blank lines at the end of the program) in the CABLE2.SCR file and regenerate the graphics.

3. Smooth the 3DPOLY line, create a surface mesh and compare the results with the mesh created by the original script files.

If you like the power of script files but find them somewhat restrictive for parametric 3D design, why not investigate a much more rewarding solution by reading *A Practical Guide to AutoCAD AutoLISP*.

An AutoLISP solution to this exercise can be found in Appendix C at the end of this book.

Exercise 9
3D in focus: graphical solutions to engineering problems

At the end of Exercise 3 in Part One, a task was set to construct a parabolic reflector and to save for future use. Revisit this drawing and the method of construction as I now wish to construct a conic in more detail.

This exercise demonstrates the value of AutoCAD in the construction of:

- Conics
- Conic focus points
- Conic tangents
- Conic reflected rays
- Conic directrix.

It also involves some advanced practical geometry.

Practical problem

It is intended in Part Three to design a suitable reflector for a microscope illumination system offering collimated light. The solution to the problem is to use a parabolic curved reflector. However, the problem facing the designer is, 'Where is the focal point of the parabolic curve?' It is at this focal point that the lamp filament must be placed in order to achieve the desired result.

Parabola

If a section plane is inclined to the axis of a right circular cone so as to pass through and to be parallel with the side of the cone (or a generator), the line at the intersection of the cone and cutting plane is called a 'parabola'.

Conic curves have been the subject of study since the Ancient Greeks.

Construction

To construct a parabola, enter:

```
COMMAND: CONE
<Centre point>: select a convenient point
```

```
            <Radius>: 50/2
            <Height>: `CAL
       expression: (50/2)xSQRT(3)
                   : see Figure 52 on page 37 for 60/30 triangle
```

Create a '3D' view and save (–1,–1,1).

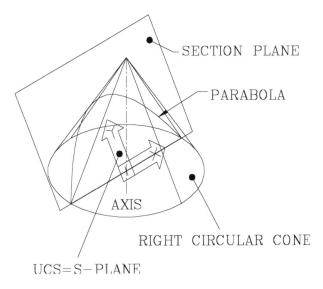

Locate the UCS at the centre of the right circular cone and rotate 60° about the 'X' axis (see Figure 239). Save the UCS, S-PLANE.

Looking down the 'Z' axis (plan), construct a rectangular polyline as shown in the figure (2D command in the current 'x,y' plane). Return to the saved view. At the command prompt enter:

```
       COMMAND: SECTION
   Select objects: select the cone
       <3Points>: select three intersection points of the polyline to
                  define the 2D plane
```

AutoCAD creates a region at the location of the section, showing a line at the intersection of the cone and the cutting plane ('parabola').

Focus

If a sphere inscribed to the right circular cone, touches the section plane, the point of contact between the sphere and the section plane is the 'focus of the conic' and the sphere is called the 'focal sphere'. (Conics are sections of the right circular cone.)

It is therefore possible to determine by graphical means the 'FOCUS point' (as well as other properties) of an ellipse, a parabola and a hyperbola as follows.

Focus point

Using the CONS layer as current (with colour), construct the four lines 'A'–'D' shown in Figure 240.

Figure 240

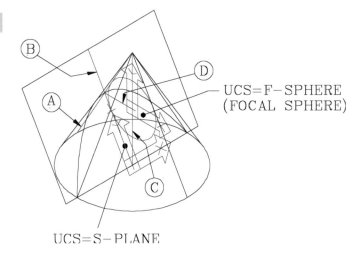

UCS=F−SPHERE
(FOCAL SPHERE)

UCS=S−PLANE

Line 'A' extends from the quadrant ('QUA') of the cone to the cone apex; line 'B' from (0,0,0) to the upper rectangle line mid-point. Line 'C' is the cone axis line (draw it), and line 'D' extends from the intersection of lines 'A' and 'B' to the perpendicular ('PERP') of the cone axis 'C'.

Move the UCS into the 2D plane of the circle and save this UCS as F-SPHERE. At the command prompt enter:

```
COMMAND: CIRCLE
<Centre>: intersection of the cone axis 'C' with line 'D'
<Radius>: tangent ('TAN') of line 'B'
        : the circle represents the 'focal sphere'
```

Place a point at the intersection of the circle with line 'B' (for future visibility) PDMODE = 3. This point represents the focus point of the parabolic curve (its 'x,y' coordinates being in the same 'x,y' plane as the parabolic curve). Freeze or erase unwanted details.

Restore the UCS to S-PLANE and move the UCS to the 'node' of the point and save as FOCUS (see Figure 241). Create a view looking down the current 'Z' axis.

Figure 241

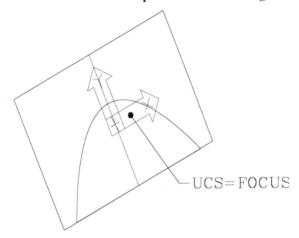

UCS=FOCUS

Collimated rays

Part One (page 73) demonstrated the relationship between incident and reflected rays. We shall now construct some collimated rays.

Figure 242

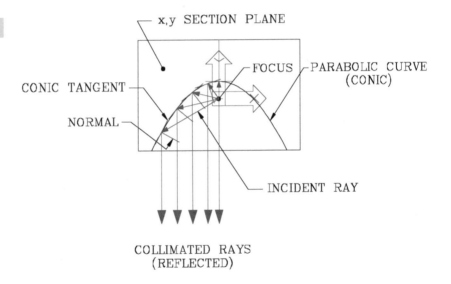

x,y SECTION PLANE

FOCUS   PARABOLIC CURVE
(CONIC)

CONIC TANGENT

PARABOLIC CURVE

NORMAL

INCIDENT RAY

COLLIMATED RAYS
(REFLECTED)

From (0,0,0) construct five lines that touch the conic as shown in Figure 242 (i.e. from the focus point to the parabolic curve). Estimate the 'conic tangent' line and construct a 'normal' from the point of tangency. Mirror the incident ray about the normal to produce the reflected ray.

All the reflected rays should now be parallel depending upon the accuracy of the estimated conic tangent lines.

If we consider the problem in reverse, by directing collimated light towards the parabolic reflector, a bright spot should appear at the focus point of the conic.

For comparison, place your coffee mug in direct sunlight such that the collimated rays of light reflect from the inner curved surface of the mug onto the surface of the coffee (it also works if the mug is empty), noting the intense area of reflected light at the point where these rays interfere (intersect each other). This very interesting curve is known as a 'caustic curve', showing the limitations of a spherical reflector for collimated rays.

Conic tangents

The more adventurous reader may wish to construct accurate conic tangents as follows.

Reproduce the construction lines 'A'–'D', as in Figure 240, including the circle. Locate the UCS in the 2D plane of the circle (UCS, restore, F-SPHERE) and, making sure that the UCS 'X' axis is parallel with the 'x,y' plane of the WCS, draw a horizontal line from the intersection of the circle with line 'A' ('F8'–ORTHO) to the intersection of line 'B'.

Figure 243

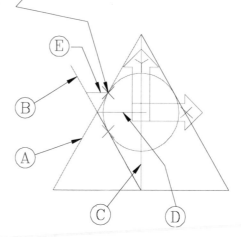

AXIS POINT of DIRECTRIX

The intersection of this horizontal line with the section plane (line 'B') is the axis point of the 'directrix' (see Figure 243). Place a point for reference at the axis point of the directrix.

Directrix

Restore the UCS to FOCUS and construct the horizontal directrix so as to pass through the 'point node' when horizontal (Figure 244).

Consider line 'E' (see Figure 243) as a 2D plane parallel to the 'x,y' plane of the cone base. The directrix is the intersection line of this plane with section plane (Figure 245).

Figure 244

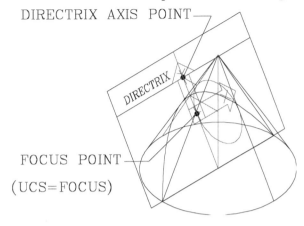

DIRECTRIX AXIS POINT

DIRECTRIX

FOCUS POINT

(UCS=FOCUS)

Figure 245

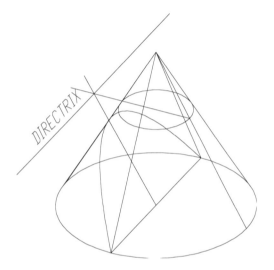

DIRECTRIX

Two properties common to all conics

■ **Property 1** – The angle subtended at the focus by a line from the conic to the focus and to the directrix forms a right-angle triangle, the hypotenuse of the triangle being the tangent to the conic at that point.

Focal chord

In *A Practical Guide to AutoCAD AutoLISP* reference was made to the construction of curves such as aerofoils and disc cams. These curves can be defined as a locus of a point, governed by specific laws.

Conics (ellipse, parabola and hyperbola) can also be defined in terms of a given law. Conics are the locus of a point ('C') which moves in a plane such that the ratio of its distance from the focus ('F') and the shortest distance to the directrix ('D') in the same plane, is a constant known as the 'ratio of eccentricity' (see Figure 246). The following relationships hold:

Ratio of eccentricity = CF/CD
Parabolic ratio of eccentricity = 1
Hyperbola ratio of eccentricity $\geq$ 1
Ellipse ratio of eccentricity $\leq$ 1

Therefore, given the conic ratio of eccentricity, it is possible to plot the loci of a point by:

1. Conventional draughting methods.
2. AutoLISP macro as above or as you have already experienced in this exercise.
3. 3D AutoCAD.

Extend line 'C' to 'F' so as to create two points on the conic. A straight line joining any two points on a conic is called a 'chord'. If the chord passes through the focus it is called a 'focal chord'.

■ **Property 2** – Focal chord tangents intersect at the Directrix (see Figure 246).

Figure 246

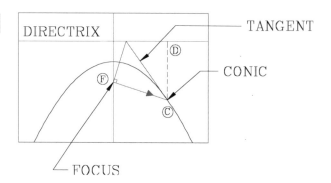

Tangent construction

Draw a focal chord intersecting the conic at two points as shown in Figure 247. (**Hint**: Use the LINE command from (0,0,0) to a point beyond the conic; this line can then be extended using the EXTEND or LENGTHEN commands. The LENGTHEN command is a useful command for the extension of lines that do not coincide with the 'x,y' ORTHO directions, making use of the following options: DELTA/PERCENTAGE/TOTAL/DYNAMIC. (I prefer DYNAMIC for the lengthening of the focal chord).

Next construct a line perpendicular to the focal chord, passing through the focus and the directrix. Draw lines from the intersection of this last point with the intersection points of the focal chord with the conic.

Figure 247

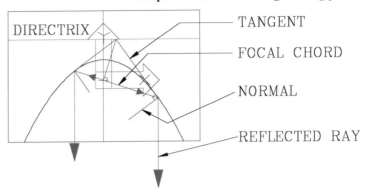

TANGENT

FOCAL CHORD

NORMAL

REFLECTED RAY

Once the 'conic tangents' are accurately constructed, the creation of a normal as the 'mirror axis' for the incident ray can be achieved without the need for estimation.

Exercise 10
Storage tank design

The object of this exercise is to construct the storage tanks to the drawing specifications using a combination of surface and solid modelling commands. The exercise allows for the opportunity to create blocks for insertion should you so wish. All of the commands necessary for the exercise have been covered previously and therefore there will not be exhaustive explanations. (**Hint**: Use layers for each of the component parts.)

Tank

Start by drawing the tank centre line and ends at 6000 centres. Construct a circle 1500 from the right-hand end to enable the filler cap to be positioned at a later stage (see Figure 248).

Figure 248

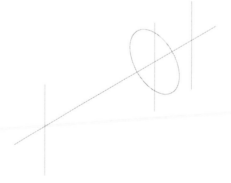

Draw the tank profile as polyline to the dimensions shown in Figure 249 and use the REVOLVE command.

Create the filler cap as shown in Figure 250 (250 DIA. × 250 length, located 950 above the tank centre line). Use Boolean operations to subtract the core.

Draw the strap to the dimensions shown in Figure 251. Extrude the base by 300 mm and the support element by 200 mm. The completed strap is shown in Figure 252. Locate the two support straps as shown in Figure 253.

Copy the tanks as shown in Figure 254.

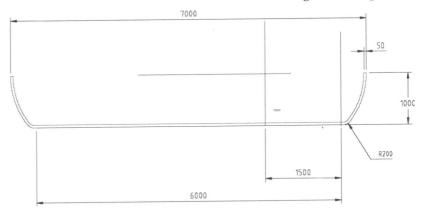

Figure 249

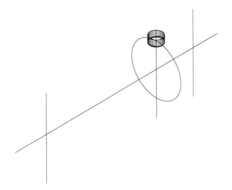

Figure 250

Figure 251

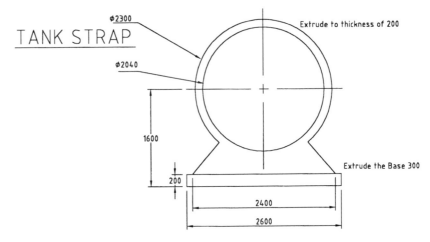

TANK STRAP

Figure 252

Next, construct a rectangle to represent the floor space (see Figure 255), prior to using the EDGESURF command. Set SURFTAB1=20 and SURFTAB2=36.

The tanks are to be provided with a platform as a walkway supported by columns for maintenance purposes. Construct the platforms and supports to the dimensions shown in Figures 256 and 257.

Figure 253

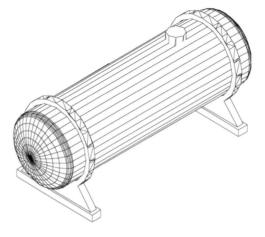

Figure 254

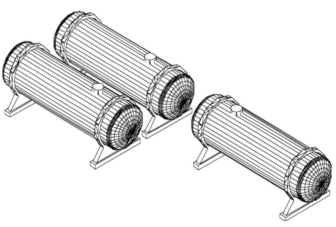

Figure 255

FLOOR   ELEV= 0

Construct with four seperate lines, then EDGESURF with SURFTAB1=20 & SURFTAB2=36

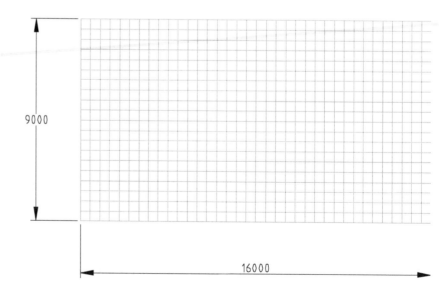

9000

16000

Figure 256

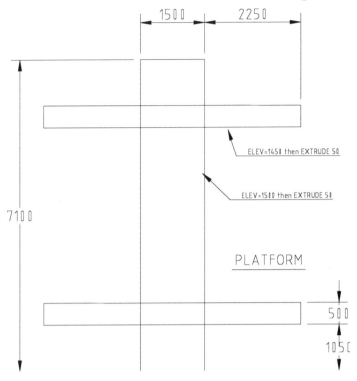

1500   2250

7100

ELEV=1450 then EXTRUDE 50

ELEV=1500 then EXTRUDE 50

PLATFORM

500

1050

Figure 257

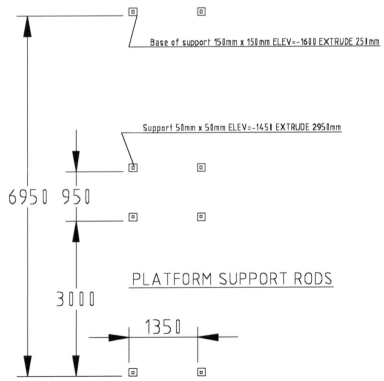

Base of support 150mm x 150mm ELEV=-1600 EXTRUDE 250mm

Support 50mm x 50mm ELEV=-1450 EXTRUDE 2950mm

6950   950

PLATFORM SUPPORT RODS

3000

1350

Tasks

1. Provide stairs to the platforms or walkways including safety rails.

2. Produce two dynamic views as shown in Figure 258.

Figure 258

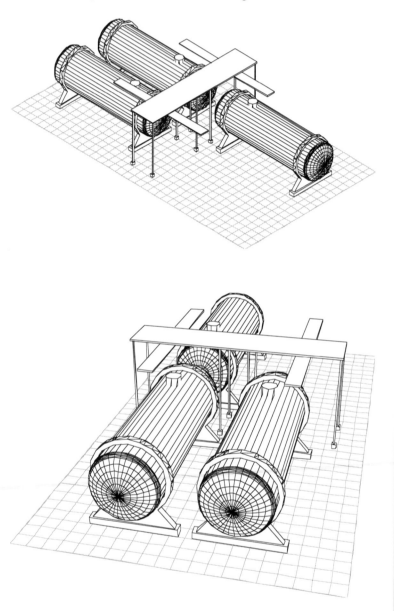

3. Time to be 'bowled over by CAD'. From the details given of the skittle profile in Figures 259 and 260, complete similar views of the bowling alley (Figure 261).

Figure 259

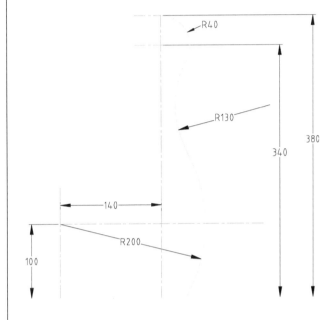

Figure 260

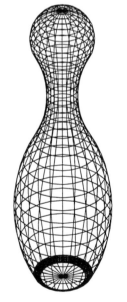

Figure 261

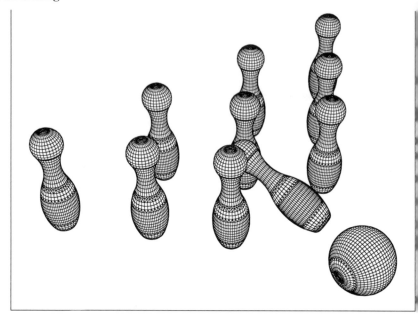

Exercise 11
Car design: mesh editing

I recall a period of my life when to entertain ambitions to be a train driver was normal for a young man. This would now not appear to be the case, the train being substituted by the car, with aspirations of personal car design. Here there is the opportunity to indulge your passions.

There are three S's when consideration is given to draughting using a CAD system:

Simplicity (of construction)
Symmetry
Standardisation

In the case of a car bonnet, the line of symmetry runs along its length, reducing the design process to one half. It is constructed as follows (refer to Figure 262).

Wire frame box

Using a construction layer, apply Rule 5 by constructing the wire frame box as shown in Figure 262. (This helps with visualisation and UCS manipulation.) Remember to apply Rule 4 when complete.

Creating mesh edges

The construction drawing shows the four edges involved with the EDGESURF command. This is the stage to apply your design flair. Each edge must be a single object such as line, open polyline (both 2D and 3D), arc or spline. Here we face the dual challenge of satisfying both functional and aesthetic requirements. Aesthetic considerations require a free-form geometry whose curves appeal to the customer, and are in many cases, in preference to functionality. These types of curve are often referred to as 'faired curves'. NURBS (Non-Uniform Rational B – Spline) curves represent a synthesis of both engineering and artistic sides of the design process.

Figure 262

CAR BONNET DESIGN

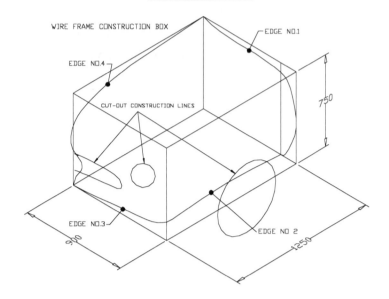

WIRE FRAME CONSTRUCTION BOX

EDGE NO.1

EDGE NO.4

CUT-OUT CONSTRUCTION LINES

750

EDGE NO.3

EDGE NO 2

900

1250

DETAILS OF THE CONSTRUCTION LAYER

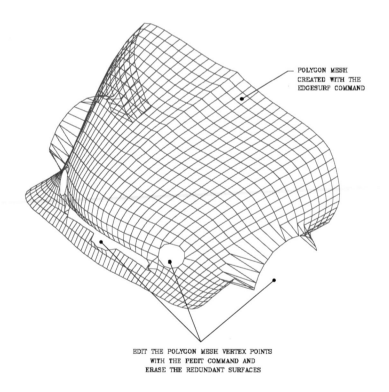

POLYGON MESH
CREATED WITH THE
EDGESURF COMMAND

EDIT THE POLYGON MESH VERTEX POINTS
WITH THE PEDIT COMMAND AND
ERASE THE REDUNDANT SURFACES

CAR BONNET DESIGN

SPLINE for car body styling

AutoCAD replaces the manual French curve technique with the SPLINE command, creating 'true splines' which are NURBS curves and resulting in curves far more accurate than edited polylines.

Interpolation

When using the SPLINE command the default setting is to produce interpolated curves. Interpolation means that the curve is generated by passing through every input point of its construction.

Approximation

You can change the tolerance of the spline. Tolerance refers to how closely the spline fits the predefined points. The lower the tolerance (zero), the more closely the spline fits the points. Approximation does *not* produce curves that pass through all the points of its construction. The fit option of the SPLINE command is very useful for smoothing exaggerated points in a curve ('curve fitting').

The SPLINEDIT command

To edit the geometry of the spline curve use the SPLINEDIT command. This is a very useful command with many options or subcommands. One extremely useful option for designers is the ability to move control points as follows:

```
             COMMAND: SPLINEDIT
     Prompt Select spline: select the spline
                         : enter F for Fit data
                         : enter M for Move vertex
                         : repeat N for Next until the required control
                           point is highlighted (curve fairing)
                         : relocate the control point
```

There are considerably more editing facilities within the SPLINEDIT command, but for the moment let us return to the creation of the car bonnet mesh edges.

Move the UCS into the 'x,y' plane of the required edge prior to the construction of each different curve (edge). In my example, all the edges were created using the SPLINE command, with the start and end tangents defined by pressing the 'Enter' key in response to both prompts at the end of the command loop.

When two or more of the polygon mesh edges have a common 'x,y' plane, consider constructing the relevant edges using a single command such as PLINE or SPLINE, prior to editing into 'individual' edges. This method ensures that the end-points of the edges coincide.

Note that edges '2' and '3' in the construction drawing share the same 'x,y' plane. These edges were constructed as a single object prior to editing the BREAK command.

Next, change to a new layer, with a different colour from the CONS layer, and set appropriate system variables for the surface mesh. Apply the EDGESURF command as follows:

- SURFTAB 1 = Tabulations between edges '1' and '3' = 'M' direction
- SURFTAB 2 = Tabulations between edges '2' and '4' = 'N' direction

The result is a '3D' spider's web appearance following the contours of the curved faces (COONs surface patch, a mathematical technique using two cubic equations).

Mesh editing

It is possible to smooth a polygon mesh by using the PEDIT command and the SMOOTH subcommand, the degree of smoothing being controlled by the 'SETVAR SURFTYPE = QUADRATIC' B-spline, where 6 = cubic B-spline, 8 = Bezier, increasing in their severity of smoothing.

Return to the CONS layer. With the UCS located in the side plane of the wire frame box, draw a circle conveniently placed to represent the wheel arch. We could have included the wheel arch as part of edge 2. However, this exercise is primarily concerned with mesh editing.

Now return to the MESH layer, with a view normal to the 'x,y' plane of the circle. Note the location of the various mesh vertex points in relation to the wheel arch. To edit these points so as to coincide with the wheel arch, the PEDIT command is used followed by E (for Edit vertex). This displays a small 'x-cursor' at the first vertex which can be manipulated to the desired vertex. Entering the subcommand M (for Move), enables this vertex to be relocated.

Warning: If the vertex point is relocated by 'screen picking', the vertex moves to the 'x,y' plane of the selected point with the 'z' value moving to the plane of the UCS. Note the exaggerated 'z' value for the wheel arch in Figure 262, shown to demonstrate this point.

Next, move the UCS parallel to the sides of the wire frame box in the 'z' direction to a more appropriate location. Use the PEDIT command to edit the polygon mesh to coincide with the circle with the aid of the apparent intersection OSNAP mode. Zoom a view to include only those vertex points in close proximity to the wheel arch (this saves time when identifying the vertex point with the x-cursor).

These polygon meshes that now constitute the inner section of the wheel arch can be erased after applying the EXPLODE command. This converts a single entity into individual 'panels' or faces (similar to exploding a polyline). Resist the temptation to explode the mesh until all vertex editing is complete.

Headlight design

Change to the CONS layer. Move the UCS to coincide with one of the inclined mesh faces and draw a circle.

Use various orthographic views to check the location of the circle relative to the curved surface. Rotate and/or move the circle in the 'z' direction if necessary. Remember to relocate the UCS if the circle location is changed by using the OBJECT subcommand of the UCS command.

Edit the polygon mesh, relocating the vertex points to coincide with the circle as above.

Front grille design

There are two solutions to choose from. The first involves the same editing as for the mesh and headlight, using a PLINE profile on the CONS layer in the front elevation. Notice the 'z' location of a number of vertex points at the centre of the lower edge of the grille. Edit these vertex points from a 3D view using different 'z' values (@0,0,z value) to give the desired result.

For a simpler approach, use the 3DPOLY command to create the construction line, by picking existing mesh vertices via the OSNAP INT mode, prior to editing the polygon mesh to suit the 3DPOLY profile.

Mesh with holes

Use the Explode command to create individual faces and erase the unwanted individual faces representing the holes.

Symmetry

Mirror the remaining individual faces about the axis of symmetry (use the wire frame box). Freeze the CONS layer.

Realisation

Render the drawing for a smoother image of your new car bonnet.

This exercise is a preparation for the construction of the armrests used in the design project in Part Three.

Surface mesh modification

If, on completion of your surface mesh, you wish to identify the value of any of the vertex coordinates, use the DDMODIFY command, picking the NEXT button in the dialogue box until the required vertex coordinates ('x,y,z') are displayed.

When selecting a 3D polygon mesh using the DDMODIFY command, the SURFU and SURFV system variables that control the surface density of smoothed surfaces in the 'M' and 'N' directions, respectively, can be modified by entering a number between 2 and 200. SURFU and SURFV system variables act in a way similar to SURFTAB1 and SURFTAB2 system variables.

Exercise 12
Piston and cylinder design

Animation

There are certain design solutions that benefit from dynamic communications (to inform and to test). The traditional solution to this type of problem is by means of a prototype or dynamic model ('mock-up'). With the advent of AutoCAD 3D design it becomes possible to animate designs or mechanisms requiring dynamic communications.

Computer animation is well known for entertainment purposes, but considerably less in terms of dynamic mechanisms. Whilst animation is beyond the scope of this book, it would be remiss of me to ignore the potential of solid modelling for possibilities in computer-animated dynamic communications, hence the choice of a piston and cylinder exercise as an example of its potential for further computer graphics development using such software as 3D StudioMax.

Solid modelling exercise

1. Construct the individual details to the dimensions shown in Figures 263 and 264.
2. Create the piston, barrel and conrod as WBLOCKs, taking care with the location of each insertion point, and not forgetting the current UCS when using the WBLOCK command.
3. When the conrod detail is complete, consider the need for chain fillets and edit as required.
4. Add the missing detail as a WBLOCK.
5. Create an assembly drawing as shown in the rendered view (ACCURENDER) in Figure 265.
6. Test the assembly for interference.
7. Use the SLICE command to complete the view.
8. Consider the potential for rendering and animation.

Figure 263

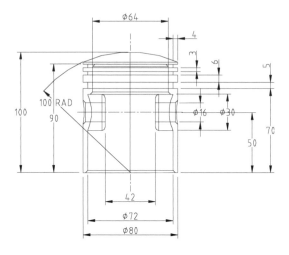

PISTON

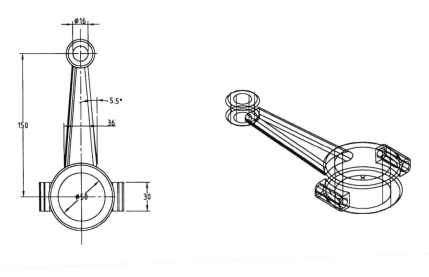

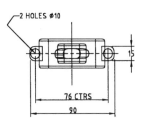

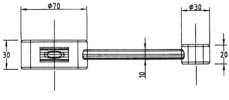

CONROD

Figure 264

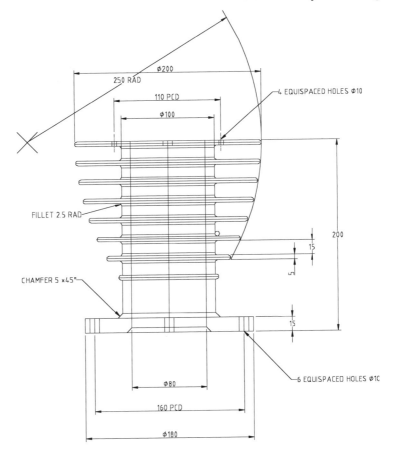

ø200
250 RAD
110 PCD
ø100
4 EQUISPACED HOLES ø10
FILLET 2.5 RAD
200
15
5
CHAMFER 5 ×45°
15
6 EQUISPACED HOLES ø10
ø80
160 PCD
ø180

BARREL

Figure 265

Exercise 13
'Up the twist' (square thread)

The object of this exercise is to create a realistic 3D image of a single start square thread with outside diameter 42 mm and pitch 12 mm as illustrated in Figure 266.

Whilst there is available a British Standard (BS 308) for conventional representation of screw threads for 2D orthographic projection, 3D representation of screw threads is a little more complex. One solution is to revolve the thread profile about the thread axis, producing a series of grooves having no 'helix angle'. This solution is not very realistic. A far better solution is to take advantage of the suggestion at the end of Exercise 7 on point translation. (See Appendix C.) **Hints**:

1. Use the CABLE.LSP macro.
2. Use both SOLID and SURFACE commands.
3. Take care with the SURFTAB2 value.

Figure 266

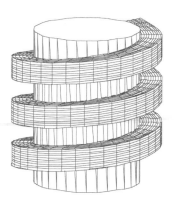

SQUARE THREAD

O/DIA= 42mm   PITCH= 12mm

Exercise 14
Steam engine design project

A complete 3D design project is included in Part Three for all those readers, who, having negotiated the hurdles of Parts One and Two, are attracted by the prospect of applying their new skills to the solution of more complex problems, in particular work-related projects for those employed in industries whose outcomes currently apply 2D design communications.

I cannot overemphasise the need to apply 3D design solutions to your current 2D work-related projects, for there is no limitation to the type of product that can benefit from surface/solid modelling.

A local model-making company has just completed a two-year task to convert all its existing 2D drawings into '2D CAD' drawings. Had it taken the opportunity to convert its existing drawings into '3D CAD' drawings, the potential for efficiency would have been much greater.

Figure 267

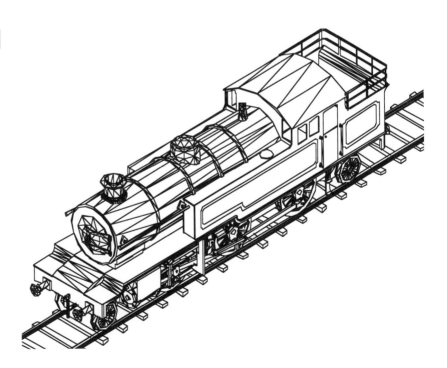

I have chosen a model steam engine to illustrate surface/solid modelling, for we may no longer wish to become train drivers, but very many people have a fascination for old trains. Figure 267 shows a surface/solid model of a model steam engine in preparation for colour rendering as an example of an alternative 3D design project.

If you do not currently have the opportunity to apply your new skills to the solution of work-related projects, can I invite you to proceed to Part Three of the book.

Part Three
3D design project

Contents

Design of a simple biological microscope

The purpose of the design project is to integrate the competences achieved in Parts One and Two of the book and to give the reader the opportunity to experience realistic design activities in the solution of a number of design problems.

The design of the project has been governed by the need to offer design realisation (design and make) for those wishing to put their design solutions into practice, hence the de-skilled nature of the design details and the 'foolproof' method of specimen focusing.

The choice of project has also been governed by a desire to extend the design activity into a series of subject research (part of the design process), more advanced geometrical constructions and the possibility of further development in rendered images.

Objectives

On completion of Part Three the reader shall have demonstrated:

- An understanding of the design specification.
- Knowledge of optical principles and ray diagrams.
- The ability to load and use an AutoLISP macro.
- The application of the following surface/solid modelling commands to the solution of 3D design problems: BOX, FILLET, CHAMFER, CYLINDER, REVOLVE, EXTRUDE, ALIGN, SPLINE, EDGESURF (PEDIT mesh), REVSURF, DOME, DVIEW, HIDE, SHADE, RENDER, SUBTRACT, UNION and INTERSECT.
- The ability to present a range of detailed design solutions, including decisions relating to the design modification of an existing design.

Optional
- Competences in mechanical/electrical/fabrication construction.
- Developments in rendering software.

Design of a simple biological microscope

Design specification

The choice of project has been influenced by experience gained over a number of years of successful design and manufacture projects in different education centres. The project is designed to satisfy the following specifications:

1. To function with standard 160 mm tube length optical accessories (i.e. eyepiece, objective and substage condenser).
2. Specimen-mounted glass slides.
3. Foolproof focusing to avoid damage to objectives and glass slides.
4. Appropriate coarse and fine focusing mechanism for up to 20× objectives.
5. Design construction by AutoCAD 3D modelling skills in surface and solid modelling, encompassing all the techniques developed in the foregoing exercises.
6. To be manufactured by simple workshop processes involving mechanical, fabrication and electrical competences.

The fully assembled microscope drawing is shown in Figure 268.

There is considerably more to the design of microscopes than this project permits. However, with limited knowledge and the use of standard optical components, experience has shown the project to be of great educational value, resulting in a workable product capable of enhancing scientific investigation. Figure 269 shows the finished model.

Teaching aid

For those wishing to refresh their basic optical theory, I have included a teaching aid that accurately draws the ray diagrams for thin lenses (converging and diverging) and reflectors (concave and convex) having a fixed object height for simplicity. Having entered the values for focal length and object distance, the program automatically draws the ray diagram to suit the input values, detecting values set at infinity and differentiating by colour real and virtual images.

Figure 268

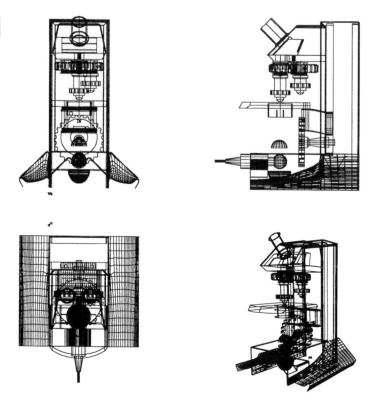

MICROSCOPE ASSEMBLY

Figure 269

Optical theory

The basic principle of the refracting microscope is to create an enlarged image of the object with full image integrity by means of glass lenses. (Remember that different colour components of light refract at different angles.)

This presents a number of problems, one in particular being the inability to achieve satisfactory magnifications from a single lens, such as a magnifying glass. Hence the need for a compound system that performs the enlargement of the object in two stages:

- **Stage 1 (objective)** – Enlarge the object to create a 'real' primary image.

- **Stage 2 (eyepiece)** – Enlarge this primary image, resulting in a 'virtual' image, having a total magnification of Stage 1 × Stage 2.

Using the learning program

Those wishing to refresh their basic ray diagram theory will need to run the AutoLISP macro OPTICS.LSP (see Appendix B for program). You will need to load individual files into your AutoCAD drawing editor before running the macro. The required files are:

- **OPTICS.LSP** – This file contains the subroutines for the choice of graphics, i.e. A, B, C or D in response to screen prompts.
- **DIVL.LSP** – A = DIVerging Lens.
- **CONL.LSP** – B = CONverging Lens.
- **CONVM.LSP** – C = CONVex Mirror.
- **CONCM.LSP** – D = CONCave Mirror.

Each one of the files A to D makes use of the subroutines OBJECT and SC.

- **OBJECT.LSP** – This routine contains the common graphics for the ray diagrams.
- **SC.LSP** – This routine places the start point for the graphics in the centre of the screen.

Using an ASCII type text editor create the above seven files. When complete, load the different files as follows:

```
COMMAND: (LOAD "A:OPTICS")
          or (LOAD "OPTICS") depending upon your choice of
          location

COMMAND: (LOAD "A:DIVL")

COMMAND: (LOAD "A:CONL")
```

And so on until all seven files are loaded. Run the program by entering:

```
COMMAND: OPTICS
```

Respond to the screen prompts.

The white arrow in the ray diagram represents the object. The real image is shown red, with the virtual image drawn yellow for clarity.

Test the macro by entering the following values for the object distance:

- Equal to the focal length.
- Greater than the focal length.
- Less than the focal length of the lens or mirror.

As an example, draw the ray diagram for a converging lens having a focal length of 30 mm with, firstly, an object distance of 80 mm followed by an object distance of 15 mm, noting the different types of image.

The compound microscope

The compound microscope has been with us since 1590 in various designs changing and improving with the advancement of science and technology up to the present time.

The modern compound microscope consists of a series of standard parts such as the 'objective', 'eyepiece' and 'substage condenser', configured to satisfy RMS (Royal Microscope Society) standards and located at specific distances in relation to each other.

The eyepiece acts as a magnifying glass to enlarge the inverted real image formed by the objective in the focal plane of the eyepiece, producing a much enlarged virtual image located at the least distance of distinct vision (see Figure 270), giving a total magnification equivalent to:

Eyepiece magnification × Objective magnification

Hence a 20× objective and a 10× eyepiece result in a total magnification of 200× when using the standard tube length.

The mechanical distance between the eyepiece shoulder and the objective shoulder is referred to as the 'tube length' and for most microscopes is 160 mm. Hence for a simple compound microscope design, the eyepiece and objective could be located at each end of a tube 160 mm in length resulting in an optical path as shown in Figure 270.

Bending the optical path

Ergonomically it is far better to 'bend' the optical path. One solution is to use mirrors (back face reflectors) to change the direction of the optical path so that the operator can use the microscope to observe specimens whilst seated.

For the project a simple eyepiece is used in conjunction with multiple objectives located in an objective changer (nosepiece) having different magnification values or 'NA' values (numerical aperture).

Figure 270

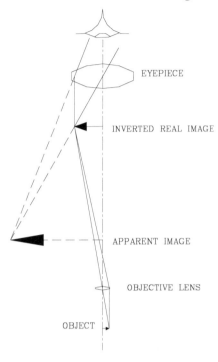

EYEPIECE

INVERTED REAL IMAGE

APPARENT IMAGE

OBJECTIVE LENS

OBJECT

COMPOUND MICROSCOPE

Figure 271

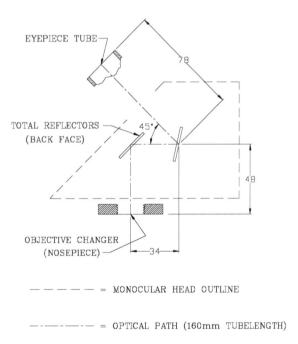

EYEPIECE TUBE

78

TOTAL REFLECTORS
(BACK FACE)

45°

48

OBJECTIVE CHANGER
(NOSEPIECE)

34

— — — — — = MONOCULAR HEAD OUTLINE

—·——·—— = OPTICAL PATH (160mm TUBELENGTH)

BENDING THE OPTICAL PATH

Instead of a simple mechanical tube, the design consists of a short eyepiece tube attached to the monocular head with the means of interchanging the objectives (nosepiece) also attached to the monocular head, all designed with the same mechanical tube length of 160 mm (see Figure 271).

The two reflectors are standard microscope slide mirrors. If a universal or metallurgical microscope is required then the 22.5° total reflector is replaced with a semi-reflector, with the lamp and lamp condenser placed behind the semi-reflector by extending the axis shown as 34 mm long in Figure 271.

Construction

The microscope design consists of three basic subassemblies:

1. Fabricated frame (fabrication competences).
2. Microscope body (mechanical competences).
3. Illumination tube (electrical competences).

1. Fabricated frame

The frame consists of four details welded together (spot weld, seam weld) to create a stable housing for the microscope body. Start with the microscope limb by drawing the cross-section including the 45° face and the safety edge as a polyline. Design a suitable safety edge using 1.5 mm mild steel sheet (see Figure 272). (**Hint**: When drawing the extrusion path, connect this path to the inside edge of the above cross-section before using the EXTRUDE command.)

Figure 272

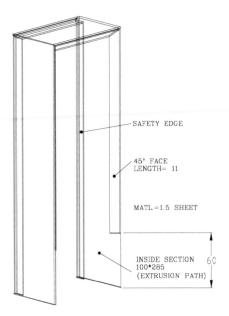

SAFETY EDGE

45° FACE
LENGTH= 11

MATL.=1.5 SHEET

INSIDE SECTION
100•285
(EXTRUSION PATH)

60

MICROSCOPE LIMB

Figure 273

Remove a 60 mm length of the 45° face by subtracting a box from the extruded section (make sure that the inside dimension is 100 mm). See Figure 273.

Fabricated top

The fabricated top presents the same problems as above but in this case the section is extruded for a height value and not a path. See Figures 274 and 275.

Armrest

The use of standard AutoCAD mesh commands (3D–3DMESH and EDGESURF) can be edited to change the location of each vertex point, to offer an infinite range of design possibilities for generated surfaces.

The following detail incorporates the standard EDGESURF command using a combination of four edges prior to vertex editing to give the required design. Control the mesh density with the aid of the system variables SURFTAB1 and SURFTAB2, using the order of edge selection to control the direction of the tabulated lines.

The armrests (i.e. left hand and right hand) offer support to the hands when operating the microscope focusing mechanism. They are also designed to offer stability to the design. If simple manufacturing techniques are required then design the armrest with uniform cross-section as shown by the larger of the two profiles in Figure 276 (section 61.25 × 55). As an exercise in edge surfing construction and polygon mesh editing, consider the design shown in Figure 276.

Figure 274   **Figure 275**

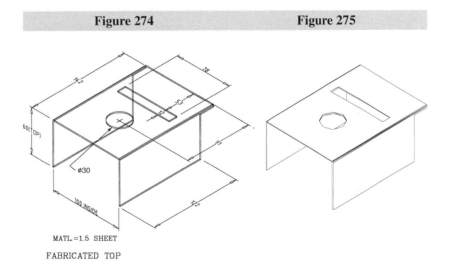

MATL.=1.5 SHEET

FABRICATED TOP

The armrest is constructed by two different but connected EDGESURF commands requiring four profiles or edges for each individual command as shown in Figure 277.

Figure 276

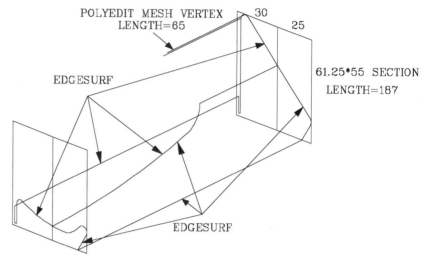

POLYEDIT MESH VERTEX
LENGTH=65

30

25

EDGESURF

61.25*55 SECTION
LENGTH=187

EDGESURF

ARMREST CONSTRUCTION LINES

Figure 277

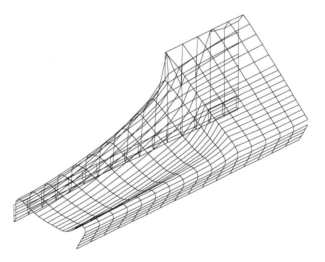

After implementing the EDGESURF command to the eight edges of the armrest, note that the section is not uniform for the first 65 mm of its length as required by the design.

To aid the editing (PEDIT) of the polygon mesh, construct lines from the quadrant points of the filleted arc for a length of 65 mm for use when moving the vertex points of the mesh (see Figure 276). (**Hint**: Don't free-hand sketch when moving the vertex points. Moving the UCS to the required 'x,y' plane of the vertex destinations is also helpful.)

If you find the editing of the polygon mesh not satisfactory for your current stage of development, consider constructing the uniform section of the armrest as an individual extrusion for the first 65 mm of its length, connecting this part to the remainder of the EDGESURF design.

Mirror the completed armrest to create a left-hand version (Figure 278).

Figure 278

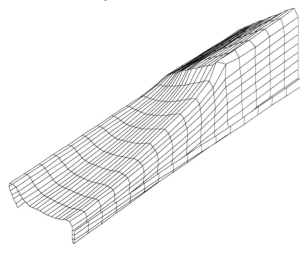

Fabricated frame assembly

Assemble the four details as shown in Figure 279 to show their working relationship in preparation for welding. Save this subassembly for further use. Figure 280 shows the perspective view.

Figure 279	**Figure 280**

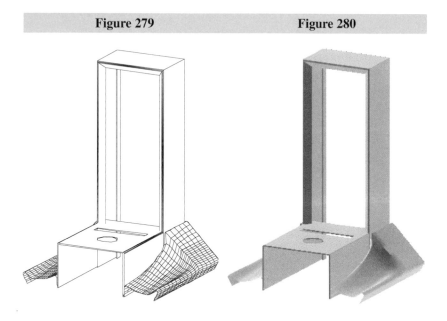

2. Microscope body

We created the aluminium limb, cam post and cam wheel as tasks at the end of Exercise 3 in Part One. Assemble the cam wheel and cam post in the limb.

Introduce this subassembly to the fabricated subassembly, locating the limb against the inside of the 45° face of the frame with the lower part of the limb in contact with the upper part of the fabricated top. Figures 281 and 282 show the assembly drawing and perspective view, respectively.

Figure 281	Figure 282

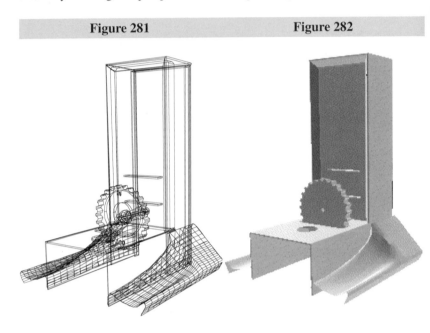

Microscope stage

The functions of the microscope stage are to:

- Hold the glass-slide specimen in a horizontal plane.
- Retain the standard substage condenser in a position relative to the specimen.
- Present the specimen to the objective by a coarse and fine motion.

The stage is constructed from the three basic groups of primitives:

- Group 1 – Classic geometrical primitive: BOX
- Group 2 – Swept primitive: EXTRUSION
- Group 3 – Edge primitive: CHAMFER

using the Boolean operation INTERSECT.

The stage coarse and fine motion is achieved by means of a disc or plate cam and follower (cam wheel), held in place by two spring plates secured to the aluminium limb. This type of design is simple but effective and offers a fool-proof method to the focusing mechanism, avoiding the problem of damaging specimens when the stage motion is allowed to make contact with the objective, as is the case with most commercial designs. Figure 283 shows a view of the stage and condenser tube in their working position.

Figure 283

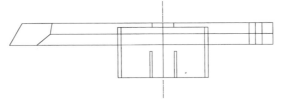

MICROSCOPE STAGE WITH CONDENSER TUBE

(SECURED WITH ADHESIVE)

Figure 284

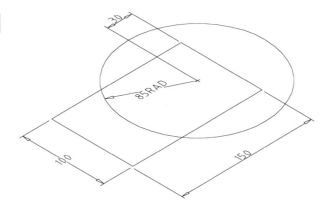

Figure 285

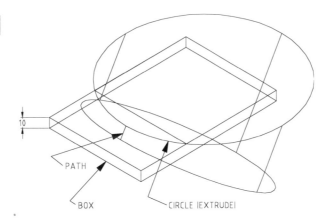

For the first part of the construction, on layer CONS construct a circle and rectangle to the dimensions shown in Figure 284.

Change layers, using the construction lines to create a box with a height of –10 mm. Draw the path at 45° to the quadrant of the constructed circle for a length greater than 10 × 1.414. Use this path to extrude the circle prior to using the INTERSECT command to create the first part of the stage (Figure 285).

Complete the stage by chamfering the two sides and by locating the three holes to the dimensions shown in Figure 286.

Figure 286

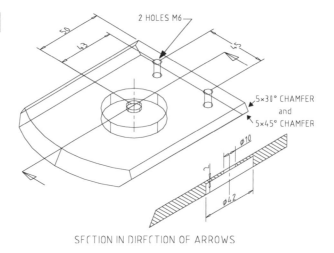

SECTION IN DIRECTION OF ARROWS

Condenser tube

The substage condenser tube is secured to the above stage by adhesive.

The two 1 mm slots in the brass tube (see Figure 287) create a tongue that is slightly depressed towards the centre of the circle offering a means of retaining and focusing a standard substage condenser such as the simple two-lens ABBE condenser, 1.2 NA (numerical aperture).

Figure 287

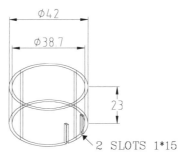

BRASS CONDENSER TUBE

The function of the condenser is to illuminate the object field of view central to the 'objective axis', hence the need to focus the resulting cone of light and to restrict the diameter of light entering the objective by means of a diaphragm.

The substage condenser diaphragm should be adjusted in diameter to suit each different objective (also its focus using cheap condensers). This means, in effect, raising the condensers when changing from low to high power objectives.

Cam follower

The cam follower is connected to the stage, causing the stage to move up and down as the cam wheel rotates about the cam post.

Create the CAM FOLLOWER to the dimensions shown in Figure 288.

Figure 288

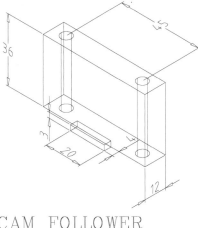

CAM FOLLOWER

Spring support

The spring support is similar to the cam follower and is located to the rear of the microscope limb between the two horizontal slots. See Figure 289.

Figure 289

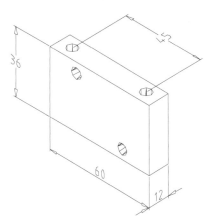

SPRING SUPPORT

Stage assembly

The stage follower and support are held together by two thin spring steel plates (secured by screws). These thin plates keep the follower in contact with the cam, with the stage horizontal as it moves up and down the optical axis. The distance between the hole centres of the cam follower and the spring support is 53 mm.

Use the SPLINE command to show the thin spring steel plates displaced 5 mm vertically, i.e. in their working or focused position, as shown in the stage assembly drawing (Figure 290) and perspective view (Figure 291).

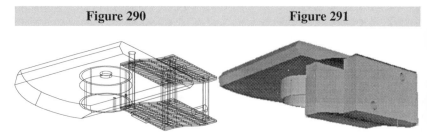

Figure 290   **Figure 291**

Assemble the stage subassembly to the aluminium limb, locating the spring steel plates and the spring support to the rear of the microscope limb and between the horizontal slots as shown in Figure 292. Try to create a similar perspective view to that shown in Figure 293 by using the DVIEW command.

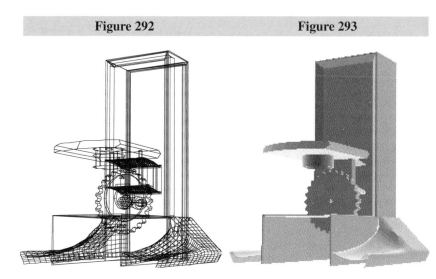

Figure 292   **Figure 293**

Monocular head

Since Exercise 2 of Part One we have been locating the eyepiece tube in the centre of the monocular head inclined face as part of an exercise. In reality, the optical axis is much higher up the inclined face, an angular distance (45° at 48.2816 mm). This need for change to the monocular head simulates real design office situations involving edit or reconstruct decisions.

Edit or reconstruct the monocular head assembly as shown in Figure 294. It would be more practical to construct the monocular head as two separate details for simple manufacturing purposes. This enables the 45° and 67.5° faces to be machined by side and face cutters (horizontal milling machine) to a depth of 27 mm. (The bottom of the 27 mm groove does not have to be flat.)

The 45° and 67.5° faces receive the two back face reflectors or mirrors (made from standard glass slide mirrors) secured by adhesive (with care).

Figure 294

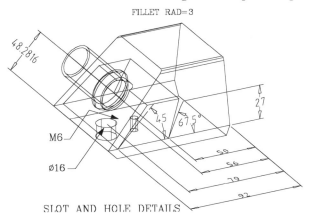

FILLET RAD=3

48.2816

FILLET RAD=3

45 / 67.5°

27

M6

ø16

50

56

79

92

SLOT AND HOLE DETAILS

These mirrors are shown in Figure 295 in their working location relative to the 1.5 mm aluminium cover. This cover sits on top of the monocular head with its back edge flush with the aluminium limb and its front edge projecting beyond the inclined face by 1.5 mm.

Figure 295   **Figure 296**

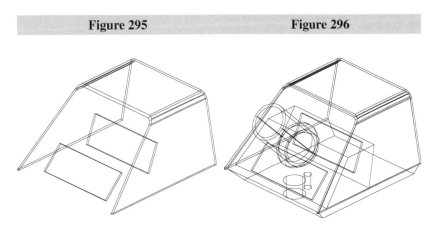

Figure 296 shows all the details necessary for the monocular head subassembly in their working locations with the exception of the eyepiece tube. The eyepiece tube is still shown central to the inclined face for clarity of illustration and to simulate a realistic situation requiring change. When the eyepiece tube is repositioned in its correct location, detail design is required to modify the monocular head. The correct location for the eyepiece tube is much nearer to the top of the cover.

Assembly relationships

When locating subassemblies, such as the microscope limb and the monocular head, in their correct positional relationship it can be very useful to use the ALIGN command. This command is used to move and rotate one object in relation to another by selecting different pairs of points: 'source' points and 'destination' points.

The first pair of points, 'P1' and 'P2' in Figure 297, cause the primary displacement of the object. Subsequent pairs of points enable the object to be rotated about this displacement point in two different planes for the benefit of '3D' objects.

In the example shown, it is only necessary to rotate the object in one plane, both objects were constructed relative to the WCS. Hence, source point 'P3' and destination point 'P4' will place the monocular head in its working location relative to the microscope limb. Point 'P0' is used as a datum point and is the mid-point of the lower front edge of the aluminium limb.

Figure 297

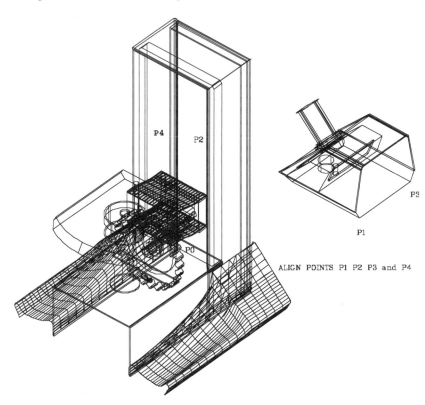

ALIGN POINTS P1 P2 P3 and P4

Aligning the monocular head

Carry out the following:

```
          COMMAND: ALIGN
   Prompt Select objects: select the monocular head
                          subassembly
      first source point: select end-point of 'P1'
 first destination point: FRO
              base point: MID select 'P0'
        of <Offset>: @39.0822,158 coordinate
                          point for 'P2'
```

```
        second source point: select end-point of 'P3'
   second destination point: FRO
                 basepoint: MID select 'P0' once more
            of <Offset>: @-39.0822,158 coordinate
                                    point for 'P4'
       third source point: press 'Enter'
 <2D> or 3D transformation: enter 3D
```

This command should result in the assembly as shown in Figure 298. The perspective view is illustrated in Figure 299.

Figure 298   **Figure 299**

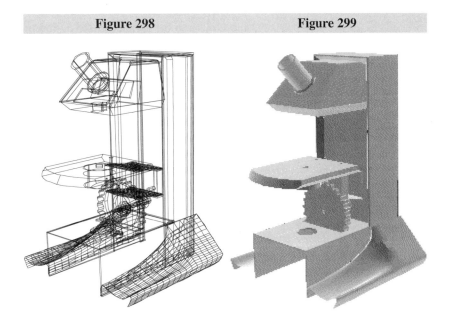

Time for reflection

Surface model

Note the wire frame image of the eyepiece tube (see Figure 298). If this detail had been constructed as a surface model, the tabulated lines would have been controlled by the system variable SURFTAB1.

Solid model (wire frame)

This eyepiece tube was constructed as a solid model. It is diplayed in a wire frame mode. The ISOLINES system variable controls the density of the tessellation lines, any change to this system variable is updated every time a REGEN is performed. (The default setting is ISOLINES = 4, as in Figure 298.)

What would be the result if the system variable was reset to ISOLINES = 0? Alter the system variable to test your answer.

The DISPSILH system variable controls whether silhouette lines are shown in wire frame mode. The silhouette lines are based on the current view, showing the outer edges of the eyepiece tube to enable you to visualise the model. Change the system variable to help with the visualisation.

Solid model (mesh)

When the HIDE, SHADE or RENDER command is invoked, the solid is converted from a wire frame to a mesh. (Returning to a wire frame whenever a regeneration is performed.)

The FACETRES system variable controls the density of the mesh. Once more observe the eyepiece tube noting the result from the default setting of FACETRES = 0.5. If you decrease the setting to 0.1, the resultant appearance would be that of a four-sided polygon (depending upon the VIEWRES value).

Remember that for construction purposes, the FACETRES value should be as low as possible to save on computing time. For photo-realistic rendered images, increase the value of this system variable at the completion of the design process.

Tasks

1. Increase the value of the FACETRES system variable to observe the smoothing effect on the curved surfaces.

2. Decrease the value of the system variable VIEWRES, noting the relationship between FACETRES and VIEWRES.

Objective changer

As mentioned previously, the simplest design of a compound microscope consists of a tube, bored at one end to receive a standard eyepiece and threaded at the other end with an internal RMS (Royal Microscope Society) thread to receive a standard 'OG' or objective glass, different objectives being used to change the total magnification of the microscope. (It must be remembered that magnification is not the most important factor dictating the ability of an optical system to resolve small details.)

For over one hundred years, an objective changer or nosepiece has been used at the end of the mechanical tube to present different objectives to the optical path, thus avoiding the need to interchange individual objectives, one at a time, by unscrewing one objective to replace it with another.

Many parts of the microscope call for a high degree of skills in their manufacture as poor workmanship leads to poor optical performance, none more so than:

- The focusing movement
- The nosepiece

In the case of the focusing movement, we used a very simple but effective solution in our design.

The design of the nosepiece has been 'de-skilled' as far as possible, avoiding the need for complicated manufacturing process and indexing systems. In the case of commercial nosepiece manufacture, accuracy is obtained by assembly machining the RMS thread and shoulder directly into the revolving member of the nosepiece on a specially designed lath using a fixture to locate the assembled nosepiece complete with the indexing mechanism.

This de-skilled design avoids such necessities by screwing a standard objective into a short steel tube which projects above the top surface of the nosepiece to form part of the indexing mechanism. It is necessary to ensure that the three holes in the nosepiece that receive these tubes are on the same pitch circle diameter (PCD), concentric and square to the axis of rotation. Equispacing of the three holes is not important as the indexing of each objective is achieved by contact with the top of the steel tubes. Parfocality is achieved by moving the steel tubes up or down to determine their precise location prior to securing with an M4 grub screw. The RMS thread in the steel tubes must be concentric and square to the outside diameter of the tube.

Nosepiece spindle

Construct the detail as shown in Figure 300. For simplicity, represent a thread on only male details by revolving a 60° profile. Whilst it is possible to construct helical threads by solid modelling, the complexity is not justified for such simple details as the M6 thread.

When manufacturing the steel objective tube (see Figure 301), make note of the geometrical requirement (mentioned previously). Manufacture the thread to suit an existing objective.

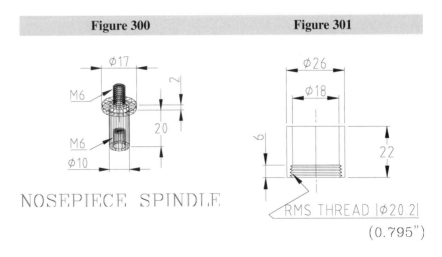

Figure 300   **Figure 301**

NOSEPIECE SPINDLE

OBJECTIVE TUBE

Construct the nosepiece as shown in Figure 302, taking care to provide maximum metal conditions for the M4 securing screws by careful spacing of the 7 mm dia. grooves. The 30° chamfers are constructed to the same depth as the circular grooves. Once more take note of the geometrical requirements. You may consider finish machining the 26 mm dia. holes when assembled to the lower part of the monocular head.

Figure 302

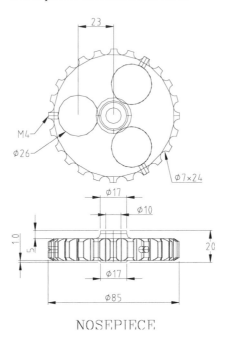

NOSEPIECE

Nosepiece subassembly

Assemble the nosepiece, nosepiece spindle and objective tubes as shown in Figure 303 (Figure 304 shows the perspective view). The objective tubes must project beyond the nosepiece spindle shoulder and are best located approximately 1 mm below this surface.

| **Figure 303** | **Figure 304** |

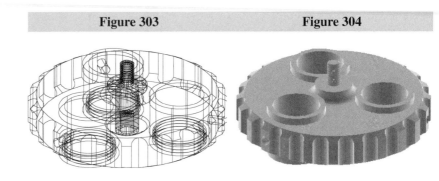

Locate the nosepiece subassembly into the monocular head such that the axis and shoulder of the nosepiece spindle M6 thread coincides with the centre of the M6 hole in the monocular head as shown in the assembly drawing (Figure 305) and perspective view (Figure 306).

Figure 305	Figure 306

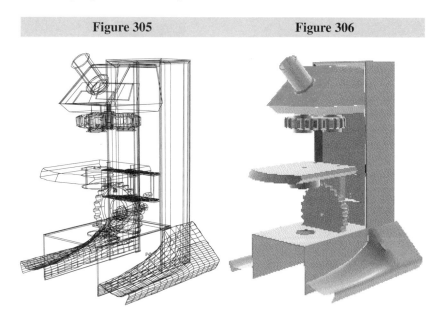

The figures show the three standard objectives located in the nosepiece in their working position when the stage is at the top of its movement. It is not necessary to construct these objectives; the drawings show standard objectives, modified by the addition of a grooved ring to complement the design style.

To complete the microscope design we need to add a standard eyepiece to the eyepiece tube and to locate the substage condenser in the tube provided, as shown in Figures 307 and 308. All that now remains is to adequately illuminate the specimen.

Illumination

In microscopical terms, you cannot see that which is not adequately illuminated. The correct illumination of an object is as important as the correct visual resolution of the object.

In very simple terms, the purpose of the illuminator is to provide an even intensity of light to the whole area of the object within the field of view, whilst at the same time the entire back aperture of the objective is evenly filled with light (controlled by an iris diaphragm). This field of view and the required light intensity varies for each objective. There are basically two ways of achieving these requirements:

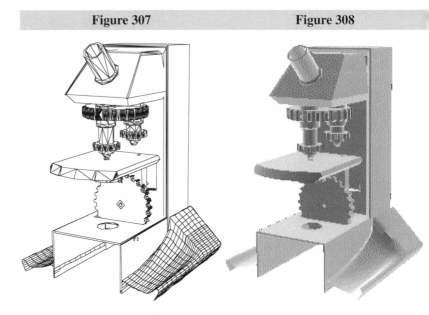

Figure 307   Figure 308

- **Critical illumination** – This produces an image of the light source in the same plane as the object.
- **Kohler illumination** – This produces an image of the condenser aperture in the object plane.

Whilst it is possible to use the sun for an even source of light, it is not very practicable in this country, hence the need for some form of high-intensity filament lamp to be projected into the object plane.

For the limited purpose of our design, a 12 volt motor car headlamp bulb is to be used to illuminate the transparent object. The type of filament used for motor car headlamps will not provide an even intensity of light but is a simple, cheap compromise.

3. Illumination tube

The standard motor car bulb is held in a 25 mm dia. body. This body is held in place (spring pressure) by the lamp support, offering two degrees of freedom (movement along the axis and rotation about the axis) for lamp adjustment purposes (see Figure 309).

Figure 309

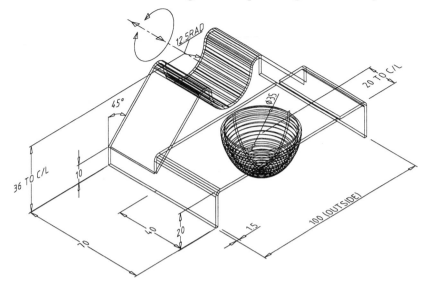

Edit the parabolic curve produced in Exercise 3 (Part One) to form part of the lamp support reflecting surface below the bulb filament. When complete, the parabolic surface is coated with silver paper or tin foil. This will increase the available light rays considerably. Select a suitable material with both elastic and ductile properties (when annealed) Alternatively, design the detail in two parts.

Illumination condenser

Figure 310 shows a hemispherical illumination condenser that locates in the fabricated frame by means of a lens cell. The lens cell is not shown as the availability of illumination condensers will determine the relative position of the lens to the lamp filament and consequently the design of the lens cell.

Figure 310

Ø27.5 DOME (3D SURFACE)

Assembly drawing

The assembly drawing (Figure 311) and perspective view (Figure 312) show all the different parts in their relative working positions with the exception of a standard eyepiece and substage condenser. To complete the project, a series of items require designing.

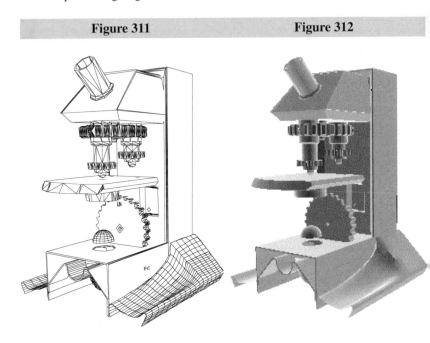

Figure 311   **Figure 312**

Final design

- **Illumination condenser lens cell** – With the substage condenser located in its working position (focused on the specimen) and the electric bulb filament in line with the optical axis, move your chosen illumination condenser lens up and down the optical axis to determine its optimum position.

    With the above location determined, design a cell capable of retaining the lens by locating the lens cell in the 30 mm dia. hole in the top of the fabricated frame. Your design should take into consideration different rates of expansion between glass and metal caused by temperature changes when operating the electric bulb.

- **Camwheel retaining screw** – This is a specially designed screw that restricts the movement of the CAMWHEEL to rotation about its axis (there is no need for a washer).

- **Nosepiece securing screw** – This screw is similar in design to the Camwheel retaining screw and must restrict any movement along the axis of the spindle to a minimum. The nosepiece spindle should remain screwed to the monocular head when the nosepiece is rotated anticlockwise.

- **Monocular head** – When constructing the solid model of the monocular head and the microscope limb subassembly, the monocular head was positioned relative to the limb by means of the ALIGN command. These two parts need securing with cheese-headed screws from the rear of the microscope limb.

  When determining the location and number of these cheese-headed screws, take into consideration any future needs for a metallurgical microscope, as the illumination axis for a metallurgical microscope is placed behind the semi-reflector (22.5° surface) extending outwards the horizontal optical axis.

  If your monocular head was designed in two parts, then these details need securing in their working position. The mirror secured by adhesive to the A5 and 22.5° faces would be improved optically by redesigning a mechanical mounting system or by placing a thin coat of rubber (flexible plastic) between the glass and metal faces. When using adhesive (take care as this will alter the optical path).

- **Microscope limb** – The microscope limb is secured to the side of the fabricated frame by means of 'pop' rivets along the 223 mm lengths. Modify the aluminium microscope limb to make this possible.

- **Illumination tube** – Using a standard 12 volt motor car bulb holder, design the illumination body having an outside diameter of 25 mm, take into consideration all the necessary safety requirements using standard parts when possible.

- **Stage supports** – The cam follower with two spring steel plates are secured to the stage by two M6 cheese-headed screws, screwed into the stage from the under side. The other ends of the spring steel plates are secured to the spring support by four cheese-headed screws, the spring support being secured to the back of the microscope limb.

- **Nosepiece spring** – The indexing mechanism to locate accurately and repeatedly the objective tubes as they rotate into the optical axis can be achieved by a spring plate that is secured to the inclined face of the monocular head and projects into the path of the rotating tubes. The spring plate can be secured using a 'V' shape profile to register against the outside diameter of the objective tube, the accurate positioning of the spring being achieved by assembly machining the screws into the inclined face of the monocular head.

  Whilst this represents one solution to the problem, there are also many other indexing mechanisms worthy of consideration. As a design principle, never accept the first idea as the solution to a problem. Develop a series of design solutions to the problem, selecting only after careful evaluation of each idea against the design specification. If after careful evaluation of all the designs, you select the first idea, you will have the confidence to support this solution as the best design with respect to the specification and conditions prevailing at that particular moment in time.

Those wishing to undertake further design problems can consider solutions to the use of standard stage clips for retaining the glass slides.

The final assembly drawing for the microscope is shown in Figure 313, and the corresponding perspective view in Figure 314.

Figure 313	Figure 314

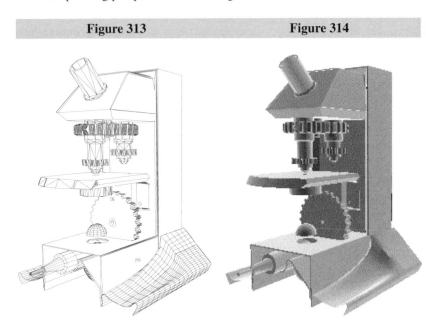

Final adjustment

Having finally assembled all the details or components (see Figure 315), consideration must be given to certain adjustments for optimum performance of the microscope.

To obtain a flat field view, bring an object into focus using the largest NA objective. If there is any part of the field of view out of focus, then an error in squareness to the optical axis exists between the stage top's surface and the monocular head. For errors in the east/west direction, slightly rotate the monocular head about the limb. Error in the north/south direction can be corrected by elongating the holes in the spring steel plates.

Parfocality means that a sharp focus is maintained as each objective is rotated into the optical axis and can only be achieved when the microscope tube length coincides with the design of the objectives.

Using the largest NA objectives (or magnification), focus onto the specimen. When the specimen is in sharp focus, rotate the remaining objects into the optical axis, moving the objective tubes up or down to achieve a sharp image without altering the position of the cam wheel. If this results in problems, move the

Figure 315

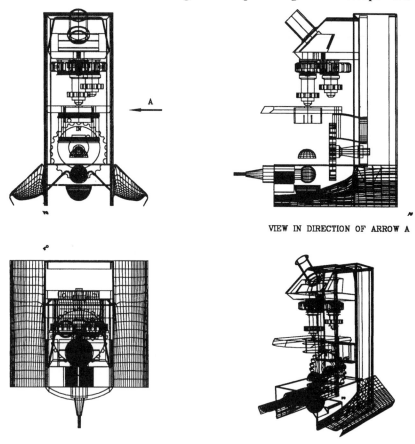

VIEW IN DIRECTION OF ARROW A

MICROSCOPE ASSEMBLY

objective tube of the largest magnification up or down and repeat the above activity until all three objectives are parfocal.

All that is now necessary is to adjust the illumination system to give the best possible results. It is worth repeating that in microscopy you don't see that which you don't adequately illuminate. Hence, for good resolution it is important to have adjusted the illumination to suit all *objectives*. Remember that with our limited illumination system it is always going to be a compromise.

1. With the specimen in sharp focus, move the substage condenser up and down to give the best result. (Close the iris diaphragm to check the iris centration.)
2. Slide and rotate the illumination tube to project as high and even a light intensity into the objective plane as possible.

   For maximum resolution, both field and aperture iris must be adjusted to suit each different objective (a fact that eludes many practising microscopists).

An ideal microscope design would connect the nosepiece to both the field and aperture iris in such a way as to cause the change in iris diameters to take place automatically as the objective changer is rotated.

3. Open the field iris to just fill the field of view. As we do not have a field iris you can ignore this stage or place a card with a series of different sized holes above the illumination condenser.
4. Remove the eyepiece and observe the back aperture of the objective by looking down the eyepiece tube.
5. Move the aperture iris (substage condenser) until approximately seven-tenths of the back aperture of the objective is filled with light.

The illumination system is now correctly adjusted for that particular objective. Stages 3, 4 and 5 must be repeated for each different objective in use.

For those readers who have negotiated their way through this design and manufacture project, a new and wonderful world awaits you as you explore the benefits of microscopy.

Icing on the cake

In my introduction to this book I asked the question, how would you like to give your potential customer a photo-realistic coloured image of the finished product without even making a prototype?

Now that we have a solid model of the project, it opens up many possibilities for enhanced communications, none more so than colour rendering. Since AutoCAD Release 13, the rendering facility is much improved. It is a simple process to attach surface materials to the individual details of the project having previously loaded the required materials into the materials list from the materials library.

The surface materials can reflect light in a specular or diffuse manner, or some combination of both. Specular light reflects as a mirror or polished surface; diffuse light spreads the light rays in all directions giving the impression of a matte or dull surface. You can also assign colours to the selected materials to give a realistic image or simply to try out different colour schemes (a most useful facility). I recall the time when microscopes had to be sprayed black. It took many years before the market would accept anything beyond black spray and chromium plating as the colour scheme for scientific instruments such as microscopes.

Use the RENDER command to render your project. Don't bother with any light settings to begin with as AutoCAD uses a virtual 'over the shoulder' distant light as a fixed default setting.

Once you have seen the results of your initial light setting you can begin to experiment with different types of lights and light locations. Adding lights to your drawing can improve the model's appearance and helps to focus the eye on certain key aspects of the drawing. AutoCAD uses four different types of light source to help with the different effects available to enhance the model. Note that at this level of rendering, no shadows are created. The four types of light source are:

- **Ambient light** – (Think of a cloudy day with no highlights or shadows.) This type of lighting does not benefit the three-dimensional effect required by rendering. It gives a flat, even intensity of illumination on all visible surfaces of the model and, as a general rule, should be set to as low a value of intensity as acceptable for the model. In the case of dark scenes, the ambient light setting should be zero.

- **Distant light** – (Think of a searchlight or the sun.) A distant light produces uniform collimated or parallel rays of light similar to sunlight and, as such, is most helpful in creating three-dimensional effects of your model. Locate a distant light at the extents of your model; this will produce collimated light rays of equal intensity on all surfaces in the direction of the light rays both in front of and behind the light source.
- **Point light** – (Think of an electric light bulb.) A point light radiates light waves in all directions from its point of origin, with the intensity of light increasing the nearer the model surface is to the light source. This type of light helps to increase the contrast between light and dark areas of the model (providing the ambient light setting is low) giving much improved 3D visualisation. Use the point light for general-purpose effects.
- **Spotlights** – (Pantomime time.) This type of light produces a cone of light from given parameters, i.e. insertion point, direction vector and cone angle. Like the point light, its intensity varies with object distance. This type of light should be used with care and only for special effects.

This is only a brief account of rendering, designed simply to encourage the reader to experiment with the AutoCAD RENDER command for there is no substitute for 'hands-on experience'. I'm sure that this experience will be very rewarding and lead you to the next logical stage of development involving more sophisticated rendering software packages involving shadows, transparency, texture maps and so on.

Appendix A
Automated solutions

This is a parametric design solution (remember Rule 15) incorporating the 3DMESH command. The program needs to be loaded into the drawing editor APPLOAD prior to use. When in use, simply respond to the screen prompts, sit back and let the computer take the strain.

```
MONO.LSP

(DEFUN C:MONO ()
 (GRAPHSCR)
 (SETVAR "CMDECHO" 0)
 (SETQ P1 (GETPOINT "\nPLEASE PICK THE L.H. CORNER OF MONO HEAD "))
 (COMMAND "UCS" "O" P1)
 (SETQ P1 (LIST 0 0 0))
 (SETQ L (GETREAL "\nPLEASE ENTER THE HEAD LENGTH ")
       W (GETREAL "\nPLEASE ENTER THE HEAD WIDTH ")
       H (GETREAL "\nPLEASE ENTER THE HEAD HEIGHT ")
       ALP (/ (GETREAL "\nENTER THE FRONT ANGLE (DEG) ") (/ 180 PI))
       BET (/ (GETREAL "\nENTER THE SIDE ANGLE (DEG) ") (/ 180 PI))
       LM (* H (/ (SIN ALP)(COS ALP)))
       WM (* H (/ (SIN BET)(COS BET)))
       P2 (LIST L 0 0) P3 (LIST 0 W 0) P4 (LIST L W 0)
       P5 (LIST LM WM H)
       P6 (LIST LM (- (CADR P3) WM) H)
       P7 (LIST (CAR P2) WM H)
       P8 (LIST (CAR P4) (- (CADR P4) WM) H)
       P9 (LIST (/ LM 5)(/ WM 5)(- 0 (/ H 5)))
       P10 (LIST (CAR P2)(/ WM 5)(- 0 (/ H 5)))
       P11 (LIST (/ LM 5)(- (CADR P3)(/ WM 5))(- 0 (/ H 5)))
       P12 (LIST (CAR P4)(- (CADR P4) (/ WM 5))(- 0 (/ H 5))))
 (COMMAND "3DMESH" 5 3 P9 P1 P5 P10 P2 P7 P12 P4 P8 P11 P3 P6
                   P9 P1 P5
        "3DFACE" P5 P7 P8 P6 "" "UCS" "P")
 (COMMAND "UCS" "P")
 (SETVAR "CMDECHO" 1)
 (PRINC)
)
```

This program can be found on the Worldwide Web at:

ftp://ftp.AWL.co.uk/pub/AWL-he/engineering/bousfield

Figure 316

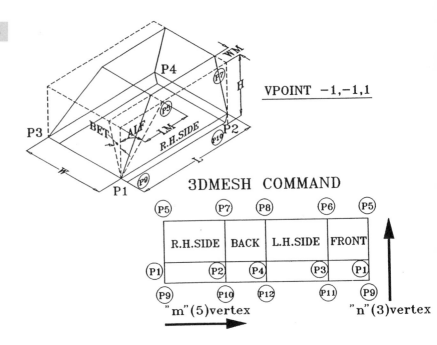

VPOINT −1,−1,1

3DMESH COMMAND

Appendix B
Teaching aid for thin ray diagrams

This program automatically draws the ray diagrams for converging and diverging lens and for concave and convex mirrors or reflectors, based on a fixed object height.

Once the program is loaded, screen prompts request values for focal length and object distance, detecting values set at infinity, and differentiating by colour real and virtual images.

```
OPTICS.LSP

(DEFUN C:OPTICS ()
    (INITGET 1 "A B C D")
    (PROMPT "\nENTER A FOR DIVERG B FOR CONVERG C=CONVEX D=CONCAVE ")
    (SETQ CHOICE (GETKWORD))
    (COND
        ((EQUAL CHOICE "A")(DIVL))
        ((EQUAL CHOICE "B")(CONL))
        ((EQUAL CHOICE "C")(CONVM))
        ((EQUAL CHOICE "D")(CONCM))
    )
(PRINC)
)
```

```
DIVL.LSP
```

```lisp
(DEFUN DIVL ()  ; DIVerging Lens
(SC)
(SETQ LOOP T)
  (WHILE LOOP
   (SETQ FL (GETREAL "\nPLEASE ENTER THE LENS FOCAL LENGTH <45> "))
        (IF (NULL FL)(SETQ FL 45))
   (SETQ U (GETREAL "\nPLEASE ENTER THE OBJECT DISTANCE TO LENS ")
        V (/ (* U FL)(+ FL U)) IH (* 40 (/ V U)) M (/ IH 40))
   (SETQ P1 (LIST (- U) 0) P2 (POLAR P1 (/ PI 2) 32)
        P3 (POLAR P1 (/ PI 2) 40) P4 (LIST 0 40)
        P5 (LIST (- V) IH))
 (OBJECT)
  (COMMAND "COLOR" 3)
  (SETQ STR (STRCAT "%%UMAGNIFICATION= "(RTOS M 2 2)))
  (COMMAND "TEXT" "C" (LIST (- U) (- 10)) 4 "" STR "COLOR" 1)
  (SETQ STR2 (STRCAT "%%UIMAGE HEIGHT= "(RTOS IH 2 2))
        STR3 (STRCAT "OBJECT DISTANCE= "(RTOS U 2 2))
        STR4 (STRCAT "FOCAL LENGTH= "(RTOS FL 2 2)))
   (COMMAND "TEXT" "C" (LIST (- U) (- 20)) 4 "" STR2
           "TEXT" "C" (LIST (- U) (- 30)) 4 "" "RED=REAL"
"COLOR" 2 "TEXT" "C" (LIST (- U) (- 40)) 4 "" "YELLOW=VIRTUAL IMAGE"
           "COLOR" 1
           "LINE" P3 P0 "" "LINE" P4 (POLAR P4 (ATAN 40 FL) 40) ""
           "COLOR" 2 "LINE" (LIST (- FL) 0) P4 ""
        "PLINE" P5 "W" 0 (/ IH 4) (POLAR P5 (* (/ PI 2) 3) (/ IH 3))
           "W" 0 0 (LIST (- V) 0) ""
        "TEXT" "C" (LIST (- (+ V 10)) (/ IH 2)) 4 "" "IH" "COLOR" 4
     "TEXT" "C" (LIST (- U) (- 50)) 4 "" "DIVERGING LENS" "COLOR" 5
        "TEXT" "C" (LIST (- U) (- 60)) 4 "" STR3 "COLOR" 6
        "TEXT" "C" (LIST (- U) (- 70)) 4 "" "OBJECT HEIGHT= 40"
        "COLOR" 1 "TEXT" "C" (LIST (- U) (- 80)) 4 "" STR4
        "ZOOM" "E" "COLOR" "BYLAYER")
   (INITGET 1 "Y N")
(SETQ E (GETKWORD "\nDO YOU WISH TO SELECT ANOTHER VALUE ? Y or N"))
   (IF (EQUAL E "Y")
(COMMAND "ERASE" "C" (LIST (- U)(- 10)) (LIST (- (/ U 2))(- 80)) "")
        (SETQ LOOP NIL))
  ) ; loop
 (COMMAND "UCS" "P")
)   ; function
```

CONL.LSP

```
(DEFUN CONL ()    ; CONverging Lens
(SC)
(SETQ LOOP T)
   (WHILE LOOP
    (SETQ FL (GETREAL "\nPLEASE ENTER THE LENS FOCAL LENGTH <30>"))
          (IF (NULL FL)(SETQ FL 30))
    (SETQ U (GETREAL "\nPLEASE ENTER THE OBJECT DISTANCE TO LENS "))
     (WHILE (EQUAL U FL)
           (PROMPT "OBJECT AT INFINITY, SELECT ANOTHER VALUE ")
           (SETQ U (GETREAL))
     )
    (IF (> U FL)(SETQ V (/ (* U FL)(- U FL)))
             (SETQ V (/ (* U FL)(- FL U))))   ; V= image distance
    (SETQ IH (* 20 (/ V U)))    ; Image Height
         M (/ IH 20))
    (IF (> U FL)(COMMAND "LINE" P0 (LIST (+ V 4) 0) "")
             (COMMAND "LINE" P0 (LIST (- (+ V 4)) 0) ""))
    (SETQ P1 (LIST (- U) 0) P2 (POLAR P1 (/ PI 2) 16)
         P3 (POLAR P1 (/ PI 2) 20) P4 (LIST 0 20)
         P5 (LIST V (- IH)) P6 (LIST (- V) IH))
(OBJECT)
   (COMMAND "COLOR" 3)
   (SETQ STR (STRCAT "%%UMAGNIFICATION= "(RTOS M 2 2)))
   (COMMAND "TEXT" "C" (LIST (- U) (- 10)) 4 "" STR "COLOR" 1)
   (SETQ STR2 (STRCAT "%%UIMAGE HEIGHT= "(RTOS IH 2 2))
         STR3 (STRCAT "OBJECT DISTANCE= "(RTOS U 2 2))
         STR4 (STRCAT "FOCAL LENGTH= "(RTOS FL 2 2)))
   (COMMAND "TEXT" "C" (LIST (- U) (- 20)) 4 "" STR2
           "TEXT" "C" (LIST (- U) (- 30)) 4 "" "RED= REAL IMAGE"
"COLOR" 2 "TEXT" "C" (LIST (- U) (- 40)) 4 "" "YELLOW= VIRTUAL IMAGE"
      "COLOR" 1)
    (IF (> U FL)
        (COMMAND "LINE" P4 P5 P3 ""
          "PLINE" P5 "W" 0 (/ IH 5) (POLAR P5 (/ PI 2)(/ IH 4))
          "W" 0 0 (LIST V 0)""
          "TEXT" (LIST (+ V 5) (- (/ IH 2))) 4 "" "IH" )
        (COMMAND "COLOR" 2 "LINE" P4 P6 P3 ""
          "COLOR" 1 "LINE" "" P0 "" "COLOR" 2
       "PLINE" P6 "W" 0 (/ IH 7) (POLAR P6 (* (/ PI 2) 3)(/ IH 4))
       "W" 0 0 (LIST (- V) 0 ) ""
       "TEXT" "C" (LIST (- (+ V 10)) (/ IH 2)) 4 "" "IH"))
    (COMMAND "COLOR" 4
          "TEXT" "C" (LIST (- U) (- 50)) 4 "" "CONVERGING LENS"
     "COLOR" 5 "TEXT" "C" (LIST (- U) (- 60)) 4 "" STR3 "COLOR" 6
          "TEXT" "C" (LIST (- U) (- 70)) 4 "" "OBJECT HEIGHT= 20"
          "COLOR" 1 "TEXT" "c" (LIST (- U) (- 80)) 4 "" STR4
          "ZOOM" "E" "COLOR" "BYLAYER")
    (INITGET 1 "Y N")
(SETQ E (GETKWORD "\nDO YOU WISH TO SELECT ANOTHER VALUE? Y or N "))
    (IF (EQUAL E "Y")
```

```
(COMMAND "ERASE" "C" (LIST (- U)(- 10)) (LIST (- (/ U 2))(- 80)) "")
              (SETQ LOOP NIL))
  )   ; loop
 (COMMAND "UCS" "P")
)    ; function
```

CONVM.LSP

```
(DEFUN CONVM ()  ; CONVex Mirror
(SC)
(SETQ LOOP T)
 (WHILE LOOP
  (SETQ FL (GETREAL "\nPLEASE ENTER THE MIRROR FOCAL LENGTH <30> "))
      (IF (NULL FL)(SETQ FL 30))
  (SETQ U (GETREAL "\nPLEASE ENTER THE OBJECT DISTANCE TO MIRROR ")
      V (/ (* U FL)(+ FL U)) IH (* 40 (/ V U)) M (/ IH 40))
  (SETQ P1 (LIST (- U) 0) P2 (POLAR P1 (/ PI 2) 32)
      P3 (POLAR P1 (/ PI 2) 40) P4 (LIST 0 40)
      P5 (LIST V IH))
 (OBJECT)
  (COMMAND "COLOR" 7 "LINE" P0 (POLAR P0 0 (* 2 FL)) "" "COLOR" 3)
  (SETQ STR (STRCAT "%%UMAGNIFICATION= "(RTOS M 2 2)))
  (COMMAND "TEXT" "C" (LIST (- U) (- 10)) 4 "" STR "COLOR" 1)
  (SETQ STR2 (STRCAT "%%UIMAGE HEIGHT= "(RTOS IH 2 2))
      STR3 (STRCAT "OBJECT DISTANCE= "(RTOS U 2 2))
      STR4 (STRCAT "FOCAL LENGTH= "(RTOS FL 2 2)))
  (COMMAND "TEXT" "C" (LIST (- U) (- 20)) 4 "" STR2
        "TEXT" "C" (LIST (- U) (- 30)) 4 "" "RED=REAL"
"COLOR" 2 "TEXT" "C" (LIST (- U) (- 40)) 4 "" "YELLOW=VIRTUAL IMAGE"
        "COLOR" 1 "LINE" P3 (LIST (* 2 FL) 0) ""
        "LINE" P4 (POLAR P4 (- PI (ATAN 40 FL)) 40) ""
        "COLOR" 2 "LINE" (LIST FL 0) P4 ""
      "PLINE" P5 "W" 0 (/ IH 4) (POLAR P5 (* (/ PI 2) 3) (/ IH 3))
        "W" 0 0 (LIST V 0) ""
      "TEXT" "C" (LIST (- V 10) (/ IH 2)) 4 "" "IH" "COLOR" 4
     "TEXT" "C" (LIST (- U) (- 50)) 4 "" "CONVEX MIRROR" "COLOR" 5
      "TEXT" "C" (LIST (- U) (- 60)) 4 "" STR3 "COLOR" 6
      "TEXT" "C" (LIST (- U) (- 70)) 4 "" "OBJECT HEIGHT= 40"
      "COLOR" 1 "TEXT" "C" (LIST (- U) (- 80)) 4 "" STR4
      "ZOOM" "E" "COLOR" "BYLAYER")
  (INITGET 1 "Y N")
(SETQ E (GETKWORD "\nDO YOU WISH TO SELECT ANOTHER VALUE ? Y or N"))
  (IF (EQUAL E "Y")
(COMMAND "ERASE" "C" (LIST (- U)(- 10)) (LIST (- (/ U 2))(- 80)) "")
      (SETQ LOOP NIL))
  ) ; loop
 (COMMAND "UCS" "P")
)    ; function
```

CONCM.LSP

```lisp
(DEFUN CONCM ()   ; CONCave Mirror
(SC)
(SETQ LOOP T)
  (WHILE LOOP
    (SETQ FL (GETREAL "\nPLEASE ENTER THE MIRROR FOCAL LENGTH <30>"))
          (IF (NULL FL)(SETQ FL 30))
    (SETQ U (GETREAL "\nPLEASE ENTER THE OBJECT DISTANCE TO MIRROR "))
      (WHILE (EQUAL U FL)
            (PROMPT "OBJECT AT INFINITY, SELECT ANOTHER VALUE ")
            (SETQ U (GETREAL))
      )
    (IF (> U FL)(SETQ V (/ (* U FL)(- U FL)))
               (SETQ V (/ (* U FL)(- FL U))))   ; V= image distance
    (SETQ IH (* 20 (/ V U)) M (/ IH 20))
    (IF (< U FL)(COMMAND "LINE" P0 (LIST (+ V 4) 0) "")
               (COMMAND "LINE" P0 (LIST (- (+ V 4)) 0) ""))
    (SETQ P1 (LIST (- U) 0) P2 (POLAR P1 (/ PI 2) 16)
          P3 (POLAR P1 (/ PI 2) 20) P4 (LIST 0 20)
          P5 (LIST (- V) (- IH)) P6 (LIST V IH))
(OBJECT)
    (COMMAND "COLOR" 3)
    (SETQ STR (STRCAT "%%UMAGNIFICATION= "(RTOS M 2 2)))
    (COMMAND "TEXT" "R" (LIST (- U) 90) 4 "" STR "COLOR" 1)
    (SETQ STR2 (STRCAT "%%UIMAGE HEIGHT= "(RTOS IH 2 2))
          STR3 (STRCAT "OBJECT DISTANCE= "(RTOS U 2 2))
          STR4 (STRCAT "FOCAL LENGTH= "(RTOS FL 2 2)))
    (COMMAND "TEXT" "R" (LIST (- U) 80) 4 "" STR2
            "TEXT" "R" (LIST (- U) 70) 4 "" "RED= REAL IMAGE"
    "COLOR" 2 "TEXT" "R" (LIST (- U) 60) 4 "" "YELLOW= VIRTUAL IMAGE"
    "COLOR" 1)
      (IF (> U FL)
          (COMMAND "LINE" P4 P5 P3 ""
          "PLINE" P5 "W" 0 (/ IH 5) (POLAR P5 (/ PI 2)(/ IH 4))
          "W" 0 0 (LIST (- V) 0) ""
          "TEXT" (LIST (- (+ V 10)) (- (/ IH 2))) 4 "" "IH" )
          (COMMAND "COLOR" 2 "LINE" P4 P6 P3 ""
          "COLOR" 1 "LINE" P3 (LIST (- (* 2 FL)) 0)""
          "LINE" P4 (LIST (- FL) 0) "" "COLOR" 2
        "PLINE" P6 "W" 0 (/ IH 7) (POLAR P6 (* (/ PI 2) 3)(/ IH 4))
        "W" 0 0 (LIST V 0) ""
          "TEXT" "C" (LIST (+ V 10) (/ IH 2)) 4 "" "IH"))
      (COMMAND "COLOR" 4
              "TEXT" "R" (LIST (- U) 50) 4 "" "CONCAVE MIRROR"
        "COLOR" 5 "TEXT" "R" (LIST (- U) 40) 4 "" STR3 "COLOR" 6
              "TEXT" "R" (LIST (- U) 30) 4 "" "OBJECT HEIGHT= 20"
              "COLOR" 1 "TEXT" "R" (LIST (- U) 20) 4 "" STR4
              "ZOOM" "E" "COLOR" "BYLAYER")
      (INITGET 1 "Y N"))
(SETQ E (GETKWORD "\nDO YOU WISH TO SELECT ANOTHER VALUE? Y or N "))
    (IF (EQUAL E "Y")
```

```
(COMMAND "ERASE" "C" (LIST (- (+ U 10)) 20)
                     (LIST (- (+ U 20)) 90) "")
                (SETQ LOOP NIL))
  )   ; loop
 (COMMAND "UCS" "P")
)    ; function
```

Examples of the results of the functions DIVL, CONL, CONVM and CONCM are shown in Figures 317–320, respectively.

Figure 317

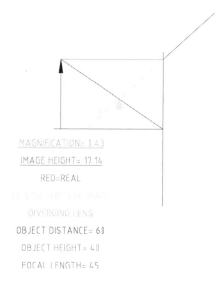

MAGNIFICATION= 0.43

IMAGE HEIGHT= 17.14

RED=REAL

DIVERGING LENS

OBJECT DISTANCE= 60

OBJECT HEIGHT= 40

FOCAL LENGTH= 45

Figure 318

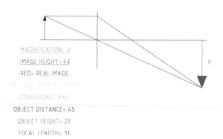

MAGNIFICATION= 2

IMAGE HEIGHT= 40

RED= REAL IMAGE

CONVERGING LENS

OBJECT DISTANCE= 45

OBJECT HEIGHT= 20

FOCAL LENGTH= 30

Figure 319

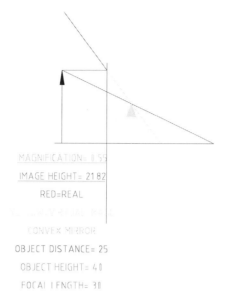

MAGNIFICATION= 0.55
IMAGE HEIGHT= 21.82
RED=REAL

CONVEX MIRROR
OBJECT DISTANCE= 25
OBJECT HEIGHT= 40
FOCAL LENGTH= 30

Figure 320

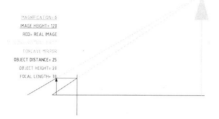

MAGNIFICATION= 6
IMAGE HEIGHT= 120
RED= REAL IMAGE

CONCAVE MIRROR
OBJECT DISTANCE= 25
OBJECT HEIGHT= 20
FOCAL LENGTH= 30

OBJECT.LSP

```
(DEFUN OBJECT () ;object for ray diagram
 (COMMAND "LINE" (POLAR P4 (/ PI 2) 4) P0 ""
        "MIRROR" "L" "" P1 P0 ""
        "LINE" P0 (POLAR P1 PI 4) ""
        "PLINE" P3 "W" 0 2.5 P2 "W" 0 0 P1 ""
        "COLOR" 1 "LINE" P3 P4 "")
)
```

SC.LSP

```
(DEFUN SC ()   ; Screen Centre
(GRAPHSCR)
(SETQ BC (GETVAR "LIMMIN")
     TC (GETVAR "LIMMAX")
     P0 (LIST 0 0))
 (COMMAND "UCS" "O"
   (LIST (/ (- (CAR TC)(CAR BC)) 2) (/ (- (CADR TC)(CADR BC)) 2 )))
)
```

Appendix C
Automatic spiral

This is a simple solution to problems such as a screw thread, telephone cable, spiral staircase etc. This AutoLISP macro is an ideal solution to the spiral cable problem of Exercise 9 in Part Two. Figure 321 shows a spiral generated by this program.

Figure 321

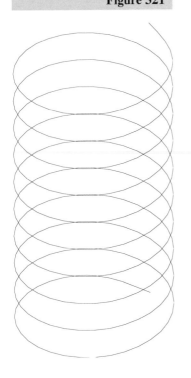

```
CABLE.LSP

(DEFUN C:CABLE () ;Start of CABLE function
 (GRAPHSCR)
  ; Parametric input
  (SETQ P1 (GETPOINT "\nPICK CENTRE OF SPIRAL ")
        D (GETREAL "\nENTER SPIRAL DIAMETER ")
        REV (GETREAL "\nENTER THE NUMBER OF REVOLUTIONS ")
        Z (GETREAL "\nENTER THE SPIRAL LEAD ")
  ) ; End of parametric input
  (SETQ A 0 R (/ D 2) Z2 (/ Z 8) Z3 0
        P2 (POLAR P1 A R) PNTS (LIST P2)
        LOOP (FIX (* 8 REV))
  )
   (REPEAT LOOP    ; Construct a LIST of points
    (SETQ A (+ A (/ PI 4))
          P3 (POLAR P1 A R)
          Z3 (+ Z2 Z3)
          P4 (LIST (CAR P3)(CADR P3) Z3)
          PNTS (CONS P4 PNTS)
    )
   ) ; End of repeat loop
     (SETQ PNTS (CONS "" PNTS)
           PNTS (CONS "" PNTS)
           PNTS (CONS "" PNTS)
           PNTS (REVERSE PNTS)
     )
    (COMMAND "SPLINE" (FOREACH P PNTS (COMMAND P)))
    (PRINC)
) ; End of CABLE function.
```

Index